Lizzie Marvelly (Ngāti Whakaue) is a musician, columnist, producer and activist, originally from Rotorua, New Zealand. In May 2015, she founded Villainesse.com, an online media project for young women. Later in 2015 she started the internationally successful #MyBodyMyTerms campaign, sparking a conversation about victim-blaming, revenge porn, consent and sexual violence. Lizzie is an opinion columnist for the *New Zealand Herald* and the co-producer of a 12-part web series called *The REAL Sex Talk*, a youth-centric series presenting credible information about sex, sexuality and relationships to young people. In 2016 and 2017, Lizzie was named as a finalist in the New Zealand Women of Influence Awards. In 2017, she won the Canon Media Award for Opinion Writing – General, the same year that Villainesse won the Canon Media Award for Best Blog. In 2017, she was a semi-finalist for the Young New Zealander of the Year Award. Lizzie lives in Auckland, although she'll always be a Rotorua girl at heart.

THAT F WORD

GROWING UP FEMINIST IN AOTEAROA

LIZZIE MARVELLY

HarperCollins*Publishers*

HarperCollins*Publishers*

First published in 2018
by HarperCollins*Publishers* (New Zealand) Limited
Unit D1, 63 Apollo Drive, Rosedale, Auckland 0632, New Zealand
harpercollins.co.nz

HarperCollins*Publishers*
Unit D1, 63 Apollo Drive, Rosedale, Auckland 0632, New Zealand
Level 13, 201 Elizabeth Street, Sydney NSW 2000, Australia
A 53, Sector 57, Noida, UP, India
1 London Bridge Street, London, SE1 9GF, United Kingdom
Bay Adelaide Centre, East Tower, 22 Adelaide Street West, 41st Floor, Toronto, Ontario, M5H 4E3
195 Broadway, New York NY 10007, USA

A catalogue record for this book is available from the National Library of New Zealand

ISBN: 978 1 7755 4112 7 (paperback)
ISBN: 978 1 7754 9143 9 (ebook)

Cover design by HarperCollins Design Studio
Cover photography by Monty Adams
Typeset in Baskerville by Kelli Lonergan
Printed and bound in Australia by McPherson's Printing Group
The papers used by HarperCollins in the manufacture of this book are a natural, recyclable product made from wood grown in sustainable plantation forests. The fibre source and manufacturing processes meet recognised international environmental standards, and carry certification.

For every woman who has ever been called
'bossy' or 'stroppy'.

CONTENTS

CONTENT NOTE

This book contains discussions of topics that some people may find distressing. Go gently. A list of support organisations can be found at the end of this book.

This book was also written from a woman's perspective with women in mind. I'm not for a second saying that it can't be read by men or by people of other genders. In fact, I greatly hope that people of all genders will pore over its pages. If you are reader of the male persuasion, haere mai. You too are welcome here. To save me a great deal of time and online abuse, however, I'm going to establish one all-encompassing disclaimer right up front. I shouldn't need to say this, but I've been on social media for too long to take the risk of leaving it to chance, so here we go, for the gentlemen in the house: when I say 'men' generally in this book, I don't necessarily mean you. I know that there are plenty of wonderful men. I also know that there are plenty of not wonderful ones. You are free to figure out whichever hat fits you.

When I speak of victims and survivors of sexual crimes and use female pronouns, please know that it is not my intention to discount male experiences of victimhood. I know that there are men who suffer, and I greatly wish that they didn't. When I use 'she' and 'her', I am paying homage to the fact that the majority of victims and survivors are female. Sexual violence is an asymmetrical horror, in which statistically one group of people (men), victimise another group of people (women) much more than the reverse, and as a woman who has experienced it herself, I speak from my own vantage point of female experience.

PREFACE

I've never shied away from a challenge. Which is lucky, because life seems to come at me hard and fast. When I pause to look back over my shoulder, I see a collection of vignettes and overarching themes.

I'm seven years old, being taught how to not 'throw like a girl'.

I'm 11, being called a slut.

I'm 18, signing an international record deal and feeling like an imposter.

I'm 21, and trying to put myself back together after a mental breakdown.

I'm 24, and being sexually abused for the umpteenth time.

I'm 25, and starting my own media company.

I'm 26, and crying after being abused online for days on end.

I'm 27, and winning national media awards.

I'm 28, and writing a book.

It's been a whirlwind. One I wouldn't change. But it's a journey that would've been very different, had I been born male.

Being born female and being raised as a girl brings with it a series of expectations that start almost from birth. Even in a life filled with joy, as much of mine has been, these expectations are always there, just below the surface, and we quickly learn that there is a price to be paid for refusing to live up to them. As a girl, and then as a woman, there are certain codes and conditions that should be respected at all times.

Or else.

I've never been very good at doing what I was told. When I was a little girl, I was told off for being 'aggressive'. It was one of the many words used to describe me. I was also 'bossy' and 'competitive' and 'not very ladylike'. Children, though we often underestimate their abilities, are avid readers of subtext and tone. From the facial expressions and the inflections that accompanied these labels, I knew that all of them were bad.

As a child, I was a cacophony of contradictions. I loved Barbie dolls, the Spice Girls and *Beauty and the Beast*. I also loved playing cricket, rescuing wild animals and wandering the fields for hours with my black Labrador, Lace. I was over-sensitive, stubborn, caring and opinionated. Part tomboy, part girly-girl, part nerd, and part ringleader; I could never seem to find a category that I fit snugly into. Come to think of it, twenty-something years later, I still haven't.

When I was ten, my teacher told my parents that I needed to be brought down a peg. She voiced what I'd already long suspected. I was too much. Too loud. Too difficult. Too different. My parents were outraged, but I was ashamed. I was set apart from the other kids, in an environment where to be 'other' is about the worst thing you can be. Today, when I speak at schools around the country, I meet girls who are going through the same thing. When I listen to their frustrations, I wonder how long it will take before being a young woman who knows her own mind is unremarkable. Have you ever heard a young man described as 'knowing his own mind'? I wonder when strong young women will finally be celebrated and encouraged rather than knocked down.

I was born nearly 96 years after women in New Zealand won the vote. I say 'won' because our foremothers fought tooth and nail to be seen as equal human beings. It's a battle I can now see that I've been fighting my entire life. It's a battle we're all part of, consciously or unconsciously, on one side or another; and whether we acknowledge it or not, we're still fighting it today.

The year I finished writing this book, 2018, marked the 125th anniversary of women's suffrage in New Zealand. Much is made of the fact that we were the first country in the world in which women could vote. It is sometimes used to argue that there's no longer any need for feminism. We've been empowered for generations now, apparently. Surely there's no reason for 'flag-waving' anymore.

Voting, however, is only the tip of the iceberg. While women in New Zealand are legally able to do almost everything men are, the idealistic equality enshrined in the law is somewhat removed from the reality of everyday life. Women have the legal right to be safe from harm, yet New Zealand has some of the highest rates of sexual violence, domestic violence and violence against women in the OECD[1]. Women have the legal right to be paid equally, yet New Zealand women are paid 9.4 per cent less than men for the same work[2]. Non-Pākehā women are further disadvantaged, with some estimates suggesting that Māori women are paid 28 per cent less than Pākehā men for the same work, and Pasifika women 32 per cent less[3].

Women make up 51 per cent of the population[4], but there is only one woman in the whole country who is the solo host of a primetime media show – Miriama Kamo. The other formidable women who are on the airwaves during primetime – Hilary Barry, Susie Ferguson, Kanoa Lloyd, and Megan Annear, among others – all have to have at least one man beside them. Women have the legal right to work, yet only one of the CEOs of the NZX 50 companies is female[5].

Can you imagine an alternative reality in which every single one of our most powerful chief executives bar one was female? A country that had been led by 37 female Prime Ministers and only three males? A country in which the Black Ferns were worshipped by every man, woman and child, playing to sold-out crowds at Eden Park, while the All Blacks had to fly home in economy class after winning the World Cup? A country in which men largely weren't trusted to anchor a primetime show alone? A country in which husbands were expected to take their wives' surnames, and stay-at-home dads outnumbered stay-at-home mums by approximately nine to one[6]?

I can't.

The idea of such a place seems ludicrous. It would be so hopelessly unbalanced that it would immediately be seen to be discriminative. Flip the genders back to reflect reality and it's simply normal. And yet women have to explain why we still need feminism.

The limitations of our ideas about gender don't just restrict girls and women, they affect boys and men too. Kiwi blokes are, of course, *real* men – whatever that means. Boys are told that they have to be strong, competitive and emotionless. Masculinity is a cloak all boys must throw over themselves, to cover up the 'weak' parts. Don't cry, don't talk about your feelings, don't be a *girl*, macho culture tells men. It is little surprise that men have the highest rates of suicide in New Zealand[7].

Our 'either-or' gender binary also creates overwhelming obstacles for people who don't identify as male or female, or whose gender identity does not match the biology of the body they were born in. Gender, providing an oversimplified framework to divide a vast array of diverse human beings into two finite categories, can be more of a prison than a place to call home.

It's realisations like these – 125 years after women won the vote – that give me pause. Quite literally. I am socialised, like most women, to stop and think about the impact of my words before I dare to say them. Should I call myself a feminist, or will that mean that I'm dismissed as an emasculating shrew? Can I say that I'm angry about the pervasive inequality that women still face in 2018, or will I sound like a humourless, nagging bitch? Should I speak up for what I believe in, or will I come across as 'aggressive' and 'bossy'? The words may change as we grow older, but the insinuations remain the same.

And yet, I am arguably an empowered woman. I am not the ten-year-old girl ashamed of standing out. I am not the young woman fighting for her life against depression. I am not the woman buckling under the weight of a torrent of online abuse. Those women are old friends who I feel protective of. I have many of them. They've been with me throughout my life, in one form or another. They are the sister selves that many women have, as we walk along the way. If there's one thing my old friends have taught me, it's that there are many interesting stops along the road to empowerment.

It's time that we took a long, hard look at our culture and the impact that it has upon all of us – men, women and people of all genders. It's time that we deconstructed the expectations, the assumptions, the representations and the generalisations ascribed to our identities.

This book is for the bossy little girl in all of us. It's time that we disrupted the fuck out of the patriarchy.

CHAPTER ONE

The making of a woman

It's a startling discovery, suddenly realising that you are a woman. One minute you're a girl, basking in girl power, then the next you're saddled with a term laden with so much baggage you're in danger of being slapped with an excess fee. Which, it should be pointed out, you most likely will be, in one way or another, for the rest of your life.

Simone de Beauvoir – a feminist icon whose seminal book *The Second Sex* I've been struggling to read for nine years now – once wrote, 'One is not born, but rather becomes, a woman.' One is clearly not born a de Beauvoir reader either, but she makes an important point. Being a woman is a journey with many twists and turns along the way. There are a few constants, however. If you're born female, there's one thing you can be certain of: there will be blood. Lots of it. Veritable fuckloads of blood. We're born (blood), we menstruate (blood), some of us get pregnant (blood tests), some of us have abortions (lots of blood) and others give birth (BLOOOOOOOOD-y hell). For much of our lives, we're only three weeks away from a good bleed. I sometimes visualise the journey to womanhood as one of those diagrams in children's encyclopaedias, though instead of a caterpillar entering into a cocoon to become a beautiful butterfly there's a girl entering a tampon and emerging 35 years later as a ghost. In my vision there are labels below each picture: Girl, Potential Baby Vessel, and Invisible. We have more blood than we know what to do with for the first 50 years (or thereabouts) of our lives, then it disappears and takes with it our identities.

I joke, but it's important to remember what we're up against.

The first part at least begins fairly well. Being a girl was fun. You could get away with being small and cute, and bossy as hell. Which I was. Growing up an only child in Rotorua, I had an abundance of pluck. At three, I marched into a room, deep in conversation and not watching where I was going, walked straight into a pillar, fell back with a stunned look on my face, and loudly exclaimed, 'Fuck!'

You could surmise that speaking my mind has never really been a problem.

I was born in 1989 to parents who had recently scraped together everything they had (and some of what they didn't have) to buy a badly rundown then 90-something-year-old hotel the year before the stock market crashed. I was most certainly not on their to-do list, which at that stage went something like this: buy a hotel and somehow survive one of the worst-ever financial sucker-punches to the New Zealand economy. Having a baby in the middle of the most chaotic years of their lives was not in the five-year plan. I clearly didn't get the memo, although, as my parents have since told me on numerous occasions, they never made the same mistake twice.

'Only child' is something of a synonym for 'spoilt brat', but there was no room for egos in our family. As a small child, my nickname was 'toe-rag', which was eventually shortened to 'rag'. I grew up around the kind of Kiwi humour that ensured that you never got too big for your britches.

Which was a very good thing. It kept me grounded. I knew from a young age that I was privileged. I remember a school trip at the end of my first year at school that ended at the Rotorua Lakefront's volcanic playground. The playground was newly refurbished, a tangle of brightly coloured, plastic-coated metal that inspired frenzied excitement among the city's youngest residents. When Rotorua's other inexpensive child-friendly attractions at the time included riding the one escalator in town (in the middle of Farmers) up and down, and playing in the sticky, smelly ball pit at Georgie Pie, the volcanic playground was basically an oasis out of our wildest dreams. My father turned up in his shirt and tie near the end of the outing to pick me up and managed to make the day even better. He bought the whole class ice creams – then priced at about 50c a pop – making 30 kids' days in one fell swoop, but some more than others. As one little boy told my father in a thank you letter – which he remembers to this day – he'd never had an ice cream before. I'd had an ice cream most days since

I was old enough to hold a cone, which likely explains why most of my baby photos appear to show a tiny sumo wrestler wearing frilly dresses. Many of the kids in my class, however, seldom received treats. Some seldom received lunch. I'll never be able to erase the memory of another small boy scavenging in the rubbish bins at lunchtime for discarded scraps. Anyone who tries to tell you that child poverty doesn't exist in New Zealand is either lying or woefully ignorant.

When you've attended low-decile state schools you almost inevitably experience a few character-building moments along the way. Especially when you're bossy, gutsy, loud-mouthed and given to meddling in situations that don't really concern you. Throughout my primary school years, I was all of those things – with an added bent for justice, so when I heard that a boy in my Year 6 class had stolen a girl's gluestick, I was having none of it. I marched straight up to the table where he sat, yanked open his desk tray and retrieved the apparently filched gluestick, whirling around triumphantly only to be met by a fist to the eye socket. You could say it was my first experience of the first law of social justice: no good deed goes unpunished. That the boy in question was suspended gives me no vindication today. I wonder what happened to him. I wonder what happened to the boy who'd never had an ice cream, and the boy who ferretted through the rubbish for food. I wonder whether they were able to overcome the odds stacked against them.

I may have been called a 'stupid Pākehā' and a 'rich bitch', had my lunch stolen and been punched in the face at primary school, but I am so grateful that I spent my childhood living in the real world. The public schools I attended – Glenholme Primary, Rotorua Intermediate and Rotorua Girls' High School – were all wonderful in their own ways. They taught me well, and not just academically. I learnt a little more about life at each school.

Whether I liked it or not.

I was nearly ready to leave primary school when I entered the Potential Baby Vessel stage of womanhood. Like most Kiwi kids in the state system, we'd had a few talks about 'what's happening to our bodies' (a phrase that still gives me the creeps today), and the information I'd received led me to believe that I was safe for a good few years yet. This whole bleeding out your vagina thing sounds horrendous, I thought. The longer it could be avoided, the better. Then one day, a few weeks before my eleventh birthday, it suddenly arrived. I'D BEEN HAD. DUPED. CONNED. I stood in my bedroom looking down at the bloodstain on the underwear I'd kicked across the room in disgust and I cried. And cried. I felt deeply ashamed, gross, and dirty.

And sick. So sick. Another thing the useless puberty talks hadn't included was any warning that my first period would be so painful and horrible that I'd wonder whether I should just quit this womanhood thing then and there. I bled for two weeks. When you're nearly 11, with a proclivity for histrionics, and clued-up enough to know that periods come once every 28 days, and you bleed for TWO WEEKS STRAIGHT, utter hysteria is the only logical reaction to the thought that you'll be bleeding out your vagina for two out of every four weeks for the REST OF YOUR LIFE (because really, when you're nearly 11, post-menopausal women may as well have a foot in the grave). What if I bled to death one night? I wondered. I was beyond relieved when the duration and severity of subsequent periods eventually reduced. Still, it seemed inconceivable that my body would spontaneously spring a leak every month for the foreseeable future. Nearly 20 years later, I still feel that it's a bloody unfair state of play.

When I got to Rotorua Intermediate the next year, I was thankfully an old hand at the whole period thing. As one of the 'early developers' (which was an actual term that adults would use, often accompanied by a knowing look and a nostalgic tone, as if we were somehow *lucky* to have commenced monthly haemorrhaging before everyone else) in the class, I would spend the next few years welcoming girls to the blood club, giving out tampons when they were caught unaware, dishing out advice about whether Panadol or Nurofen were better for period pain. It was at Rotorua Intermediate, too, where I would find my first five boyfriends, kiss a boy for the first time (in the back of a bus on a school trip), kiss a girl for the first time (in the back of another bus on another school trip) and rack up the school's record for the most achievement badges received during a student's two-year tenure. It was an eventful time.

While primary and intermediate school taught me important life lessons, Rotorua Girls' High School *made* me. It challenged me, extended me, knocked me around, bloodied my nose, held me close and wrapped me in its security blanket. It remains to this day the most girl-power-fuelled environment I've ever had the pleasure of existing in. I didn't need feminism at Rotorua Girls' High. Girls' High *was* feminism. With then around 1000 students and a mainly female staff body, it was a place where girls could be loud, stroppy, clever, strong and relatively free to be themselves. In short, it was something of an alternative feminist reality.

That's not to say it was a utopia. We were not immune to bitchiness and clique warfare, bullying and gossip. We had social hierarchies, which, now I look back, all too often established themselves as rankings descending from the girls that boys liked the most to the girls that boys liked the least. Thankfully, most of the time the boys were absent and we could freely talk about cramps, compare hickies, play truth or dare, make and break confidences, and roll up our skirts as high as we pleased – no matter the size of our thighs – while we sunbathed at lunchtime.

Girls' High was the kind of school where the student council voted upon the design of the uniform. It held democratic elections, and the Head Girl, Arts Captain, Sports Captain, Board of Trustees Student Representative and House Captains were selected by their peers. It had a wellness centre where you could go to get contraception, to see a doctor, nurse or counsellor, or – if you were me – to drag your friends every time you found yourselves in the middle of a fight and needed to talk things out. Homeroom was called Whānau, the four houses were named after prominent Māori women, and New Zealand history was taught both from a Māori and a colonial perspective. There was even a school for young parents attached to the main school, with an early childcare centre across the playground. Though I didn't realise it at the time, it was about as progressive as a high school could be.

It cut a staggering juxtaposition to the environment I would discover at King's College when I won a scholarship to attend the prestigious Auckland school for my last two years of schooling. King's College was essentially everything that Rotorua Girls' High School was not.

When I was driven through the gates of King's College in 2006, the last chapter of my girlhood came to a close. I'd been scouted by the school as an exceptional student, as I had been by Rotorua Girls' High three years earlier, and I now found myself a young woman 200 kilometres from home in an environment where I knew no one. At King's I was a talent to be sculpted in the hope that I would bring glory to the school. I was expected to fit into the King's way of life without upsetting the balance of 'the way things should be'. The problem was that the way I thought things should be was certainly not the way things were at King's.

When I moved to King's, I may as well have moved to another planet. All of a sudden I found myself in an environment where boys held up pieces of toast with numbers drawn in Vegemite on them to rate the attractiveness of the new girls out of ten as they walked into the dining hall. It wasn't as if having girls at King's was a new thing either. By the time I arrived there, King's had been accepting female students for 26 years. Not that you'd have known it from looking at the prefect body. Of the top 16 'blue jersey' prefect positions (at King's, for some reason that escapes me to this day, the top prefects wear blue jerseys, while the other students wear maroon), only three were designated for female students. The one Head of School position had an insurmountable prerequisite – you had to have a penis – and of the four Deputy Heads of School roles, only one could go to a girl, who then became responsible for helping to organise the social functions. I'm not kidding.

For the first time in my life, my gender had become a barrier. I took it exactly as you'd expect. I picked fights with boys who made in-the-kitchen jokes. I had long and frustrated conversations with the female staff, who knew exactly where I was coming from, because they'd been trying to subvert the patriarchal system for years. I marched straight into the Associate Headmaster's office to demand he update the leadership materials we were given when we became prefects – which in 2007 still exclusively used male pronouns, and contained gems like 'A good leader must be tough enough to win a fight, but not tough enough to kick a man when he is down. Good human relations develop out of strength, not out of weakness.' God forbid a leader could be non-combative. God forbid a leader could be a she.

I became, in short, a teenaged feminist activist. I hadn't felt the need to do more than simply identify myself as a feminist until I found that I actually needed feminism. Sometimes it takes smacking up against the glass ceiling to realise that it exists. In the months leading up to my departure for King's I'd often heard that success was celebrated at the college. When the Headmaster's wife travelled from Auckland to Rotorua to watch me sing and convince me to come to the school, I'd been told that striving for excellence was encouraged not only by the staff, but also by the student body.

Success, I would eventually learn, *was* celebrated at King's – if you were male, succeeding at traditionally male endeavours. A lot has changed since my time at the college – it needed to – but boarding at King's in 2006 was a unique challenge when you were opinionated, smart and female. Standing out as a female student marked you as something of a target in the student community, and a nuisance to a few of the more traditional staff.

My experience at King's wasn't helped by the fact that I was never allowed to fly under the radar. During my first week at the school I was asked to sing at the school assembly, a request that I could hardly decline, given that I'd received the most significant scholarship available to a female student. I can remember it vividly, standing at the front of the Great Hall in my brand new (extortionately expensive) uniform, attempting to stifle my fear by telling myself that it was just another performance rather than a very public introduction to a room full of teenagers who I didn't know, and belting out 'On My Own'. I couldn't have chosen a more appropriately titled song if I tried. I was immediately known as 'that singer girl', though I was given a more permanent nickname soon after, by the Head Prefect no less. He dubbed me 'Little Miss Perfect' after noticing that I was the only girl in the line waiting to enter the dining hall for dinner who was standing in a ray of sunlight. The name stuck so firmly that it was eventually (mercifully) co-opted by my friends, shortened to L.M.P. and emblazoned on my leaver's jersey.

The feeling I overwhelmingly remember from my time at King's was one of being watched and measured. As a scholarship student, I felt obliged to constantly earn my place, so I set out to achieve everything I humanly could while I was at the college. I played the lead in three school productions, became the captain of the Girls' First XI soccer and cricket teams, received full school colours in academics and culture, and half colours in sports. I became the head of my house, the cultural coordinator, a school prefect, a member of the elite scholar's common room, and the leader of the senior debating team. I also studied for my teacher's qualifications in Speech and Drama, toured New Zealand with Sir Howard Morrison and Dame Malvina Major, signed my first record deal and recorded my first album. I was an insufferable overachiever, yet through it all I constantly wondered whether I was good enough.

I also fretted about whether I was pretty enough, thin enough, and cool enough, as many teen girls do. At King's, however, almost every social gradient – gender, race, sexuality, appearance and socio-economical status among them – was marked and judged. Truthfully, I'd never encountered such a hostile environment. Snark, bitchiness, ridiculing and bullying were common in the student body, and I quickly became aware that I didn't fit in. Over my two years there I felt most comfortable when surrounded by those who were also on the fringes – the music geeks, the nerds, the truly nice kids, the quirky kids, and the debaters. Socially I was a drifter, floating from one group to another and missing my Rotorua friends terribly.

When I was on campus, I would escape to the music block to play the piano whenever I could, and took to going for runs around the perimeter of the school grounds, which now makes me think of a caged animal, searching for a way out. I spent as little time at school as was possible for a boarder. From the middle of Year 12, an allowance was made for me to have a car at school (a privilege usually reserved for a small number of prefects) and I left the campus to attend singing lessons two afternoons a week. I'd sit for hours in heavy traffic, but those trips from Otahuhu to my singing lessons in St Mary's Bay kept me sane. I would sometimes stop in at Sylvia Park to buy something for dinner on the way back to school and feel deeply relieved to be out in the real world, outside of the King's bubble, with normal people.

I very nearly left the college at the end of Year 12. I had university entrance, and frankly couldn't wait to leave an environment I'd almost come to regard as a prison. Then I was made the head of my house, and a school prefect. Despite my misgivings about the school, I was passionate about my house, so I chose to stay. I wore a blue jersey and stood out like a sore thumb. I continued to work myself into the ground. As it turned out, I effectively ended up leaving school early anyway to record my first album, taking off before study leave started and returning only to sit exams or attend unavoidable events.

The end couldn't come quickly enough.

When it did, I left with mixed feelings. I have friends from King's still, people who I love and feel deeply grateful to have in my life, but I've certainly never grieved or pined for the college. If anything, I was relieved. I know that there are students who love their time at King's, but it was a terrible fit for a person like me. I'm lucky, in a way, that I learnt the lesson of incompatibility so early in life. I've made a conscious effort to avoid environments like it ever since.

With the power of hindsight, however, I'm forced to conclude that there is some truth to the cliché that what doesn't kill you makes you stronger. King's offered me an insight into an environment I'd never seen before. In a way, I'm thankful. It prepared me well for the backlash I'd later receive as an outspoken young feminist in the public eye. It also gave me a strong sense of just how wide the inequality gap is in New Zealand. While many of the kids I went to primary school with were from families that were just scraping by, my King's friends were jetting off to Europe, Africa, Asia, and the United States for the school holidays. The contrast could not have been more apparent.

When my time at King's ended, I had no time to process the experience. I released my first (eponymous) album on 3 December 2007, and flew out to Hong Kong to perform at the premiere of Hollywood movie *The Golden Compass* a week later. There was no time left to be a kid. I was expected to be an adult, travelling the world at the ripe old age of 18. Over the next few years I'd see more hotel rooms than I can count, and often pass through countries in a matter of hours. For example, although I performed a concert there, I cannot, for the life of me, remember what Antwerp looks like. Other than cloudy. I woke up there on the tour bus one morning and by the time I went to sleep the next night we'd already driven back across the border. I performed 40 shows in 11 different countries on that particular tour, supporting

Britain's Got Talent winner Paul Potts, and I remember it in flashes and snatches. Much of that time of my life is blurry, almost as if it happened to someone else.

Music was my first love. I began playing the piano when I was three years old, started singing when I was eight and quickly became obsessed with all things musical. My childhood dream was to become a professional singer (after I got over my phase of wanting to become a dolphin trainer, that is) and I was one of those rare people for whom a pie-in-the-sky fantasy became a reality. I dedicated most of my childhood and teen years to music, and began performing professionally at 15. I often missed out on parties during weekends because I was performing somewhere, which I actually didn't mind at the time. The allure of the stage was much stronger than the desire to go and get drunk. Looking back, I wish that I'd been a bit more focussed on having a typical teenager social life, if only in the hope that it would've had a taming influence on my wild early twenties, but the stage was my favourite place in the world. It still is. The music industry may have had its ugly way with me over the years, but I'll always love music.

Being a young woman in the music industry, however, can be extremely difficult to navigate. While I'm grateful for the many extraordinary career highlights I experienced and the great people I met, I had been sexually harassed, taken advantage of, and slut-shamed for it by the time I was 20. There was an ill-advised fling with a much older colleague who should've known better, sexual harassment at the hands of other older co-workers, and the jeers and gossip of male colleagues who either insinuated or bluntly insisted to others that I was a whore. It's one thing to be learning about life and love with people your own age at university; it's another thing entirely to find yourself a pawn in a game you don't yet understand properly, dominated by players far more experienced and less scrupulous than you.

My time in the music industry came hard and fast. I performed in Australia, Europe, Asia, and the Middle East, released two top-ten albums and a top-15 EP, and lived in a world few have the chance to see. The moments I spent blinded by the spotlights, staring out into the darkness from centre stage, were blessings. There is nothing like standing behind a microphone and sharing the magic of music with a room filled with people, whether they number in their tens, their hundreds, or their thousands. The music industry, however, is a package deal. The magic and glory come accompanied by steep learning curves, rollercoaster highs and seemingly bottomless lows. If you're not careful, it'll eat you alive. It nearly got the best of me. But that's a story for another chapter.

For better or for worse, each challenge along the way has shaped me into the woman I am today. They've each played their part in the making of the woman.

And what a procedure that is.

It's a process that begins with good intentions, although something seems to go awry along the way. Now that I look back, I can see that a girl is not regarded as a threat. Girls, even when they're strident, can generally be tolerated and humoured by a system that affords them little power.

That's not to say that girls are unimportant, or powerless. They are the opposite. Girls can, and do, stand up for their beliefs, organise, and agitate for change. They sometimes take advantage of their widespread underestimation in the eyes of others and pull off incredible feats. Girls and young women are the main reasons that I became a feminist advocate. They inspire me and give me a purpose, but they are among the most likely to be underestimated and overpowered by a system that wants them to be pretty and compliant. A system, in short, that is hilariously out of date and in desperate need of an upgrade.

Women are seen to be much harder to control. Women cannot be silenced by a teacher. They cannot be sent to the principal's office for speaking out of turn. Women have the power to upset the balance in a drastic way, and they are beginning to do so with ever increasing frequency and ferocity. It is profoundly exciting to watch a growing movement of women beginning to seize the power that is their birth right – born out of generations of oppression and suppressed anger – and deploy it with precision.

I began to truly become a woman in my mid twenties. While each woman's journey is unique to her, my metamorphosis started when I began to say 'no'. No, I will not stifle my passionately held beliefs just to keep the peace. No, I will not starve myself to fit into society's narrow standard of beauty. No, I will not apologise for vehemently disagreeing. No, I will not allow you to touch me when I don't want you to. No, I will not pretend to be anything other than exactly what I am … The difference between being a girl and being a woman is that now no one has the authority to shut me up.

I make my own rules, and set my own parameters. As I've begun to test my limits, I've committed to speaking up even when it scares me, and in doing so, I've slowly taken back my voice.

When I began my music career at the ripe old age of 15, I had a team of men around me telling me what to do and who to be. On one memorable occasion, in London when I was 18 and wide-eyed and trusting, I even had men telling each other who I should be. In front of me. My parents and I had been flown to London by my record label to discuss my second album. I'd been wined, dined, taken sailing on a yacht, whisked away to Salisbury to record demos and all that remained of the trip was a meeting with a hotshot manager who the president of my label had in mind to manage me.

His office was in Soho. My father accompanied me, and I seem to remember getting lost on the way, alighting at the wrong tube station and walking a reasonable distance down Oxford Street before finally finding the right side road. This was in the days just before Google Maps. How the hell did we ever get to where we were meant to be on time before Google Maps? I can't remember. I don't think I managed it often.

Arriving at an unremarkable building, we trooped up the stairs, probably not speaking to each other as a result of the walking uselessly around the centre of London for 45 minutes, and were greeted by the manager, who introduced us to his staff before we sat down to talk. He was the kind of man who filled a room with his presence. A long-time industry veteran, he had lived through the glory days. He was accustomed to success. To an 18-year-old kid from Rotorua, he was more than a little imposing, but I'd been working around and for imposing adults for most of my teens, so I steeled myself to play the game.

He cut through the small talk fairly quickly, and began asking a series of questions about my career and ambitions. What had drawn me to music? How had I come to be signed to an international record label? What were my goals and dreams? I set about answering him, feeling strangely like I was auditioning for a role I wasn't sure I wanted. I was mid-way through a sentence when he raised his hand to me like a traffic cop at a broken intersection, wordlessly silencing me. I hesitated, my mouth hanging open in shock, and watched him turn to my father and engage him in conversation. My time was up. It was time for me to stop talking. He addressed his questions mainly to my father for the rest of the meeting.

It's an experience I've never forgotten. There are many others like that. Another that sticks in my mind is being told that a boardroom discussion was held while I was at school about what my professional name should be – a discussion in which I had no say over my own identity. When they settled on the name 'Elizabeth', it was presented as a done deal. I didn't think much of it at the time, but five years later, when I reverted to the nickname my friends had been calling me by since intermediate school, 'Lizzie', it felt like my identity was finally my own.

Identity is important. The idea of being who you are may have been slapped across a picture of a sunset and posted on someone's Instagram so many times that it seems like a tired truism, but it is the ultimate expression of originality. As a girl, I stood out but wanted to fit in. As a woman, I stand out, I know it, and I don't give a fuck. I have very little time to waste on caring about what other people think of me. If I have any leftover musing time at the end of my long days I'm certainly not going to spend it worrying about whether I meet someone else's arbitrary standards.

As a woman, no one can tell me who I should be. They can try, but equally, I can laugh in their faces. I don't mean to present an image of womanhood as having to be constantly combative, but it is a simple fact of my existence that when I've asserted agency over my own decisions, they have been challenged. Men don't face the same questions. They are not asked, for example, when they are going to have babies, as if it is assumed that they will want to do so. They are not warned about coming across as too 'angry'. They are not penalised for being ambitious. They are not told that they'll change their minds and 'come around eventually'. They are taken at their word. Men make decisions that are respected, even when they're disagreed with. Women make decisions that are assumed to be changeable, should the right circumstances arise.

Enough.

As women, we are not Potential Baby Vessels, and we are sure as hell not Invisible. We are formidable, unique, magnificent beings with the potential to reshape the world in ways we may not even yet be able to fully conceive of. We may start out as products of our experiences, but we also possess the power to transcend them.

One is not made a woman. Rather, one makes a woman of herself.

CHAPTER TWO

Boys don't cry

When I was five years old, the boys at my school would spend their lunchtimes playing 'catch and kiss'. The general gist of the game is pretty self-explanatory, but for the uninitiated, the basic premise was that packs of unruly little boys would sprint around the playground chasing after groups of squealing girls with the intent of capturing one, pinning her down and kissing her. I remember feeling a certain wariness when we were sent out to play, hoping against hope that I wouldn't be the one caught and kissed. The horror. Public humiliation *and* boy germs.

As it turned out, one lunchtime during the first week that I was at school, I was chased by a group of said boys, and fled into a classroom to hide, where I was discovered by a teacher and punished for violating a rule I had not known existed about children not being allowed inside classrooms during break times. I was marched to 'the cross' – a series of Xs painted on the concrete at the edge of the netball courts where the naughty children were forced to sit and contemplate their sins while suffering the curious gazes of their peers – and told to think about what I'd done. I hadn't the foggiest. So I wailed, solidly, in great heaving sobs, until my sentence was served and I was allowed to go. It's fair to say that catch and kiss sunk even lower in my estimation after that.

One of my greatest primary school memories was witnessing a role reversal that upset the catch and kiss league for quite some time. A girl in my year, fed up with being endlessly chased, decided that enough was enough. She charged at the boys like a rocket, pinned one down and smooched him as he rolled around howling in the dirt. Then she got up and marched away. Needless to say, they never bothered her again.

Funnily enough, bullrush had been banned long before I reached the school gates, and tackle rugby was similarly outlawed, but catch and kiss still happened during many a lunchtime. Games in which boisterous kids could hurt each other: bad. Games in which boisterous kids could terrorise and sexually harass each other: meh.

Though catch and kiss could technically go either way, the game was almost always started by the boys, who would barge into the middle of our games, screaming 'catch and kiss!' at the top of their lungs while we scattered. Eventually, they graduated to playing touch rugby at lunchtime and finally left us alone.

Kids' games are generally pretty innocuous, but I struggle to think of a more interesting microcosm of societal conditioning than catch and kiss. When the fun of the game relies on hunting down a member of another sex and violating their personal boundaries without their consent, there are certainly a few thought-provoking social messages in the mix. It should be noted that I never, in all of my primary school years, saw a boy chase after and kiss another boy, nor a girl kiss another girl.

There has been plenty of research that has shown that ideas about gender roles and behaviours begin to have an impact on children even before they get to school. From the segregation of 'girls' toys' and 'boys' toys' in stores to the ridiculous practice of assigning colours to genders, kids grow up absorbing ideas about gender like oxygen. Particularly – in New Zealand at least – boys. One thing is for certain, if you are a boy in New Zealand, you sure as hell better be tough. Because boys don't cry, son.

I'm not sure whether it comes from our settler past, our adoption of the British stiff upper lip, our Māori warrior DNA or a mixture of all of them, but Kiwi men are expected to be staunch. The stereotypical Kiwi guy drinks beer, lives for his mates, cracks jokes in almost every situation, avoids serious discussions like the plague, resorts to violence when provoked, is petrified of having to talk about his feelings, and, it could be argued, has the emotional range of a sledgehammer. There are many great things about Kiwi men, but there is also an undeniable dark side to a culture that views any show of vulnerability or emotional expression as something to be mocked, ignored or discouraged.

Kiwi masculinity can act like a virus. It infects the masses, mutates when under threat, and, if left unchecked, it has the ability to maim and kill. I'll be called misandrist for characterising it in that way, but I mean it compassionately. I have seen many men hurt by the restrictive bounds of masculinity over the years. I've seen it take the life of a friend tortured by the unattainable idea of what he thought he *should* be. His story is not mine to tell, but after witnessing someone spend years struggling to contort themselves into a box they would never fit into, I realised that men are just as locked into destructive and arbitrary gender ideals as women are. Only those ideals tell them that showing any emotion and reaching out for help are signs of weakness, and that violence is the manly way to deal with problems, even when that violence is turned inwards. In the years since his funeral I've found myself wishing that my friend had known that he was loved for exactly who he was. What he saw when he looked in the mirror and what we saw when we spent time with him were markedly different things.

Boys are expected to be strong, dominant and aggressive from the outset. Whether that aggression and dominance is somehow 'natural' is, in my opinion, moot. In early human societies, cannibalism was once common. The fact that we don't go around eating each other anymore seems to demonstrate that nurture is at least as influential as nature. In fact, I'd argue that nurture – the way in which we are raised, the environment we are exposed to – can be exponentially more powerful than nature. Take, for example, the kinds of messages regularly aimed at boys and young men in New Zealand:

'Kia kaha!'
'Don't be a girl.'
'Harden up.'
'Boys don't cry.'

'Be a man.'

'What a sissy.'

'Man up.'

'Grow some balls.'

'What a little bitch.'

'Wimp.'

'Pussy.'

'Sooky-bubba.'

'Fag.'

'Poof.'

'Suck it up.'

'Get over it.'

'Move on.'

'She'll be right.'

'Bros before hoes.'

'Treat 'em mean, keep 'em keen.'

'Real men ride women.'

Showing vulnerability, weakness or any kind of emotion is not really an option if you're a Kiwi man, not unless you want to be accused of being that absolute worst of things – a girl. Or, nearly as bads – gay. Respecting and standing up for women, or calling out male mates that say sexist or homophobic things, are similarly discouraged. Any display of behaviour that doesn't meet the standards of manliness expected in New Zealand society will typically be either ridiculed or forcibly shut down. As Kiwis, we don't traditionally give our boys the tools to navigate their internal emotional landscapes, or to form respectful, meaningful and fulfilling relationships. We instead give them a pair of rugby boots.

The fingerprints of masculinity are as much etched upon catch and kiss as they are on rugby, the game New Zealand collectively adores. Boys grow up idolising professional rugby players, who are lauded for their toughness. If they are fortunate enough to make the First XV at high school, particularly at boys' schools, they will often be treated as heroes by much of both the staff and student bodies.

The rugby player is a staunch man. He puts his body on the line, relying on brute strength, physical fitness and the support of his teammates to 'smash' his opponents. Many of the terms we use to describe rugby are either aggressive by nature, or have taken on violent meanings outside of the game: 'kick', 'tackle', 'maul', 'blood bin', 'sin bin', 'charge down', 'knock on', 'scrum', 'ruck', etc. Rugby is indisputably a rough game.

I say all this as a long-time rugby fan. When I was a child, my father was the business manager for the Bay Of Plenty Steamers. I'd go along to the games and sit on the terraces with a tub of hot chips – a culinary tradition I continue to this day when my anthem duties have been fulfilled (only now I sit in the stands stuffing my face in full hair and make-up while people gawk at the bizarrely overdressed woman who arrived carrying a small suitcase at half time).

Like many New Zealanders, rugby has played a huge role in my life, even though I've never played the game myself. My love of rugby started early. In 1996, I became a fan of the brand new Super 12 team for Waikato/Bay of Plenty, the Chiefs. I went to every home game, wearing my too-big Chiefs jersey with pride, blowing a plastic horn until my lips swelled to twice their normal size. I'd jump around the lounge when they played away games, joining in the familial tradition of pointlessly screaming advice at the screen, willing 'our boys' to win. I stuck with them every year that they bombed out in the play-offs. And there were plenty of those.

I was similarly passionate about the All Blacks – especially Andrew Mehrtens and Jonah Lomu, who were my favourites. Like many Kiwi children, I idolised the men in black.

Rugby is an incredible force in this country. It is woven into our national tapestry as a vital thread of our identity. I've only ever felt such national pride as when I stood beside our team in front of a sell-out crowd at Eden Park to sing the New Zealand national anthem at the semi-final of the 2011 World Cup on one other occasion – the night New Zealand legalised marriage equality. For many of us, me included, rugby is sacred, which makes any discussion around rugby culture fraught.

It also makes those conversations all the more important. When my beloved Chiefs hit the headlines for all the wrong reasons in 2016, my heart sank. As a female fan who'd supported the side for 20 years, I felt betrayed that my team would hire a stripper, using the objectification of women as some kind of consolation prize to mark the end of a lacklustre season. When Scarlette, the dancer engaged by the Chiefs, went public with allegations of inappropriate behaviour and non-consensual touching, I was appalled. The allegations themselves were horrific, and the reactions they inspired in the public narrative ('she's a stripper, what does she expect?') were similarly bad.

Whether you choose to believe Scarlette or not – and make no mistake, that decision is intrinsically tied to centuries of slut-shaming, misogyny and protecting powerful men at the expense of vulnerable women – the blunt truth is that a group of idolised men gathered together to leer at a woman for fun. Men who were role models for thousands of kids – boys *and* girls. Men who'd done the same the year prior – an occasion that was also called into question when a second dancer, Laura, came forward to make allegations similar to Scarlette's. At the very least, what these events demonstrated was that the culture within the Chiefs allowed for women to be viewed as sexual objects – a phenomenon that is hardly rare in exclusively masculine spaces.

So-called 'locker-room talk' and behaviours are a part of masculine bonding for reasons that I struggle to understand. There is social capital to be earned in those spaces from demeaning and objectifying women. When there are only men in the room, women can quickly become pawns in a macho game of one-upmanship, even when the men doing the denigrating have sisters, mothers, girlfriends, or wives who they would defend to the death. When a woman has no relation to a man, and is simply a kind of caricature or means to an end, she is easily dehumanised. Many of the men who have made sexist comments would bristle at the suggestion that they are in any way misogynistic. They'll point to their wives or their daughters and suggest that they couldn't possibly be sexist because there are women in their lives who love them. Many of them, despite their lewd comments and actions, do actually have respect for the women they know. So why do they partake in misogynistic rituals with their mates? Are the women outside of their immediate circles somehow different to the women they love? When a man has no emotional involvement with a woman, does that somehow make her fair game?

These are questions that I can't answer, but they must be asked. It shouldn't just be accepted mindlessly that 'boys will be boys'. What does that even mean? When 'boys being boys' results in demeaning behaviour towards women, their actions should be put under the microscope. There are other hard questions that must be posed. Why does male bonding so easily turn into denigration of women, whether it's in the locker room or a private Facebook group? What is it about masculine culture that encourages the objectification of women?

I'm not saying that masculine behaviours are inherently bad, nor am I suggesting that all men are brutish idiots who have no feelings. Though masculinity and being a man seem to be intrinsically tied together, they become easily separable when you ask who decided that a certain trait was a 'masculine' one in the first place. How, for example, did strength and toughness become masculine traits when it is women who are forced to endure the greatest physical pain imaginable during childbirth? Likewise, friendship (or, in its hyper-masculinised forms, 'mateship' or 'brotherhood') is often seen as a masculine behaviour – reinforced by rugby captains talking in grunts and gasps at the end of the game about 'the boys' and 'the brothers' – despite the fact that women are just as likely to form deep and long-lasting platonic bonds with other women. Only when women talk about their 'sisters', they're either shrieking feminist banshees hell-bent on establishing a matriarchy, or they're gossiping girls tittering about fashion and celebrities.

The categories and stereotypes established by masculine/feminine paradigm are not rooted in any biological proof – in fact, recent research into neuroplasticity has shown that only six per cent of brains (from a sample of 1403 brains studied) have rigidly 'male' or 'female' structural profiles, or an even mix of the two[1]. Most of our brains are instead a mish-mash mixture of male and female brain characteristics that may lean to one side or the other. Basically, whether you're biologically male or female has very little to do with how your brain is structured. As the researchers reported, 'we cannot predict the particular array of "male/female" brain characteristics of an individual' by their sex.

When even scientists can't tell a person's sex from their brain structures, gender begins to look more and more farcical. Both masculinity and femininity are arbitrary constructions. They are fusty old rulebooks, authored by such entities as the Catholic Church. They are easy ways to categorise human beings who are in reality far too complex and nuanced to fit neatly into two 'opposite' groups. It should come as no surprise that they're creaking and cracking in a colourful and multi-dimensional modern world.

Counter-intuitive though it may sound, masculinity is not the exclusive domain of men. Stereotypically 'masculine' behaviours are exhibited by a number of women, while 'feminine' traits are demonstrated by a number of men. The insistence on attributing certain behaviours to a particular gender creates expectations of how individuals should act, and what yardsticks they should be judged against by society. Radical though it may seem, femininity and masculinity don't actually exist. They are made-up ideas that place one gender in the dominant role and one in the submissive. The truth is that human beings exist along a spectrum that includes more gender identities, traits and behaviours than I could possibly name.

The idea that gender ideals are arbitrary can be deeply threatening to some people, however. Particularly the staunchest proponents of masculine culture, which is why recent years have seen a surge in interest in the so-called 'men's rights movement'. For 'men's rights activists', 'neo-masculinists', 'meninists' and the like, a world in which men are not automatically dominant over women is an enormously unsettling idea. Any discussion that casts masculinity in a negative light is seen as 'demonising' men, while any call for the advancement of women is part of 'the feminazi plot'. For these men, their idea of masculinity doesn't allow for equality with women. Being equal with women, to them, means a downgrading of their status as men. Or at least that's what I assume they mean when they go around the internet calling people 'cucks'. Sometimes it is difficult to keep up with their made-up words.

While masculinity isn't necessarily negative in and of itself, when taken to the extreme it can certainly become toxic. When strength, aggression, dominance and competition are the ideals boys are encouraged to emulate, whether they have 'natural' or 'genetic' foundations or not, they are the pillars that they will subconsciously fall back on.

When we make sexist jokes around our boys, minimise disrespectful behaviour, objectify women, turn a blind eye to the kinds of hardcore pornography many of our boys are accessing, or perpetuate the idea that women are somehow intrinsically submissive and open to domination, we create an environment where catch and kiss can morph into something much more dangerous.

The problem with the 'boys will be boys' logic is that you can equally apply the same theory to this phrase: 'rapists will be rapists'. By suggesting that boys and men are doomed to act in certain undesirable ways we are both selling them short and setting an alarmingly low bar for young men to aspire to. Call me idealistic, but I want to live in a world where boys will be decent human beings with a sense of compassion and respect for others.

I can hear the cries of 'NOT ALL MEN!' reverberating around my brain as I write this – a qualifier that should, to my mind, be obvious – but my own experiences, and those of the many thousands of Kiwi women represented in some of our most embarrassing national statistics, tell me clearly that we have issues with masculinity in this country. I don't think that we can be surprised any longer when sexist scandals hit the national and international media. It's time for us to move past reactions of shock and disbelief, and to ask serious questions about the role that masculinity plays in our society. We need only look at the Chiefs, Tony Veitch, Paul

Henry, the Roast Busters and Wellington College to see what happens when masculinity goes wrong. We have problems that are taking on a whole new life in the digital age, coupling with good old-fashioned misogyny and creating a clusterfuck of toxic ideas about what it is to be a man. We tiptoe around discussing toxic masculinity, looking for other excuses and explanations, when the elephant in the room is quite likely the cause of the carnage around us. We'd rather not talk about it, thanks. Because talking about it would require us to examine our homegrown 'bloke culture', and doing that would cause some blokes to feel deeply uncomfortable.

Talking about it would also set us on a trail that winds perilously close to examining the role sport might play. To be clear, these issues aren't the sole responsibility of rugby, or any other sport. They are the responsibility of society as a whole. One of the most difficult self-fulfilling prophecies of masculinity, however, is that 'manly men' don't traditionally like to be 'nagged' by women. Women can talk until we're blue in the face and we'll simply be muted in the brains of those who we most need to reach, like the Briscoes lady on mute, voicelessly smizing and gesticulating from the screen. As frustrating as it may be, some men only really listen to men. Which is why sports like rugby play such a vital role in this conversation. As the heroic Sir John Kirwan has proven through his life-saving work on mental health, it takes a seriously manly dude to be able to not only display vulnerability, but to be respected for it. It takes great courage to step outside of the bounds of acceptable masculine behaviour to shine a light on the elements of masculine culture that are causing harm.

It's time that we neutralised the virus – inoculated ourselves against it and committed to studying it in a way that would allow us to understand it better. There is no problem with boys being strong, brave, tough and confident. There is a huge problem with boys not knowing how to be anything else.

CHAPTER THREE

Sugar and spice and all things nice

Once upon a time, in a faraway land, there was a sweet, young, pretty, porcelain-skinned, able-bodied, skinny, heterosexual, cisgender princess. She was born to a loving and benevolent father and a mother who could only possibly become more saintly if she snuffed it – which she promptly did.

Not long after the hallowed Queen's death, the King was taken in by a wicked, ugly, unwomanly, cunning shrew; or, depending on the particular version of the story, a vain, self-obsessed femme fatale. The poor man, almost certainly bewitched by the darkest of magic (or more likely a potent mix of testosterone, dopamine and oxytocin), became besotted with this woman of ill repute and tragically married her. (Funny, isn't it, how men who make bad marital decisions have been 'bewitched' or 'conned', while women who marry the wrong men 'should've known better'.)

The King's new wife was wildly jealous of her stepdaughter, resenting her youth and beauty. From the day she arrived on the scene, the malicious woman set to making the Princess' life a misery; forcing her to scour pots and pans, sweep the floor, cook, clean and wait upon the household (or, you know, do the kinds of things that most non-aristocratic women have had to do for centuries) and depriving her of her usual important daily engagements, like frolicking with cute animals, playing the lute, and settling down in the parlour for a spot of embroidery.

Somewhere along the line, the King died (no doubt so the audience could be sure that he was not in any way responsible for the cruelty the Princess suffered at the hands of *that evil woman*) and so our poor princess was confined to the living hell of domestic drudgery (whimpering piteously whilst not doing a single thing to save herself) until, depending on the tale in question, a. her envious stepmother sent her into the woods to be killed or b. suddenly a young prince materialised out of nowhere (almost as if he'd typed 'nearest pretty princess waiting to be rescued' into Google).

The arrival of alternatively 1. a young, strong, and handsome prince, or 2. the news that her stepdaughter was still alive and kicking – and yes, still the fairest in the land – was not part of the evil stepmother's master plan, so she set out to do everything in her power to royally screw our sweet damsel over. (And thus create the obligatory danger/conflict/obstacle that the Princess needed a man to help her to overcome.)

At this stage in our story, things got rather out of hand. I won't go into great detail, but let's just say that our damsel found herself in quite some distress. Luckily, however, the brave Prince was able to sweep in at exactly the right moment to rescue our fair maiden, so they celebrated with a quickie wedding, rode off into the sunset and lived happily ever after.

Because of course the best way to recover from being the target of an assassination plot, or years of child labour, is to get married to someone you barely know. Especially when you're a teenager (Cinderella was 19, while Snow White was 14). As long as it involves a pretty dress and a tiara, what more could a girl want?

And we read this shit to our children.

Fairy tales have a lot to answer for. As a child, I adored them. I had an actual (cardboard) treasure chest full of *The Little Mermaid* books, *Beauty and the Beast* on VCR (I'm old), the soundtrack to *Pocahontas* on tape (again, old) and various other bits of merchandise from the Disney films of the late 80s/early 90s. Like legions of girls who came before me, I thought princesses were pretty cool. *Beauty and the Beast*'s Belle was my favourite – that beautiful, clever, spirited victim of Stockholm Syndrome. I sympathised with the poor, misunderstood Beast (conveniently glossing over the fact that he imprisoned Belle against her will and forced her to remain separated from her family), and felt elated when they fell in love. It's extraordinary how early in life we are presented with the narrative that men who act like monsters should be given the benefit of the doubt. And that damaged men can be saved by the selflessness of good women. And we wonder why society has until very recently bent over backwards to absolve and redeem men accused of sexual misconduct.

* * *

From the ancient original stories to Disney's modern-day princess empire (which brings in billions every year), generations of children have grown up listening to fairy tales. Tales of heterosexual love overcoming potentially fatal barriers to result in the ideal nuclear family have been influencing young girls particularly for centuries. While Disney seems to have turned over a new feminist [lite] leaf in recent times, with films like *Moana, Frozen* and *Brave*, it's hard to know where to begin in the unravelling of centuries of folklore. There's the fact that most of the stories hinge on hysterical female rage and jealousy as a major plot device, from the affronted Maleficent, who turns herself into a fearsome dragon to prevent the rescue of Briar Rose, to the evil queen who first orders the slaughter of Snow White, then, when that doesn't work, condemns her to an enchanted sleep breakable only by 'true love's first kiss' because she desperately fears the day when she will no longer be 'the fairest of them all'. According to fairy tales, there is no force more fucking terrifying than a jealous witch.

Then there's the idea that a single woman is an aberration. Think about it. If there's one thing almost all evil fairy tale characters have in common it is that they're husbandless or widowed. If there's one thing almost all fairy tale princesses have in common it's that they cannot live happily ever after without a man by their side. It wasn't until 2012 that Disney created a princess whose goal in life wasn't solely to become a bride. Long live Merida.

The trope that most needs to die, however, is that of the damsel in distress. As brutal as it sounds, we need to exorcise her like the demon she is. If you were under the impression that the patriarchy wouldn't be caught dead wearing a princess dress, just take a look at Snow White. Behind that docile smile is a perfect patriarchal checklist of all of the things a woman 'should' be: young, beautiful, slim, adept at cooking and cleaning, caring, sweet, mild, innocent, demure, and requiring the protection of men (even if they are smaller than she is) so that they feel needed and masculine. In short, not the kind of bird who'd burn her corset.

The damsel in distress is the perpetual victim – maltreated and oppressed, and then saved by men who she in return dotes upon. She is a frenemy to young girls, sending them the message that they will never be strong enough to save themselves. She's also no friend of young boys, filling their heads with rigid ideas of what girls and women are like and how they should be treated. The damsel in distress may be hundreds of years old, but she remains a powerfully influential figure in society.

Despite their age, fairy tales are like the stubbornly affixed shagpile carpet that some idiot glued to the floor of our society. We may have ditched the corsets and tiaras, but 'happily ever after' isn't going anywhere in a hurry. Nor is the idea that girls are made of 'sugar and spice and all things nice.' The narratives and ideas found in fairy tales are in many of our modern-day stories. Take *The Bachelor*, for example. Behind the manufactured melodrama and constant tinkling of chimes is a bizarre modern version of competitive *Cinderella*. Only with 21 ugly stepsisters instead of two.

In which it is somehow *worse* to be single than to date a man who is publicly dating 21 other women on national television. Because happily ever after.

And woe betide any woman who is suspected of the heinous crime of not-being-there-for-the-right-reason. I'm not sure that any reason to go on *The Bachelor* could reasonably be judged as 'right', but of course every *Bachelor* contestant worth her salt is supposed to say that she's there for 'true love'. When I first forced myself to watch *The Bachelor* (the things I do to research for columns) I was astounded by how often contestants made reference to fairy tales. More than a few contestants were there to meet their 'prince' – and seemingly thrilled to live in a modern-day harem while he decided who was the fairest of them all.

It sounds like my idea of hell, but I can understand, from a theoretical standpoint at least, why women would sign up to be a part of it. There is no widely known version of happily ever after that features a single woman strutting into the sunset, hair blowing in the wind, living life to the fullest and kicking ass every step of the way. The only ever after that we can conceive of for single women involves buckets of wine, a house filled with cats and an extensive collection of vibrators.

To be honest, given the choice between televised competitive *Cinderella* and a wine, cats and vibrator combo, I know which I'd choose.

The apparent horror of the single-ever-after situation is also reinforced in Hollywood romantic comedies. Sandra Bullock, for example, has played more 'difficult' single ladies than I can count. In *The Proposal, Miss Congeniality* and *Two Weeks Notice*, Bullock's characters (Margaret Tate, Gracie Hart and Lucy Kelson respectively) are, in essence, rescued from themselves by men. All three are passionate women, with goals, aspirations, careers, and, as the films are quick to point out, not much else. They are the difficult and opinionated women; the shrews who have yet to be tamed. Yet their achievements are only the background for the main event – the eventual kiss with a man who thought they were unattractive before unexpectedly spending a significant amount of time with them and finding that they were actually not as bad as first thought.

While some recent additions to the genre have begun to subvert established conventions, in the vast majority of romantic comedies, the fairy tale narrative is replicated with a few modern additions. The plot generally revolves around two white, straight, attractive, cisgender, able-bodied characters who have to overcome a series of obstacles (her dedication to her career, another woman, another man, different social backgrounds, etc.) in order to live happily ever after. Love, the romantic comedy tells us, will conquer all. Love is all that matters. Love is all you need. The single girl in the romcom is simply the girl who has yet to meet her prince. What she's doing with her life while she waits for him is just filling in time. For my generation of women particularly, these are the stories that we grew up hearing.

Even the few female characters in pop culture that are famed for being single – Carrie Bradshaw, Bridget Jones, and

Ally McBeal are the ones that first spring to mind – are often preoccupied with changing their relationship status. Carrie provides a particularly memorable illustration of the lengths some women will go to in the quest to find a man. It's not until she breaks out in hives after trying on a hideous 80s wedding dress that she finally begins to acknowledge that there's something wrong with her relationship. Even then – after having an allergic reaction to the idea of marrying Aidan – she blames herself: 'It's not him, it's me. I'm missing the bride gene.'

I spent much of my early twenties head-over-heels in love with Carrie and her friends – strangely, as the series finished in 2004, when I was 15. I saw the much-maligned film first, loved it, then bought the box set of DVDs on a whim a few months later. I can't tell you how many times I've watched the whole thing from start to finish. Too many to count. As a piece of television, *Sex and the City* was revolutionary, revelationary and problematic. As much as it is criticised now, over 20 years since its debut, it was one of the first shows to tell women's stories unashamedly – even if those stories represented only an extremely narrow stratum of society. For all its failings, it smashed taboos, embraced female characters that eschewed any kind of good/bad dichotomy, and made us laugh. I don't think I would've bought my first vibrator, for example, if the women of *SATC* hadn't talked about masturbation not just frankly and unapologetically, but enthusiastically. I would've fretted about the number of people I'd slept with for a lot longer than I did if I hadn't seen four single 30 to 40-something women unashamedly having sex with whomever they wanted, whenever they wanted, for whatever reason. In some ways, *Sex and the City* was a late 90s/ early 00s fairy tale that wasn't quite self-aware enough to be a deconstruction of the age-old genre. While the women of *SATC* all lived their own interesting lives, they too – or at least Carrie and Charlotte – were, to varying degrees, obsessed with finding their happily ever afters.

Carrie, Samantha, Miranda and Charlotte felt like friends-of-friends. They were recognisable and familiar, likely because they were – as much as it pains me to admit it – archetypes. These were not the women that you were supposed to look up to. These were women who made terrible decisions, acted badly, said the wrong thing and yet still made us laugh. Yes, there were about a thousand problems with the series – the lack of any significant characters of colour and the objectification of black men when they were included in the storyline, the way in which Carrie could afford to live a fabulous life on a columnist's income (speaking from experience, that bit's a massive con), Carrie's disempowerment when it came to the men in her life, her infidelity, Charlotte …

Ironically, one of the main problems of *Sex and the City* is one Miranda identified during an early episode. 'How does it happen that four such smart women have nothing to talk about but boyfriends?' she asks during 'Take Me Out to the Ball Game' in Season Two. The characters' obsession with finding a man – or in Samantha's case, men – wasn't particularly surprising, however. A manless woman is something that we still haven't come to terms with. A bachelor can quite happily go about his life without needing a woman to validate it, but a 'spinster' needs a man to authenticate her existence – and to rid her of that hilariously dated label. When all of the stories you grow up with end in coupledom, being a single woman can be a difficult path to walk. Even, apparently, in Manolo Blahniks.

I know I've certainly felt pressured to throw off my spinsterhood – a feeling that has only intensified over time. I wasn't always a perpetual spinster. Being a person of extremes, I spent most of my teens entangled in various relationships, then most of my twenties in self-chosen solitude. Over the past decade, however, whenever I've entered into a relationship, I've often found myself longing to be single again. When I finally decided to be honest with myself, I realised that most of the short-lived dalliances I'd entered into had been motivated by internalised social expectations.

Throughout my twenties, I tried to squeeze myself into relationships that were blatantly wrong because I knew that I was supposed to want to be coupled up. There are a few memorable disasters. When I was younger, I had many problematic ideas about relationships, which can best be summed up by something I'd said to a group of close friends under the influence of three too many glasses of wine. 'Sometimes a woman just wants a caveman to drag her back to his cave by the hair,' I'd said. It was probably something I'd read in *Cosmopolitan*. I probably thought it marked me as the kind of woman that men really wanted. One who was quite happy to be dominated and humiliated. (And, now I think about it in hindsight, possibly raped? Where was I going with that statement? What was I thinking?)

The man I was dating was my caveman in shining armour. While there was no hair-dragging, there were other shows of dominance. Some that I loved, and others that made me feel uncomfortable. About a month in, that discomfort started to outweigh the attraction. In the background of our relationship, I was trying to make sense of an incident of sexual abuse that had happened to me a few months before I'd met him. There was a lot going on in my life, and I was struggling to cope, so I started to distance myself.

He didn't like it.

One night, after an evening of partying, I ended up a drunk and tearful mess, finally confessing the sexual abuse to close friends. The man I was dating wanted to come around. He showed up at the gate and my friend told him I was not in any state to see him. He was furious. He called me the next day and told me that he was coming to my house and that we would talk. It wasn't phrased as a question. It was phrased as a statement of fact. I was not thrilled with this idea, and I knew that there was no way that I would be letting him into my house, so we ended up sitting in his car in the rain.

When I stepped into the car he interrogated me, then he lectured me. How rude I was to treat him in such a way. How inconsiderate. Then he released me, as if to send me inside to think about what I had done.

I felt like I was three feet tall.

I continued to date him for another month.

A few months later, cured of my caveman obsession, I'd embarked on a summer romance with a sweet, creative man who I quite liked. You could call him my manic pixie dream boy. He had the kind of eyes you could get lost in, and had perfected the art of looking simultaneously deep in thought, troubled, and heartstoppingly handsome. We'd been dating for a month or so, after which the speed and strength of his feelings were starting to make me feel unnerved. Eventually, he wrote me a long, feverish poem that went on for several pages and was probably the last straw. I ended it. Gently. I wasn't ready for anything serious, I told him, quite truthfully. I didn't mention the poem.

He showed up outside my house and refused to leave until I spoke to him. I had nothing to say. He sat in his car for several hours, making sure I could see him through the window, but never actually stepping foot on the property, making it impractical to call the police. He didn't leave until I called a male friend, who drove to my house to keep me company.

I look back on those relationships (and others) and shake my head. For someone who is otherwise so confident and outspoken, I excused a lot of bad behaviour and contorted myself into something I wasn't with alarming regularly in my personal life. I felt societal pressure keenly. My friends had slowly entered into serious relationships, while I remained single. My extended family had started asking me about my love life. I stood out from the crowd, bucking the trend. I began to feel a bit like a misfit. So, in a show of breath-taking rationality (I jest) and, I fully admit, selfishness, I entered into relationships with men that I quickly realised I had little interest in – sexual or otherwise – just for the sake of having a partner. Then I wondered why I felt trapped and miserable. *Cinderella*, *Snow White* and *The Little Mermaid* don't prepare you for the possibility that you might find that Prince Charming is boring or needy or an arrogant fuckwit.

The narratives I grew up with – in fairy tales, books, films, on television and in the media – did very little to prepare me for the fact that I genuinely enjoy being single. They were also woefully inept at readying me for the realisation that I was equally interested in both Prince and Princess Charming. When it turns out that your fate might not result in a man, a picket fence and 1.87 children, a certain amount of recalibration is required. Which is not to say that there is anything wrong with love – straight, gay or otherwise. If I were to find myself in a relationship, I would of course hope it was one built on 'true love' (even feminazi bitches have hearts). I will say, though, that being in a relationship without love – whether of the happily ever after variety or the non-sensationalised mere mortal version – is, in my experience, excruciatingly hard work. Which is why women feeling pressured to conform or 'settle' causes me such concern. Over the years I've known many women who have thrown themselves into unsatisfying relationships simply to avoid the terror of being alone. Or, in my case, to live up to societal expectations. I've learnt the hard way what a terrible idea that is. It's better to be single than to be in a relationship with someone who doesn't flick your switch, so to speak. Or, if you're just looking for companionship, to at least be open with yourself about it, rather than hoping that an unsatisfying relationship will eventually turn out to be the kind of magical love you once dreamed of. That's the problem with fairy tales. They tell us that love will conquer all obstacles. Then we grow up and realise that they're not real.

There's nothing wrong with desiring human connection, however. Most human beings are social animals. As people, we undeniably need human contact in our lives, but it doesn't necessarily have to be in the form of an intimate partner. Our social lives can be rich, satisfying and filled with love without revolving entirely around a significant other. Contrary to what Maleficent and Ursula may have led you to believe, you're not suddenly going to turn into a dragon or a be-tentacled sea demon if you spend a few years on your own. In fact, it's astounding what you learn about yourself when you spend time being single. I'd wholeheartedly recommend it.

While you could argue that fairy tales are intended to be cautionary tales, warning of the monstrous things that single women become, I wonder whether Maleficent, Ursula, Lady Tremaine et al. have the better lot in life. They are unencumbered, in control of their own destinies, and – at least in the case of Maleficent and Ursula – have way better costumes. They are allowed to be complicated and flawed beings, and they are taken seriously. No one would dare pat a villainess on the head – not if they wanted to live to tell the tale.

When women who have been expected to be sweet, pliable princesses turn around and become capable, intelligent and independent women, the tendency to label them witches, though regrettable, is perhaps understandable. While the fairy tale narratives that still permeate our society today encourage little girls to identify with princesses, I hope that at least some of them will try to understand the witches and the villainesses – or at least to glean the idea that there are other paths and possibilities. Not every little girl is made of sugar and spice and all things nice – and in my humble opinion, witches are much cooler than princesses anyway.

It will likely come as little surprise that Hermione Granger from the *Harry Potter* books was (and still is) my favourite role model. Hermione came into my life at a time when I needed her most – when I was nine and bossy and beginning to stand out. She was the anti-princess. In her I'd finally found a character I could look up to.

Hermione is a patron saint of bright and bold girls. Her true magic lies in the way she makes smart girls feel. In my experience, she may not have made it *cool* to be brainy, per se, but she made it okay to be intelligent, passionate and a bit stroppy. Which was a profound relief. As I had about as much chance of ceasing to be those things as I did sprouting a tail.

Characters like Hermione Granger, George Kirrin of *The Famous Five* books, Katniss Everdeen of *The Hunger Games* trilogy, Jessica Jones of the same-titled TV series, (and the many other bold heroines that are emerging as our society becomes more aware that girls and women deserve to be the protagonists of stories that don't just revolve around finding a man to validate them) have more in common with Maleficent et al. than they do with Snow White and Sleeping Beauty. They are their own women, imperfect and unapologetic. The point of their existences is more than to become a wife and a mother (although they may well go on to become one or both). They know the difference between needing and wanting a relationship. They get to be funny and sassy and a bit odd, and no one cares if their hair isn't perfectly coiffed. They are the antidote to Princess Syndrome. We need more of them. Because our lives are not fairy tales. We are the protagonists of our own stories, free to do as we like and we certainly don't need anyone to 'complete' us. We owe it to ourselves to write our own plotlines, rather than trying to squeeze ourselves into princess-sized holes.

Not every story has to end with a prince, a white steed and a sunset.

And who knows what happens after ever after anyway?

CHAPTER FOUR

Herstory

History hasn't been kind to women, which is perhaps unsurprising, given that the story of humankind has generally been dominated, written, revised, edited, and published by men. He, the collective male scholar/writer/publisher who has been tasked with recording human progress for the last, well, forever, has ensured that man has been the protagonist of his story, while women have often been little more than a footnote. Mansplaining may be relatively new to our vernacular, but it has existed for millennia. The fact that up until very recently the official record-keepers of our lived experiences were almost exclusively male – and almost exclusively white – presents a conundrum closely related to the old adage that the victorious set the rules. When it is overwhelmingly white men who determine what a society remembers and what it forgets, what's to prevent a little selective amnesia?

One fact that cannot be objectively denied is that women have been treated in a manner ranging from unfairly to appallingly for an alarmingly long time. And it's not over yet. While it's easy to dismiss examples of ill-treatment from hundreds of years ago – like, for example, the way that women were viewed by society and the law as possessions; owned first by their fathers and then by their husbands – there is plenty of horrific shit that has happened well within living memory. Marital rape was legal in New Zealand until 1985. Until 1995, protection orders sought by women escaping domestic violence were often refused by judges because they were seen to present a barrier to reconciliation between partners[1]. In 2011, a 13-year-old girl reporting a sexual assault was asked by a police officer what she was wearing[2]. In 2016, a woman was asked in a New Zealand court what she'd meant when she said 'no'. In 2017, the man who was accused (and later acquitted, during his second trial) of raping her went on to become a Black Cap[3]. Also in 2017, the Court of Appeal handed down a judgment that suggested that the Family Court had been misinterpreting domestic violence law for years[4]. When it comes to the treatment of women, it seems that history all too often bleeds into the present day.

History – his story (and yes, mansplainers, I know that the root of the word, 'historia', has nothing to do with the possessive 'his') – has a tendency to gloss over the prickly parts (of which there are many), but just because something is uncomfortable doesn't mean that it should be minimised or forgotten. The idea that we should simply 'move on' and 'forget about the past' has, however, gained traction in recent years, often when people are encouraged to consider uncomfortable recollections. A classic Kiwi example is provided by Waitangi Day. 'Move on!' Māori are told. 'Stop living in the past!' Ironically, those who are most vocal in their rejections of the importance of Treaty history are often those who claim that Anzac Day is our true national day. The fact that the signing of the Treaty of Waitangi and the beginning of the First World War happened less than a century apart and both over a century ago seems to be entirely lost on them. Māori remembering 1840, and the nearly two centuries afterwards in which the Treaty was repeatedly violated, are accused of stealing unacceptable backwards glances while people remembering the events of 1914–1918 are good patriotic citizens commemorating a vital part of our history. It's funny how the story changes, depending on your point of view. Some histories are still seen to be more important than others – particularly those that tell tales of victorious wars on faraway shores. Likewise, histories in which men feature prominently are taught and retaught endlessly, but while most people will have at least a cursory knowledge of the World Wars, the Great Depression, imperialism, and perhaps a revolution or two, ask your average person on the street about the history of the women's movement and you'll likely be met with blank faces. How many Kiwis could tell you off the top of their heads which year women's suffrage was achieved? How many could tell you the date of Suffrage Day or the story behind exactly how women came to be able to vote in New Zealand? History has a lot to answer for, if you are a person who is not a cisgender white man. It's time that we held it to account.

Alongside history, there has been another narrative quietly looking on and analysing events from an entirely different perspective. Herstory may not be recognised by the dictionary, she may be marked with an angry red line when you type her name, but she exists. She presents an alternative account, relayed not from the vantage point of a powerful man, but of a curious woman, and she's not afraid to disagree.

In my humble opinion, at this point enough has been written about history to last us at least another hundred years. It's herstory that I want to know more about.

Aotearoa New Zealand's herstory is particularly interesting. For a start, and as I've already alluded to, we were the first women in the world to win the right to vote. I've seen many historical accounts suggesting that women were 'given' the vote, as if the men in Parliament just woke up one day and collectively decided that it was time to let the little ladies have a say, as long as they remembered that their husbands knew best and made sure that they still had a meal on the table for their families at the end of the day. Hilarious. No source of power was ever 'given' to women by men without struggle.

When I first heard the story of New Zealand women's suffrage as a child, I wondered why they called it something that sounded so much like 'suffering'. As a grown woman I now think that the name is blisteringly apt. There are very few women's rights campaigners who haven't suffered in some way as a result of their work, and suffragists carried a particularly heavy load.

Our foremothers weren't 'given' the vote, they fought relentlessly for it, presenting petition after petition to Parliament, holding rallies, sending slews of telegrams, and refusing to give up after a series of defeats. Their eventual victory, which we today celebrate as a symbol of our national progressiveness, hinged on the desire of two male members of the now-defunct 'upper legislative chamber' to embarrass Premier Richard Seddon. The two representatives changed their votes from opposition to support of enfranchising women out of spite[5]. We got the vote because of one-upmanship. The majority of the men in charge may not have had the foresight to see women as eventual equals, but they did have good old male pride and combativeness. Thankfully it worked in the suffragists' favour.

The strength and determination of Kiwi women existed long before the suffrage campaigns of the late 1800s, however. As a nation of women, we are descended from wāhine toa on one side and settler women on the other. We've been tough as nails for generations – we've had to be in order to survive. It also takes a certain kind of toughness to embark on the journey of learning about our past, acknowledging the wrongs committed just a few generations ago and understanding the ways in which they have reverberated down the years.

Whenever I read about our colonial history, I feel faintly sick. My stomach becomes tense and I find that my eyebrows have creased and furrowed without my consciousness of their little act of defiance. It is hard to put into words the emotions that the stories of our colonial beginnings raise within me. It is clear to me that modern-day New Zealand functions on the back of a widespread ignorance about our past, and I say that without occupying any position of superiority. That ignorance is mine too. Until Parliament acknowledges the education system's particular and vital responsibility in the construction of our nationhood, and moves to ensure that every Kiwi student has a proficient understanding both of te reo Māori – one of our official languages – and the uncensored history and herstory of Aotearoa, that ignorance will be the birth right of the vast majority of New Zealanders.

It is no accident that some Kiwi stories are widely known while others are not. Such a situation has come to pass as a result of generations of Pākehā prioritising their own narratives at the expense of Māori stories and, often, the truth. How widely known is it that 1600 armed men invaded the peaceful settlement of Parihaka at the behest of the New Zealand Government, imprisoning its leaders without trial, destroying crops and buildings and raping the women left behind? How many people know about the history of Bastion Point? The New Zealand Wars? The Land Hīkoi?

That racism still exists in New Zealand today – and if you don't think it does, I encourage you to take the time to actually speak to Māori, earn their respect, and listen closely to the stories they have to tell – is a direct consequence of the ignorance of New Zealanders about our past. There are many stories that are deeply uncomfortable to learn about, but acknowledging them is the cruel gift we as a nation must give ourselves in order to be able to move forward with kindness, mutual respect and understanding.

Our past belongs to all of us, and it holds the answers to the accusatory 'why?' that has echoed down the decades. Why are Māori disproportionately represented in prison statistics? Why do Māori die younger than Pākehā? Why do Māori protest on

Waitangi Day? Why are Māori disproportionately impoverished? Why are Māori angry? Why can't they just 'move on'? The answers are all there, if those who posed the questions weren't too lazy – or afraid – to seek them.

The herstory of women in New Zealand is also inextricably tied to the history of colonisation. You cannot simply learn the settlers' version of events and claim to understand New Zealand's past. Nor would you want to. As a nation, we have so many fascinating stories to tell, many of which you likely won't have learnt about at school. It would be fair to say, for example, that most New Zealanders don't know much about the herstory of Māori women, which is a great shame, particularly for anyone interested in women's rights. In pre-colonial times, Māori women held a great deal more power in their communities than their British counterparts did in theirs. Among the signatures on te Tiriti o Waitangi there are the marks of a handful of high-ranking Māori women, who signed on behalf of their people. One such woman, the daughter of Te Pehi of Ngāti Toa, was prevented by Major Thomas Banbury from signing the treaty, a move that prompted outrage among other Māori women[6]. Thirteen women did sign[7], however, demonstrating the high status some Māori women commanded within Te Ao Māori (the Māori world). As the late, great Michael King explained:

> *Both sexes could inherit rangatira status, mana and tapu from male and female antecedents, and among some tribes, such as those on the East Coast of the North Island, women were visible among the front ranks as tribal and community leaders*[8].

Under the traditional Māori system of communal land ownership, some Māori women also had ownership rights in tribal land. The idea that women could possess such power and hold such rights would've been unimaginable in British society, perhaps with the exception of aristocratic widows and Queen Victoria.

Female rangatira (chiefs) were reasonably rare, however, and some women were treated harshly by their iwi, especially if they were 'low-born'[9]. The skills and special roles of women were, however, enshrined in Māori tikanga (customs): the welcome karanga (calls) of respected kuia (older women); the unique ability to restore people and places from tapu to noa (from being in a state considered too sacred to touch – tapu – to resuming a non-sacred state – noa); and the harakeke (flax) weaving skills that women used to create precious woven technologies for their whānau and hapū, for example, were valued highly in their communities.

Throughout herstory, Māori women have contributed much to their iwi, to Māori people and to New Zealand as a whole. As the years rolled on after colonisation, Māori women became more and more prominent in the struggle for Māori rights, with wāhine like Te Puea Herangi and Dame Whina Cooper leaving iconic legacies that should ensure their status as Kiwi legends for generations to come. I say 'should' because I'm quite sure that a number of New Zealanders have absolutely no idea who they were and/or what they were famous for. And that makes me sad. So, just in case you're scratching your head …

Te Puea Herangi was born Te Kirihaehae Te Puea Herangi in 1883, the granddaughter of the Māori King, Tāwhiao. Destined to become a leader, 'Princess' Te Puea (a title bestowed upon her by Pākehā that she never used herself) was noticed by her elders as being particularly capable, and began to advocate for Māori early in life. In an early stand, she fought for her people to not take part in the Pākehā conflict presented by the First World War. 'They tell us to fight for King and country,' she is recorded as saying. 'Well, that's all right. We've got a king. But we haven't got a country. That's been taken off us. Let them give us back our land and maybe we'll think about it again.'[10]

During her lifetime, Te Puea would be responsible for such feats as rehoming 100 children orphaned by the influenza epidemic of 1918, masterminding and driving the establishment of the Tūrangawaewae settlement and marae at Ngaruawahia, revitalising the Kīngitanga movement, establishing farms in the Waikato to provide an economic base for her people, championing unity among Māori people of all different iwi and hapū, forming relationships with powerful politicians and leaders – both Pākehā and Māori – to advance Māori interests, establishing a clinic at Tūrangawaewae marae where Māori felt comfortable receiving treatment, and becoming the first patron of the Māori Women's Welfare League[11]. Her personal mantra, delivered to the press when they interviewed her on the illustrious occasion of receiving her CBE, was 'Ka mahi au, ka inoi au, ka moe au, ka mahi ano' (I work, I pray, I sleep, I work again)[12].

Dame Whina Cooper, born Josephine Te Wake in 1895, was the daughter of Heremia Te Wake, an eminent Te Rarawa chief. She inherited his mana and acquired an enormous amount of her own, becoming a staunch advocate for Māori and working to improve the plight of her people for the length of her life. She is perhaps most famous for being the first president of the Māori Women's Welfare League in 1951, and later, as an elderly woman, leading the historic Land Hīkoi in 1975[13]. Cooper was still alive in my lifetime (she died in 1994 at the age of 98) and I remember often seeing the iconic photograph of her walking with her three-year-old mokopuna Irene Cooper on the road to Wellington during my childhood. Women like Te Puea Herangi and Dame Whina Cooper exemplify the power of mana wāhine – the fierce, indomitable spirit of Māori women.

New Zealand's herstory also includes many strong Pākehā women. Two who stand out to me are Ettie Rout and Kate Sheppard (a name every New Zealander should recognise, or hang their heads in shame).

Ettie Rout is a name that has largely been lost to us, and that was never properly acknowledged to begin with. Ettie Annie Rout was born in Tasmania in 1877, and immigrated to New Zealand with her family in 1884. From her youth, she stood out, first as a talented scholar, then as a young woman who refused to submit to the mores of the day. She eventually became a prominent campaigner for safe sex, collaborating internationally with renowned doctors of the time to create her own safe sex kits, which she distributed to New Zealand soldiers during the First World War, after observing both an alarming rate of 'venereal disease' (as sexually transmitted infections were called in those days) and a complete unwillingness by the New Zealand authorities to do anything about it, likely because taking action would've required them to acknowledge the glaringly obvious truth that New Zealand servicemen were frequenting foreign brothels. Rout, who had views about sexuality that were seen to be frighteningly radical during her lifetime, campaigned tirelessly for the Government to provide servicemen with prophylactics and other (primitive) contraceptives, notably writing a letter to the *New Zealand Times* about the issue that helped to convince the Defence Minister to adopt Rout's kits and distribute them to all New Zealand soldiers. Ironically, after that letter was published, the New Zealand Government censored all mention of Rout, threatening publications with a fine that would amount to over $10,000 in today's money if they dared to even mention her name. Rout was largely demonised by the New Zealand public and eventually committed suicide in Rarotonga in 1936.[14]

Kate Sheppard was born Catherine Wilson Malcolm in Liverpool, England in 1847, and moved with her family to New Zealand in 1869. She is famous as the leader of the New Zealand women's suffrage movement, campaigning tirelessly for women to have the right to vote, a fight she and her fellow suffragists won in 1893. In 1896, she was elected the first president of the National Council of Women, an organisation that survives to this day[15]. She remains the only woman other than the Queen to appear on a New Zealand bank note.

Women like Ettie Rout and Kate Sheppard embody the determination and stubbornness of Pākehā women. Indeed, without the staunch will and resolve of early Pākehā women, it's debatable whether the early settlers would've survived at all. In Te Ao Pākehā, settler women found themselves in a markedly different situation to the one they'd left behind in England. Colonial New Zealand was a harsh and uncompromising place without the support of friends and family, and women were largely the engines that kept the colony running. British settler women often had to learn to be hardy[16], helping their husbands to clear land, making do with whatever homes they managed to build with their husbands and giving birth with the assistance of their female friends. Many settler women died in childbirth, while others grieved for the homes they'd left behind.

New Zealand could also, however, offer a kind of independence British women could only dream of. One such woman, Mary Taylor, arrived in New Zealand in 1845. A single, unmarried woman, Taylor worked as a teacher, bought land and engaged in cattle dealing until her cousin joined her in 1849. After that, Mary and Ellen Taylor opened a woman's clothing and drapery shop[17]. There were many women, both Māori[18] and Pākehā, engaged in business in colonial New Zealand. In a developing society, the desperate demand for just about everything meant that women could bring income into their families by churning butter, hosting lodgers, sewing, weaving, scraping flax fibre and selling firewood, fish, and fruit, among many other activities. Kiwi women have been enterprising from the outset, aided by an environment in which the traditional barriers to women's involvement in wealth-creation were superseded by the needs of growing communities. In a young colonial country where demand for labour well exceeded supply, women could also earn relatively decent wages working as barmaids, domestic servants, 'nurse girls' and the like. With a huge gender imbalance in the new colony, New Zealand women also had their pick of suitors[19].

For all of early Aotearoa's progressiveness, however, women still experienced considerable hardship and discrimination. A quick and incomplete timeline of the moments in New Zealand herstory when Kiwi women began to slowly win the right to be treated as human beings goes something like this:

1860 – The Married Women's Property Protection Act gave women the right to own property and any assets gained by them after being deserted by low-life husbands. It meant that they and their assets couldn't be held accountable for the debts of the dude who'd fucked off and left them[20].

1867 – The Divorce and Matrimonial Causes Act meant that women could divorce their husbands, although if they sought a divorce on the grounds of adultery, it had to be combined with cruelty, incest, bestiality, rape, bigamy, sodomy or desertion[21]. Just being a cheating prick wasn't enough. Men, of course, could divorce their wives on the grounds of adultery alone[22].

Also in 1867 – The Municipal Corporations Act meant that female ratepayers could stand and vote in local body elections[23].

1870 – The Married Women's Property Protection Act (another one) gave a woman the right to have exclusive custody of her children and receive child support if her husband was – how shall I put it? – a scumbag[24].

1871 – The first high school for girls opened in Dunedin, 15 years after boys were granted access to secondary education[25]. Women were also admitted to the University of Otago from the year of its opening – also in 1871.

1877 – The Education Act clarified that both men and women could be seen as 'householders', and thus eligible to stand in elections for school committees[26]. One would've thought that after gaining the right to stand in local body elections, school committees would be a no-brainer, but apparently not.

1884 – The Married Women's Property Act had the effect of bringing about the individual legal existence of married women. I'm not kidding. Before this, married women were basically legally absorbed by their husbands. This act gave women the right to own property, make contracts, sue and be sued[27].

1893 – Women won the right to vote, becoming the first women in the world to gain full suffrage. While we celebrate this as an auspicious occasion, it's worth noting just how astounding it is that before 1893 women had absolutely no official say in the way the world was run. We should never forget that just 125 years ago, men thought so little of women that they refused to extend to us even that most basic of human rights.

Also in 1893 – Elizabeth Yates was elected as the mayor of Onehunga. She became the first female mayor in the British Empire[28].

1896 – The age of consent was raised to the age of 16. It had previously been 12, allowing lecherous older men to take advantage of young girls[29].

Also in 1896 – The National Council of Women was established, a women's organisation that endures to this day. Its first president was suffrage hero Kate Sheppard[30].

1897 – Māori women won the right to stand and vote for the Māori Parliament[31].

1898 – The Divorce Act finally removed the gender disparities in the grounds for divorce contained in the earlier 1867 Act[32].

1900 – Incest was criminalised, but any prosecution for the rape of an underage girl had to be brought within one month of it happening. The New Zealand Justice System, ladies and gentlemen: protecting rape victims since … never mind[33].

1919 – Women won the right to stand in general elections.

1933 – The first female MP, Elizabeth McCombs of the Labour Party, was elected. She won the seat of Lyttelton[34].

1947 – Mabel Howard, a Labour MP, became the first female Cabinet Minister[35].

1949 – The first female Māori MP, Iriaka Rātana of the Labour Party, was elected. She won the seat of Western Māori, one of the four former Māori electorates[36].

1960 – The Government Service Equal Pay Act gave women working in the public service the right to equal pay for equal work[37].

1966 – Te Arikinui Dame Te Ātairangikaahu succeeded her father King Korokī to become the first Māori Queen.

1972 – The Equal Pay Act gave women working in the private sector the right to equal pay for equal work[38]. While the Act enshrined the right to pay equality in law, gender pay discrimination has continued to the present day, perhaps best demonstrated by

Kristine Bartlett's historic legal battle for equal pay, in which she won a pay rise for over 50,000 aged care workers in 2017[39].

Also in 1972 – Whetū Tirikātene-Sullivan, MP for Southern Māori, became the first Māori woman Cabinet Minister[40].

1976 – The Matrimonial Property Act meant that women were entitled to half of the marital property and assets in the event of divorce[41]. The same right wouldn't be extended to women in de facto or same-sex partnerships until 2002[42].

1977 – The penalty of 'seven years' imprisonment with hard labour'[43] for having an abortion was removed from the Crimes Act[44]. The act of having an abortion itself was left in the Crimes Act, where it remains to this day. The Contraception, Sterilisation and Abortion Act was also enacted, introducing the ridiculous framework for abortion that also survives to this day[45]. More on that later.

1982 – The Domestic Protection Act was implemented, aiming to protect women from violent partners[46]. Domestic violence has a long and shameful history in New Zealand, that sadly continues to the current day. As *Te Ara* explains, 'domestic violence was common, and in the 19th and early 20th centuries was seen by many as a man's right.'[47] It should also be noted that at this stage, marital rape was still legal.

1985 – Marital rape was finally outlawed[48]. This was only four years before I was born. Before this, under the Crimes Act 1961, the law clearly stated: 'no man shall be convicted of rape in respect of his intercourse with his wife.'[49]

1989 – Helen Clark became the first female Deputy Prime Minister of New Zealand.

1990 – Dame Catherine Tizard became the first female Governor General of New Zealand.

1997 – Jenny Shipley became the first female Prime Minister of New Zealand.

1999 – Helen Clark became the first *elected* female Prime Minister of New Zealand.

2001 – Under Helen Clark's Government, the top five most powerful positions in New Zealand were held by women: Prime Minister Helen Clark, Leader of the Opposition Jenny Shipley, Governor General Dame Silvia Cartwright, Attorney General Margaret Wilson, and Chief Justice Sian Elias.

2003 – New Zealand became the first country in the world to legalise prostitution as sex work for those over the age of 18[50].

2009 – Former Prime Minister Helen Clark became the first woman to lead the United Nations Development Programme[51].

2016 – Dr Farah Palmer became the first woman ever to be elected to the board of New Zealand Rugby[52]. She is still the only woman ever to have served as a board member in the organisation's 125-year history.

Also in 2016 – Paula Bennett became the first female Māori Deputy Prime Minister of New Zealand.

2017 – Jacinda Ardern became the youngest ever Deputy Leader of the New Zealand Labour Party. Later that year she became the youngest ever Leader of the New Zealand Labour Party, before becoming New Zealand's third female Prime Minister (and the second youngest Prime Minister in the country's history).

All of this goes to show that over the past two centuries, Kiwi women have fought a long and difficult battle to achieve equality with our male counterparts. Slowly, incrementally, we have secured basic rights, and are now viewed, at least in the eyes of the law, as equal. While the successes of the past should be remembered and celebrated, however, we still have a long way to go. We often speak proudly of our unique position as the first nation in the world in which women won the right to vote, but what does that accolade really mean when women could still be legally raped in their marital beds 90 years later? What does that achievement mean 125 years later? I can only answer for myself. For me, it means that I'll never forget that my foremothers were fierce, staunch and determined ladies. It means that whenever I feel the wrath of the patriarchy as it fights back against me, I'll remember how far we've come, and how hard my elder sisters fought to get us here. The patriarchy is a many-headed beast that fights back with fury whenever it is threatened. When I look back at our herstory in its entirety, I know that every milestone along the way was met with resistance, but that every battle was won eventually.

Herstory is never ending. There are many conflicts still raging, glass ceilings still to shatter and unconscious biases to drag into the spotlight. Luckily for us, the stage was set many generations ago, by the extraordinary Kiwi women who came before us. Those bloody (great) women built the foundations upon which we stand today. It's our turn now to fight the good fight, and our duty to do them proud.

CHAPTER FIVE

The media told me that I was fat

'Bread is the enemy,' was my teenage mantra. I'd whisper the words to myself as I stood hovering at the pantry door, engaged in an internal battle of wills in which self-discipline would usually win out over hunger. Bread contained carbs, and carbs – so I'd been told – made you fat. And being fat was to be avoided at all costs.

I spent most of my teenaged years waging war against myself. In my efforts to be perfect, hunger was to be denied, exhaustion fought off, fun enjoyed only occasionally, sadness squashed. Nowhere did my personal battles play out so strongly, however, as at that pantry door. While I felt out of control, drowning under the weight of an over-full schedule and punishingly high (and largely self-imposed) expectations, restricting my food intake became the one thing that I could manage – and manage it I did, with military precision.

There was a time when I could've told you almost exactly how many kilojoules were in most common foods. During that era, I could also have told you exactly how much I weighed on any given day – and you could be sure that the information was correct, because I would've already spent hours agonising over the 0.1 of a kilogram that I'd gained since yesterday. During my teens my weight went from 62kg at 13 – a fairly normal weight for a girl of average height – to 56kg at 15, and continued to nosedive from there. At 20 I weighed a scary 49kg. My ribs and my hipbones jutted through my skin when I looked in the mirror. I was desperately unhappy, but I also felt a perverse sense of satisfaction. I was finally 'skinny'. When people would tell me they were worried about how thin I'd become it would only feed my obsession. I'd become so fixated on being thin that their concern felt like positive reinforcement. There was plenty of negative reinforcement too, however – like the constant pressure I felt to be thin for photoshoots, or the words of a young man who'd just seen me naked for the first time. I was at my thinnest, and even then terrified of becoming 'fat'. 'I'm not normally this thin,' I said to him. 'That's a shame,' he replied.

I was never diagnosed with an eating disorder, largely, I suspect, because I continued functioning until suddenly I didn't, and by the time I didn't, my eating issues were the least of my problems. Looking back, however, it seems pretty clear that I was grappling with eating behaviour that was significantly disordered, though the shame I felt about my body meant that I went to great lengths to mask any warning signs that may have given my secret away and tipped people off about my horrendous 'fatness'. Going to boarding school made it much easier to control my food intake, as did travelling the world alone as a musician. Left to my own devices, I developed an addiction to thinness. Though, like any addict, I was never satisfied. If I could only lose another kg …

I'm not going to go into weight-loss methods here, even to denounce them, because I know from experience that I would take notes from tell-all anorexia recovery stories during that time of my life, hoping to glean new insights into how to shrink my monstrous thighs. I have no intention of adding to someone else's perfect storm. God knows they have enough to contend with. Self-loathing and dramatic self-flagellation doesn't happen in a vacuum. Kids don't suddenly wake up one day and start thinking that they're disgusting. It happens gradually, after an accumulation of negative experiences and influences, although it can start alarmingly early.

I can't exactly pinpoint the moment when I became convinced that I was fat. I can remember a mother of one of my school friends pulling me aside at the end of the school day when I emerged from my classroom one summer afternoon to tell me that everyone could see my 'bosoms' in the dress I was wearing. I can even remember the dress – it was one of my favourites, yellow, with navy blue frills, and no sleeves. I felt humiliated, and interpreted her statement to mean that the dress was too small for me and that I must be monstrously fat. I was six. I wouldn't have any 'bosoms' to speak of for another four years. It wasn't the first time I'd felt like I was a revolting creature, however. I can remember being taunted for being 'fat' in the playground, and feeling much bigger than the other girls in my ballet class. I can also remember my mother fretting about her own weight. All of these things were small and insignificant, but when combined, they created the foundations of a deep sense of insecurity that would later turn into a well of self-loathing.

And then the media came along.

From my early teens until my early twenties, I bought magazines every single month. At first, my mother bought me *TV Hits, Creme Magazine, Girlfriend,* and *Dolly*, then I graduated to *Cleo* and *Cosmopolitan.* Later, I would buy *Harper's Bazaar* religiously. Magazines filled many functions in my life. They provided entertainment in the form of celebrity news, hard-to-get information that seems gorgeously quaint these days – does anyone else remember Dolly Doctor and the *Cosmopolitan* sealed sections? – and a window into what kind of girls and women were fashionable, beautiful, and desirable. Magazines provided me with a kind of guidebook, for better or for worse, on how to be a woman.

As a teen I would pore over them hungrily, reading the stories, but spending more time simply gazing at the pictures. I would compare my body to those of the airbrushed, photo-shopped glamazons on the page, making a mental checklist of all of the ways in which it was defective and inadequate, and musing on the merits of various ways to 'fix' my 'problem-areas'. There is a whole language built around weight loss, and the media and advertisers co-authored it. As a result, I worried about cellulite, bat wings and spare tyres before I knew whether I had them. I punished myself for not having a thigh gap and, after watching the news one night and noticing that Wendy Petrie's ribs were visible beneath her collarbones, wondered what I could do to make my décolletage look like hers.

Both directly and indirectly, the media told me that I was bigger than I should've been. In featuring an over-representation of very thin women, in editorial, programming and advertisements, it fostered, and continues to foster, a warped view of womanhood. This misrepresentation of women continues today, although it often goes unnoticed. We've become so accustomed to seeing thin, white women in print and on screen that we rarely question it. The problem is not that thin, white women are represented in the media, it's that women who are not thin and/or white are overwhelmingly under-represented. Statistically speaking, the women that we see on television are not likely to be the kinds of women that we see walking down the street. The 'average size' of a Kiwi woman (as problematic a measure as that is) is apparently 12–14[1]. The average size of women seen in advertisements, on television, in magazines, newspapers, films, games and other media would most likely be a size 8. To be clear, there is nothing wrong with being a size 8, but it's important to question why we see more size 8 women in the media than size 14 women, when there are many more of the latter than the former.

It's exactly this paradox that has brought about the explosion of so-called 'plus-sized' (whatever that means) blogs, vlogs, social media accounts, tumblrs and channels, through which women who don't fit into the mainstream media's organic-fat-free-vegan cookie cutter mould become celebrities by reaching the millions of women who have been neglected, bullied and taunted by traditional outlets for decades. Online, women are able to find role models who look like them. They're able to find supportive groups and forums where people build each other up rather than giving them new things to hate about themselves. That's not to say that the online environment is an empowering, body-positive, safe haven. For every plus-sized vlogger, you'll find many more #fitspo stars, 'pro-ana' websites (the ana meaning anorexia), weight-loss advertisements, 'how to get the bikini body of your dreams' articles, and millions upon millions of horrendous, soulless fat-shaming comments. For every step women take towards self-love and acceptance, there is some faceless dickhead behind a Twitter account just waiting to tell them that they could do with losing a few pounds. The backlash that comes with a decision to make peace with your body is both fascinating and depressing.

Over the past few years, I've made a conscious effort to let my body be exactly the size it wants to be. I've stopped crash-dieting before photoshoots. I've taken a more moderate approach to exercise. I've started eating the delicious food I would usually deny myself. Whenever I speak about my decision to flip the figurative bird to society's ridiculous beauty standards, I'm often met with looks of surprise and confusion. After many such reactions I finally realised that there were two main themes at play. The first was that some people were surprised that a woman who is on the thinner side of the spectrum would struggle with body-image issues, and the second was that many people simply don't know how to deal with a woman who actually loves her body. The idea that, 'You look like you've lost weight!' is most certainly not a compliment is just foreign to some people. We're so used to women hating their bodies that we've forgotten what it's like to speak to women who have a deep and hard-won respect for themselves, regardless of what others may think about their appearance.

I suspect that there is a patriarchal undercurrent to the backlash against body positivity. To put it simply, when women decide to love themselves on their own terms and to reject external pressure to live up to a heteronormative, societally sanctioned ideal, their value becomes self-gifted, rather than bestowed by men. They decide that they are beautiful, without having to wait for a man to validate their attractiveness. When women love their bodies, the opinions of men become obsolete and unwelcome, and – surprise, surprise – men accustomed to centuries of mansplaining tend to find an environment in which their opinions are redundant fairly uncomfortable. When men who have spent their lifetimes thinking that calling a random stranger 'beautiful' is going to win them brownie points have their opinion thrown back in their faces by said random 'beautiful' stranger, they often react angrily. The woman who refuses to be the object of their sexualising gaze will be maligned as a 'stuck-up bitch' or the like. Similarly, when a man who calls a woman 'fat' or 'ugly' is either ignored, laughed at or taken to task for his own looks, he has no idea how to deal with such a reaction.

And then there are those people who go to great lengths to explain that they're 'not fat-shaming, but at some point you have to acknowledge that body positivity is dangerous because people are fatter than ever and obesity is killing people'. I have a confession to make. I used to be one of those people. Especially when I was a group fitness instructor (fun fact: I taught an exercise dance class in my early twenties. Yes, I wore a lot of Lycra. And yes, I have tried to bury those memories in the far, far back corners of my brain). From my perspective as someone who found it relatively easy to lose weight by following conventional advice (consume fewer kilojoules and exercise more) and had the financial security to be able to buy nutritious foods and pay for a gym membership, I believed that if people simply did what I did then they'd lose weight. In my mind, I'd turned a complex situation in a simple one, and at its core my belief system relied on the 'will' to be healthy. Somehow, in my rush to be holier-than-thou, I forgot that I'd had a food-related addiction myself – probably because I was in the grips of an exercise-related one at the time – and that when I was at my thinnest, simply telling me to go and eat a pie would have done diddly-squat. My addiction, however, brought about a socially rewarded outcome – skinniness – whereas the inverse addiction brings about the wrath of a society obsessed with appearances. Of course, being thin is no guarantee of 'health'. There are plenty of thin people who are horrendously unhealthy, but that doesn't stop every man and his dog weighing in on the subject of obesity. Especially when the people daring to take up space are women.

Here's a revolutionary idea: perhaps we should all just shut the fuck up about other people's bodies? With the exceptions of health professionals treating patients within the bounds of doctor-patient confidentiality, and the support networks of people seeking health treatment, there is absolutely no need for anyone else to comment on someone's appearance. Doing so because you 'care' about their health is no excuse. If you really care, treat your fellow human beings with dignity rather than casting them as poor uninformed or stubborn dolts who need help to see the errors of their ways. What could you possibly have to say to them about their weight that they haven't heard before a million times? I have never been a size that has drawn random stares in the street, so I would never claim to have any personal understanding of the lived experiences of people who are bigger than I am, but I did go from 49kg to 69kg within the space of just over a year when I was in the darkest depths of depression, which certainly didn't go unnoticed. Unsurprisingly, I felt deeply self-conscious about my weight, and any comments – however well intended – about how I should do more exercise or perhaps not eat that fifth Tim Tam were more likely to make me feel so miserable that I reached for the sixth and seventh Tim Tam than to propel me off the couch and into my trainers. When I eventually ended up back somewhere in the middle of my yo-yo extremes, it was because I started exercising for my mental health and, after a few years of therapy (more about that later) I no longer needed to rely on comfort eating as a crutch to take my mind off how miserable I felt. Ironically, it was through a commitment to treating myself kindly, not beating myself up, that resulted in me losing weight – which was not even the goal in the first place. From this vantage point, when my weight has bounced in all directions, I can say with some confidence that no comment anyone ever made about the size of my body ever did anything positive for me. What I weigh is no one's business other than my doctor's and my own.

The obsession with weight isn't helped by the promotion of 'fitspiration' and the like. While I was an early proponent of 'strong is the new skinny', lapping up a sentiment that fed my ego and masked my insecurities, I now see the idea as deeply problematic. Posting pictures of your ripped body as 'fitspiration' for others has to be the lamest justification for hubris ever. And I say that as someone who has done just that in the past. There comes a time when it's important to think about why we're posting pictures of our bodies. Why does it matter what our followers think about the way we look? When it comes to the kinds of selfies that often feature either a gym or a bathroom in the background, and a taut, toned twelve pack in the foreground, I've come to the conclusion that it would be a lot easier if people sharing such selfies simply captioned them, 'I'm super-hot', so we could get on board with their self-love up front, without having to read some long, deep and meaningful post that has absolutely nothing to do with the fact that they are half naked in front of the bathroom mirror, or feeling obliged to go out of our way to give them the validation they need but don't want to ask for explicitly. I say that with no judgment. It's hardly surprising that we seek validation online when our appearances are policed so stringently by society's arbitrary beauty standards. I'm not opposed to selfies generally, and I understand the revolutionary shift in perspective that comes especially from young women turning the lens on themselves. In a culture in which photographs of young women have historically been taken by and for men, shot either as a manifestation of the male gaze or with male consumers in mind, the idea of women having agency over how they're portrayed is in itself radical, though the amount of self-objectification I see in women's selfies gives me pause. The fact that we self-objectify – and I do it myself – when we take pictures of ourselves demonstrates just how deeply we've internalised views about how we're meant to look. If we all believed that we were beautiful just the way we are; if thinness wasn't prized and strong wasn't 'the new skinny' (I can't help but wonder what happened to the old skinny), I doubt we'd feel the need to suck in and position our bodies in exactly the right poses in the most flattering lighting while holding our phones in awkwardly outstretched arms, searching for the best angles. If we all believed that we were beautiful there'd be no need for such performance and pretence.

The thing is, for women particularly, we've spent our whole lives being told how we should look, and many of us have spent far too many years trying to make ourselves smaller in order to squeeze into the little pockets of air that society has allotted to us. We don't need fitspiration, we need self-love. We need to be given the space to find ways in which to fall deeply in love with ourselves; not to feed our egos but to soothe our souls. The most important thing our bodies can do is serve us well, to do the best they can to keep us healthy and functioning. What do we have to gain from hating the very things that keep us alive? Nothing.

But it is a struggle. It is a struggle I know intimately. I speak about my body in ways I'd never speak about another human being. I can be cruel, uncompromising, demanding, demeaning and downright nasty in the space of one internal conversation. I've got better over the years, which I am eternally grateful for. Every small victory represents a conscious refusal to beat myself up, which, to me, is cause for celebration. For example, I no longer fantasise about scalpels and suction moulding me into the kind of woman I thought I should be.

My obsession with plastic surgery started young. I must've first heard about liposuction at around age eleven, and for years after that I became preoccupied with the idea of having a machine suck all of the fat out of my thighs. I'd no longer have to punish myself for my indiscretions at the pantry door, I thought, if I could suddenly melt the two slabs of flesh that sat atop of my legs down to a more acceptable size – which, given I was raised in the time of heroin chic, was about the size of a broomstick. Liposuction was a regular fantasy throughout my teens, though I knew it could never become a reality. It was expensive, and I knew that my parents would never agree to such a drastic procedure (bearing in mind that it was also an utterly ridiculous fixation, and I was well within a healthy BMI). As I grew older, however, I shifted my fixation to another surgical alteration that would eventually be within my capability to make a reality. When I was 16, I decided that I wanted breast implants. I didn't dislike my breasts, but I knew deep down that they weren't the kind of breasts that boys fantasised about. I wanted to have bigger boobs – not huge, like the images of porn stars that

I'd seen, but larger than what I had. A D-cup perhaps, instead of my 10-Bs. This idea followed me into my twenties, and I began investigating different kinds of procedures – the difference between saline implants and silicon, how long they lasted, how much they cost. I told men that I was dating that I wanted to get a boob job. None of them tried to talk me out of it. One did memorably say, 'Well, I'm not paying for it, and I'm not looking after you once it's done.' It didn't matter – at that stage I could've scraped together enough money to pay for it myself.

Eventually, after years of dreaming of bigger boobs, I realised that getting a boob job would mean going against everything I stood for. By this stage I was on a pathway towards trying to love myself. It would be some time after that before I managed that extraordinary feat, but even then I knew that paying someone to cut me open and shove bags of liquid inside my chest would not be an exercise in self-kindness.

I wholeheartedly support women seeking plastic surgery that is medically necessary or would minimise suffering after illness, accident or injury, and I'm not here to judge women who have had elective cosmetic surgery. I understand the desire to alter your appearance, to 'fix' a part of yourself you've long disliked, or to feel more attractive. I understand how difficult it is to live with the pressure of society's restrictive beauty ideals. I have friends who started botox treatments in their early twenties. I myself have had laser hair removal. I desperately wish, however, that we lived in a world where our bodies were just allowed to exist as they are. I wish that we could talk openly about the shame and anguish that sometimes informs our decisions to seek cosmetic surgery. I wish that women didn't have to feel that they had to hand over thousands of dollars to a surgeon in order to feel beautiful.

One of the most disturbing plastic surgery trends I've heard about in recent years is cosmetic labiaplasty. For the uninitiated, cosmetic labiaplasty is a procedure in which the labia minora and/or the labia majora (or, to put it plainly, the inner and outer lips of the vulva) are surgically altered, most often to make them smaller. Essentially, your vulva is sliced open, the offending lips are cut shorter, and you are stitched back up. I'm sure there are surgeons who would describe the increasingly popular procedure with much more elegance, but I don't think the horror of it should be adorned or obscured. Counter-intuitively, although I am alarmed by the very thought of the practice, I can absolutely understand the motivation to get it done. Female genitalia is so taboo that the vast majority of the population can't even name it correctly. The vulva (not the vagina – that part of the anatomy is inside our bodies) is seen only very rarely in mainstream culture, although the penis rears its head (pun intended) with increasing regularity, and naked breasts are seen so often that they hardly raise an eyebrow. Think about the last scene you watched in a film or on television where you saw a vulva. In the couple of examples I can summon to mind, *The Reader* and *Sex and the City,* both Kate Winslet and Kim Cattrall's vulvas were obscured by merkins (pubic-hair wigs). When we do see a vulva on screen, it's likely to be from a distance, or hidden beneath a wig of fake pubes. Even during lesbian sex scenes in films and shows like *Carol, Orange is the New Black*, *Orphan Black* and the like, you'll be unlikely to see anything more than a suggestion of the general direction in which a vulva is located. You might see a (generally pretty, most often white) head disappearing behind a gracefully bent knee, but that's about it. Which is not really the fault of filmmakers and showrunners, as featuring a vulva on screen can lead to a restrictive rating or worse, censorship. Funnily enough, the penis isn't subject to the same draconian rules. The message being sent loud and clear is that a vulva is simply too controversial to be shown on screen, despite the fact that roughly half of the population possess one. When we grow up in an environment where we have very few vulvas to compare our own to, where they are hidden away as if they are shameful, misnamed or referred to by euphemisms, it's no great surprise that women grow up with some anxiety around their pussies. When that anxiety morphs into a dislike of our vulvas, however, and a desire to cut them so that they fit into our idea of what a vulva should look like, something has gone terribly wrong.

In 2015, 63.4 per cent of labiaplasties performed in the United States were on women younger than 35[2]. Four hundred of the procedures were performed on women younger than 18[3]. The majority of the women seeking such procedures are young. They often tell stories about hating their vulvas for much of their lives. In one anonymous account published in *Miss FQ*, a 31-year-old described her feelings thusly:

> *Looking back now, I realise I was in a sort of denial. I think I knew deep down that if I'd had a good look at images of other vaginas, I'd have found mine wasn't so bad. That it was normal, even. But that would have meant facing the reality that I'd wasted years sacrificing love in favour of physical self-loathing. I couldn't face that prospect, so I held onto the idea that I would find my confidence in surgery. It wasn't until my consultation that I saw pictures of other women's vaginas. It turned out my instincts were right and mine was normal. But, my desperation to have the procedure remained.*[4]

She eventually went through with the surgery. 'I'm not exactly proud of it, but I don't regret it,' she concluded.

In another anonymous account published by Fairfax, a woman who had undergone a labiaplasty at age 16 told the story of how one side of her labia was longer than the other. She described her feelings at the completion of the procedure:

> *My only feeling was relief; that I was not ill or disfigured and relieved that I could one day be intimate without being afraid of rejection.*

Later, however, she realised that her uneven labia were far from unusual:

> *When I did start having sex, with women, I soon realised no two vaginas are the same. It was a simple fact I wish I'd known sooner.*

And, while I have no regrets about the surgery (it helped pull me from a dark and lonely place), I do regret that I was not told more about women's bodies and that I did not have access to information that would have told me I was within the spectrum of normal.[5]

Both of the women in these accounts described themselves as feminists, and both cited a lack of exposure to images of other vulvas as a reason for their eventual decision to have surgery. While the vulva has been censored for generations, now seems to be a good time to ask whether erasing female sex organs is protecting women or harming them.

Anxiety about vulva appearance is also making women self-conscious in the bedroom. Some women feel too embarrassed about the appearance of their vulva to allow themselves to engage in or enjoy oral sex. I can't put into words how much those women are missing out on. In the absence of any meaningful, widespread discussion or appreciation of female genitalia, women are given more and more reasons to feel that their vulvas are somehow defective or disgusting if they don't look like a Barbie doll. Take, for example, outrageous trends like the 'vagacial', which aims to brighten (what?) and smooth the labia; potions, douches and other products that claim to mask the smell of the vagina; the 'V-Lighten', which uses a laser to lighten the skin of the labia; or the 'V-Tighten', which involves inserting some kind of laser wand up your vagina, which then proceeds to shred the vaginal canal with a number of tiny cuts to stimulate collagen production. Ladies. What the fuck? How did we get to this point?

Our vulvas and our vaginas are under attack; they are the final frontier. Every other inch of our body has been analysed, critiqued and shamed into patriarchal submission, and our fannies are simply the last holdout. In 2018, tanning, waxing, botox, dieting, hair extensions, brow shaping, exercise classes, facials, manicures, pedicures, liposuction, breast implants and lip fillers are no longer enough. Now you must have a tight, bright, light, sweet-smelling, neat and tidy minge in order to be thought of as attractive.

The most ludicrous thing of all is that in many cases we've been conned into being our vulvas' harshest critics. I have never, in a decade of sexual activity, received any criticism about my vulva from sexual partners. Which is just as well. If someone had the audacity to insult my vulva they'd find themselves kicked out of my bed before they finished their sentence. Our vulvas, vaginas and surrounding organs are designed to do incredible things, from bringing new life into the world to delivering immense pleasure. They deserve respect and reverence, not snipping, zapping, and shaming. If women felt half as proud of their vulvas as men do of their penises, the 'designer vagina' business would go bust.

If I were to write a list of all the ways in which the media, advertisers, cosmetic surgeons and the beauty industry have told women that their bodies are defective, it would fill a book of its own. I'm going to put it baldly: we've been had. We have been bullied, shamed, taunted, exploited and disrespected for decades, relentlessly and masterfully, until we started to believe what we were being told about our 'thick thighs' and 'ugly vaginas'. The truth is that our only 'problem area' is now the control room between our ears, which has been under attack from malignant external forces hell-bent on getting us to either part with hard-earned cash or make ourselves more suitable for some guy's boner. There is no easy cure for a brain that has been relentlessly bombarded with nasty, negative messages since childhood. The best we can do to protect ourselves is to be conscious of the relentless offensive waged upon our minds and try to counteract its malevolent impact. To fight valiantly so that our younger siblings, cousins, friends, daughters, nieces, students and followers don't believe the crap they're told about themselves. The truth is that nothing will change until the money dries up. It's the perfect con. We're the perfect marks. What more can I say? It's fucked.

CHAPTER SIX

Take back the media

Let's be clear. As women, the media has never belonged to us. We may be masterful storytellers – so much so that we're known as 'gossips' and 'chatter-boxes' – but the official story has always been in the hands of men, shaped and legitimised by them and then broadcast through distribution channels they have always owned.

We can't take it back, as it never belonged to us, but we can take back our own narratives. We can wrest control of our own stories, and insist that we be the ones to tell them. We can take back the truth and demand that it be told in full, uncomfortable as it may be. We can, and we must, because the media is the lens through which we view the world.

The media is everywhere. We are living in a time when escaping it takes more effort than seeking it out. While the media's revenues may have shrunk, its power has arguably grown, as every topic is up for discussion, every screen is a broadcast platform and every person with a smartphone is a potential citizen journalist.

We are surrounded by news, views and everything in between; we're addicted to information, living in a digital liquor store with a thirst that is never satiated.

I've been involved in the media, in one way or another, since I was a child. I wrote my first letter to the editor when I was 12 years old, to register my disgust that Osama Bin Laden masks were being sold as Halloween costumes. It was published in the *Rotorua Daily Post*, coincidentally a newspaper that now syndicates my *New Zealand Herald* column every Saturday. You could say that my destiny to rant in print was clear from the outset.

Talking about the media sometimes seems trivial, when I think about all of the injustices in the world, but it is an important conversation because of the great power television, radio, print, digital and social media have to influence the way that we think as a society. The media is the mouthpiece of humanity, and the stories it tells become the stories of humankind. Unsurprisingly, some stories are prioritised over others, and some are not told at all. Still others are told from one perspective, framed in a way that consciously or subconsciously places one version of events above another. Historically, the vast majority of editors and producers were older white men, a trend that hasn't been entirely stamped out yet. Indeed, you only have to look at the current broadcasting landscape, where there is currently only one woman in the whole country who hosts a solo primetime national show (Miriama Kamo, who hosts TVNZ's *Sunday*), to see that there's still a long way to go. (When I started writing this book, there was also Alison Mau, who hosted the RadioLive Drive Show, but she left at the beginning of

2018. She was replaced by a lop-sided male-female pairing, with vastly experienced senior journalist Lisa Owen put beside young male journalist Ryan Bridge.) While there are other shows with solo female hosts (Kim Hill, Wendyl Nissan and Kathryn Ryan spring to mind) they are broadcast outside of primetime.

Out of curiosity, I conducted a non-scientific study in December 2017, in which I tallied the numbers and configurations of male and female announcers on the radio stations owned by the two major commercial radio networks, NZME and MediaWorks, simply by visiting their websites. The results were sobering. At the time, NZME had 36 men and ten women working as named announcers on nationally distributed shows across NewsTalk ZB, Radio Hauraki, Radio Sport, ZM, The Hits, Coast and Flava. MediaWorks had 70 men and 22 women working as named announcers on nationally distributed shows across Radio Live, Mai, The Edge, George, The Rock, More, The Breeze, The Sound, and Magic. Radio Sport and Magic had no women at all in announcer roles, while significant discrepancies occurred at NewsTalk ZB (nine men and two women), Radio Hauraki (seven men and one woman), George (18 men and two women), The Rock (eight men and one woman), and Radio Live (18 men and six women). Across all stations, there were 52 shows hosted by solo male hosts, while there were only 15 shows hosted by solo female hosts. There were also 13 shows hosted by teams of male hosts. There were no shows hosted by female teams at all. It will be of no surprise that the number of Māori announcers, of any gender, was also depressingly low.

While radio lags behind, other media has at least made steps to improve its representation. Most of the television current affairs shows feature a mix of men and women (although discrepancies can be seen in shows like *The AM Show* and *The Project*, which are helmed by two men and one woman in the regular host positions) and many newspapers and magazines have a number of female journalists and columnists. The picture becomes hazier, however, the further up the chain of command you go. There is no data available, for example, to show how many editors, producers, heads of news, programmers, commissioners, executives and the like are female. There is some data available about overall representation. For example, the latest Global Media Monitoring Project report, produced in 2015, found that 47 per cent of New Zealand reporters were female, but that only four per cent of female presenters were aged over 50, compared to 52 per cent of male presenters. On the other side of the story, women made up only 18 per cent of news subjects (people seen, read about or heard in the news), well down on the global average of 24 per cent. In New Zealand, this trend has been consistently downward facing, from 26 per cent in 2005, to 23 per cent in 2010, and finally to 18 per cent in 2015[1].

There's no publicly available information about what kind of gender pay gaps exist in the media, although the fierce denunciation by powerful male members of the media of any calls to make gender pay levels public seems to suggest that disparity is likely. There's no scientific data available about genders of announcers, presenters, or columnists, let alone their cultural backgrounds. While organisations like the Women's Media

Center in the United States publish reports every year measuring the diversity (or lack thereof) of major media organisations, New Zealand has no such transparency.

In the course of writing this book, I spoke to several high-profile media personalities – Alison Mau, Miriama Kamo, Miriyana Alexander and Hilary Barry – about their experiences of being female in the media. From the need for diversity, to the experience of sexual harassment, they had plenty to say.

Why does the diversity (or the lack thereof) of media personnel matter? There are many reasons. The first is that as much as they may fight against it, reporters, broadcasters, columnists, journalists, producers and editors approach stories with their own lived experiences in tow. They frame questions according to the way they see the world, which is informed, often unconsciously, by their position in it. Men, women and people of other genders – and people from different cultural backgrounds – often see stories in very different ways, and imbalances in the demographics of media practitioners can result in one particular viewpoint being prioritised over others.

Alison Mau describes the situation thusly:

> *Most journalists, male and female, would swear black and blue that [their gender] wouldn't affect their reporting at all, but we know that all of us have some kind of unconscious bias. I also think that some stories about women – not all – need that deeper understanding. For example, when it comes to abortion, really, no uterus, no opinion. That doesn't mean that you can't put together*

> *a news story about it that's informative but I think sometimes that deeper understanding is necessary.*

Sometimes, people who have no experience of a particular issue are sent to cover complex stories that have a significant impact upon people who are unlike themselves. 'You're going to miss something in the translation,' Mau says. From a pure reporting standpoint, a media landscape dominated by any one group can result in coverage of issues that is infected by bias and ignorance, despite the best efforts of journalists to be impartial. It's difficult to control biases that you don't even know you have.

An area where this can be particularly problematic is in the reporting of sexual violence cases. Miriyana Alexander, recently the editor of both the *Weekend Herald* and the *Herald on Sunday*, and currently the editor of premium content at the *Herald,* believes that the New Zealand media doesn't always do a great job of reporting such cases:

> *I think that there's a traditional way that the media works – report a court case and here's this accusation, this is what was said in court – so suddenly that is the big headline because of course it's astonishing, and people will go 'wow', and people will read it because of that, but then where is the nuance? What happens if people miss the other side of that headline? Where is the examination of the issue? And where is the feature on how the court deals with sexual assault trials, rape trials?*

Alexander, like Mau, believes that any journalist worth their salt will be able to identify an important story and report on it accurately, but when it comes to probing issues like sexual assault, debunking myths, and exploring the context in greater depth, not all journalists and editors will think to do that. 'It's that thing of making yourself think about what else should be a part of that coverage,' Alexander says:

> *The senior male editors that I work with are very open to that kind of coverage, and utterly recognise the importance of such, but that hasn't always been so. It hasn't ever been a case of blocking such ideas or coverage around the issue, it's more that they haven't been in the space themselves of actually thinking about those issues that way in the first place.*

All of which wouldn't be a problem, if there were enough women in senior roles to ensure that all sides of the issue were considered. In many newsrooms around the country, that is not the case. While it is difficult to discuss the demographics of the media workforce without access to statistics on the subject, anecdotally, the junior end of the media professions is often dominated by women, and female journalism and broadcasting graduates far outstrip their male counterparts, but, as Mau says, the further up the ladder you go, the fewer women you'll find. 'The numbers of females graduating media courses and journalism courses – that's been very high for years, decades, since just after I did my cadetships,' and yet, 'women are missing from the key roles.'

Alexander, who was the only female editor of an NZME publication for some time, agrees:

> *Ever since I've been a journalist there's always been a lot of women wanting to be journalists and in the industry, and for whatever reason that doesn't always then translate into a lot of women in top jobs all the time. I don't think women are underrepresented, without knowing the total numbers, in newsrooms overall, but I do think that when it comes to the positions of senior leadership, there aren't as many women.*

The age-old conundrum of balancing work and family life may be a factor in the dearth of women at the top of the food chain, Alexander believes:

> *Journalism is a very hard career to balance with family because news is 24/7. We run a 24/7 newsroom, so it's not really a job where we can say – 'sure, you can work these hours because that works for you'. We can where we can, but actually there are some roles and jobs that have to be done across the day 24/7, and so some people might choose to opt out of them.*

In the 21st century, it shouldn't have to be pointed out that men have families too, but women still appear to shoulder most of the caretaking burden. 'Outside my son's school, there's still a majority of women [waiting to pick up their children],' Alexander says. For many women, having children impacts upon their careers in a way that their male partners don't experience. The dual burdens of caretaking and 'emotional labour' often fall mainly to women. 'There's a whole lot of personal stuff that comes into play,' Miriama Kamo says:

> *There are just so many things that women are trying to balance and think about all at once. Is it easier for men? I'm going to brazenly say yes.*

In light of the extra responsibilities working women have, Miriyana Alexander says, organisations need to adapt:

> *I think that there are a lot more progressively social things that we should be doing for people and families. Apparently TVNZ used to have a crèche on site and I think those kinds of things in big organisations should just happen, because it makes it a lot easier for you as a working parent.*

Kamo believes that organisations are not necessarily opposed to adaptation, but the lack of women in roles of power may play a role in the lethargic rate of change:

> *I think there's more will than we give men credit for in wanting to [accommodate mothers]. I don't think men are necessarily against it across the board, but if you don't have that personal challenge yourself, of having to balance all those different things – like breastfeed a baby – then you're not necessarily going to be thinking*

> *of solutions for it. But there are amazing innovations around the world – some of those Silicon Valley companies are doing really amazing things to make it easier for women to have a family and work. We could definitely do with more of that, and New Zealand's the ideal place for that sort of innovation. We're a perfect test population. Maybe we do need more women in power. Just to at least get those ideas across the line.*

Until the workplace changes to be more family-friendly, however, many women make career choices that may result in a step backwards or sideways professionally so that they can keep up with the demands of family life.

In some situations, however, it is clear that women are held back by forces outside of their control, especially when others make choices for them. Broadcaster Hilary Barry found that having children had an impact upon her career that she hadn't foreseen, and that was entirely beyond her control. She says:

> *I think after having children you definitely suffer the effects of that in the workplace, and it's often from a well-meaning male boss who doesn't offer you the same opportunities as your male colleagues because in the back of his mind he knows that you've got kids and he doesn't want to put extra pressure on you, so it's that benevolent sexism. But we want to be asked. We want to be given the opportunity. We'll be honest about saying if we can or can't do that, but just ask us. We'll soon let you know.*

She recalls a time when she approached the Human Rights Commission because she wasn't being offered the same opportunities her male colleague was. While her male colleague was out reporting on news as, when and where it happened, Barry was stuck in the studio:

> *I had to stand up for myself because I was losing confidence because I felt I wasn't a valued member of the team. And for my own self-respect. It wasn't good for me to feel like I was a second-class citizen and not given any opportunities when my male colleague was.*
>
> *After I'd had children it got to a point where I did seek out talking to the Human Rights Commission to talk about going to arbitration, because it had got to a point where I'd tried to talk to my boss and just say, 'Look, this isn't fair and I'm sure you're not being sexist' – while looking at him thinking, 'You're totally being sexist' – but I was just banging my head against a brick wall. I did for a long time and then it was just ridiculous, so I went to the Human Rights Commission and had a chat with somebody there who said 'Look, we can help you with this process, it's not a legal process, we simply sit down and go through arbitration.'*
>
> *So I went to my boss and I said 'Look, this is what I think we should do because obviously the message isn't getting through and I feel like we should go to arbitration' and he completely freaked out just at the words 'Human Rights Commission'; absolutely panicked and got our in-house counsel at the time to*

> *see if we could just have a chat together, which I was 100 per cent behind, because she is an absolutely fantastic woman.*
>
> *So we had a chat about the situation and she was completely on my side and said [to my boss] 'Oh my gosh, how has this gone on for so long? Pull your head in.'*
>
> *It was great, and it worked out fine and it was settled by a good conversation, but it shouldn't have got that far and I shouldn't have been the one suffering so much angst over it. I wasn't asking [my boss] for a pay rise, I wasn't asking for more leave, I wasn't asking for anything that was going to materially affect him at all, I simply was asking as a journalist to be sent out of the building on a similar number of stories as my male colleague, and I simply wasn't – I never left the building, because the little lady had to stay at home keeping the home fires burning and not put on a pair of gumboots and go out and report on a flood. Imagine – what about my hair and makeup? The audience wouldn't be happy, I'd look a mess, oh my gosh!*

Even after Barry's conversation with her boss about the Human Rights Commission, however, the most maddening moment was yet to come:

> *The then boss, after I'd said, 'Look, I think we need to go to arbitration with the Human Rights Commission', came out of his office one afternoon and said, 'I've got a story for you to go and do! Why don't you go and be the royal correspondent for the tour of Charles and Camilla?' And I looked at him and I said, 'I don't*

think you've got the point.' He wasn't even trying to be funny. And I said, 'Tell me this, would you ask Mike McRoberts to go and report on the royal tour of Charles and Camilla?' and he said, 'Yes I would.'

And I said 'No you wouldn't.'

Often you're dealing with individuals who you really love and respect as bosses and you know in your heart of hearts they can't possibly be sexist, they're decent human beings, and yet it's just so part of society, of workplaces, that that mind set exists. I guess that's the hardest thing – that you kind of take it because you like the person, you like your male boss, they're good people, and you go, 'There's so much good about you but this is just unacceptable.'

All of the women that I spoke to while I was researching for this chapter acknowledged that the lack of women in positions of power in the media is a problem. Until women are more equally represented at the top of the professional hierarchy, it's likely that benevolent sexism – behaviour that may appear positive but is actually damaging to gender equality – will continue to exist in the media industry. It's also unlikely that old perceptions will change, both for women working in the news business and for the women on the other side of the story. On top of that, there's also a high likelihood that there'll be pay disparities within media organisations, as women remain clustered in lower-paid positions and men sit atop the food chain.

In media, like most other businesses, men have routinely been paid more than women for decades. When Miriama Kamo subverted that long-held trend, she was swiftly reminded of how unusual such a situation was:

> *I worked in a job once where I was told in a pay discussion that if I received what I was asking for, then I would be earning more than my male counterpart. I was shocked because I didn't feel my workmate had any place in discussions around my own remuneration, any more than I should have in his – how that became an issue in that conversation to this day does my head in. Given my seniority, I was surprised that I wasn't already earning more than him. I think the bar is set higher for women and even higher for Māori women, and we have a long way to go to achieve pay equity.*

Other prominent women in the media have also had frustrating experiences with pay negotiations. Alison Mau famously wrote in 2017 about how, when she was asked to take over Mike Hosking's job on *Breakfast*, the then Head of News at TVNZ laughed in her face when she asked to be paid what Hosking had been earning. Even worse, she says, it's still happening now:

> *After I wrote that Sunday Star Times column on the pay gap, I had a rollercoaster week of quite senior female journalists direct messaging me and pouring their hearts out, saying, 'Oh my God I'm so glad you wrote that, you'd never guess what's happened to me'. Funnily enough I probably would guess. And it just went on and on. I was so depressed by the end of the week because I just saw capable people, high profile people that you would never guess*

> *were being treated [unequally] in 2017. The example I gave was almost 15 years ago, but it's still happening.*

Even women who have not experienced pay disparity believe that it is important to take steps to combat it. Hilary Barry says that she has always been paid the same as her male colleagues, but she is well aware that others have not been so lucky. Not that being paid what you are worth should have anything to do with luck.

> *I do think that we need to within workplaces be more open about what we earn because we can solve the problem. It may not be publicly available or printed by the company what people earn, but if you build up trust within a group of people I think people should feel that they can talk about what they earn and what their expectations are in terms of salary, what other people think they should be asking for. We could all use being a bit more open about it.*

Just as the undervaluation of women has been the norm for generations, other trends are also stubbornly entrenched in our collective psyche. As just one example, the typical perception of a senior editor, producer or programmer remains what it has always been: that of a middle-aged man. The male editor of a major newspaper is such a powerful stereotype that it is still prevalent today. Indeed, as Massey University's Dr Catherine Strong told me, in 2017, 74 per cent of the editors of daily newspapers in New Zealand were men. Alexander still receives letters and emails addressing her as 'Dear Sir'.

> *That fucks me off. Can they not even dream that there might be a female editor who they're writing to? Lack of imagination. And they will come equally from women and men because, again, 'Oh my goodness, if you're a newspaper editor you must be a sir.'*

Mau doesn't think that the trend against women's advancement is accidental.

> *I think that there is a level of management in my industry that is actually almost actively holding [women] back. TVNZ, for example, four years ago, was so proud of its team of female executive producers, and one [high-ranking] news and current affairs woman, that they did a glamorous four-page spread in* Next *magazine … All of those women have been either sacked or let go or have moved on. None progressed to management. And as far as I know, right now [in December, 2017], the only female executive producers there are heading non-primetime shows, or are in acting executive producer roles.*

When there are no women involved setting the agenda, there's no balance of viewpoints and life experiences informing the major decisions of a news organisation. There's no high-level check on unconscious biases.

A lack of diversity becomes even more dangerous when it comes to opinion writing, editorialising and punditry. A media landscape that amplifies the opinions of predominantly white men can only ever claim to truly represent white men. The views presented in such a landscape will never be able to tell the full story, and as a result, the public suffers.

In her former role as editor of the *Herald's* weekend titles, Miriyana Alexander made diversifying the voices in her papers something of a personal mission:

> *It's no secret that I wanted more female columnists, which I've done across both of our weekend papers, because there were just too many old white men, and there still are a lot of them across our seven days. My view is that we needed to get more female voices into our publications.*

It seems her instinct for diversity (among other things) paid off. While other papers were shuttering, feeling the pinch of the digital age, the *Weekend Herald* significantly increased its readership during her reign.

But even while the New Zealand media takes important steps towards diversity within its group of commentators, it still has a long way to go. As far as I know I am one of only two Māori opinion writers with a regular column in the national mainstream print media (alongside my *Herald* colleague John Tamihere). Tamihere and I often have different points of view, but we simply cannot represent the breadth of Māori experience in New Zealand. Nowhere near it. The situation is better in digital media, but there still remains a large discrepancy throughout the media as a whole. The lack of Māori commentators and journalists remains a significant blight upon our media landscape, and contributes to a continuing widespread lack of understanding of Māori issues. While Māori media is vibrant and obviously presents a number of Māori viewpoints, our current media landscape is currently largely segregated; a situation that hardly serves readers. 'It isn't a reflection of our readership and our society,' Alexander says of the lack of cultural diversity of New Zealand's opinion writers. 'And that's on us. We should be looking for that. I'm sure there are great non-Pākehā opinion writers and we need to be going and looking for them.'

Mau agrees:

> *I think representation of all non-white ethnicities is pretty poor in this country. That's an area we could all do much, much better at. There must be talented people of other ethnicities coming through journalism schools, surely. Maybe they're too smart and they're all going into industries that actually pay and are not dying.*

Young Māori considering joining the media professions are likely well aware of the problems both surrounding the financial future of the media and with Māori representation. When Miriama Kamo speaks to young Māori broadcasting students, she says, some understandably report feeling apprehensive about the mainstream media:

> *When I've spoken to Māori journalism students or young broadcasters, what the feedback has been in years past is, 'We're worried that if we come into mainstream media we will be*

> *isolated and that people won't understand our worldview and that we'll feel that we're cut off and we're not appreciated and understood', and really the only way to solve that is to get more [Māori journalists] in.*

Māori in the media often have to face unique challenges. Like the ridiculous notion that Māori broadcasters and journalists should act as spokespeople for the entire Māori population, a phenomenon Kamo has experienced first-hand:

> *When I first started out, actually even before I began, all my life I had been the [spokesperson]. If you turn up to a meeting and you're Māori and a Māori issue comes up – oh well, you'd better talk to it, because you know everyone and everything. Being Māori, you must know. And if you didn't know something, people were wont to say, 'How can you not know about this?' I often found myself having to be the spokesperson for things Māori, having to stick up for things Māori; it was very isolating actually, for a long time. But the bigger issue is the implication that one person can speak for all things Māori, as if there is only one Māori view. It is much better now, but there are still echoes of it.*

Over and above that, being a Māori woman in the media adds an extra layer of complexity. 'There are very high expectations of Māori women in positions of influence and power,' Kamo says. 'There are politics that come into play as a Māori woman, whether you're a broadcaster or you're a politician – whatever it is – there's a lot of pressure.'

Despite that, Kamo believes that the New Zealand media is 'at the beginning of the right path' when it comes to Māori representation and storytelling in the media:

> *I think there's an acceptance that we need to have diversity in our newsrooms and that actually that isn't about doing the right thing, it's about doing the best thing. It's ridiculous that some are still 'thinking' about how to create diversity – we should have moved on from that, but the fact that we are actually taking action and making that happen is great.*

On television, however, the main opinion leaders are still – surprise, surprise – mainly white men. Barry points out the sexist landscape that women in the media are faced with, which she believes is at least partially driven by audiences:

> *I would love to see some audience research on [a female host-led show] because I suspect that the audience wouldn't cope with it. As wrong as that is on so many levels, I would put money on the fact that if you got a focus group and played them a programme with an intelligent, coherent woman at the helm and then played them a show with a man at the helm doing exactly the same job, that they would absolutely feel more comfortable with a man because that's the way it's always been. That's been the paradigm, that's been the way it's always done, 'When I tune in in the*

> *mornings, I want to hear the authoritative tones of a male voice.' That was the criticism of early female newsreaders as well. When the BBC had its first female newsreader the criticism was, 'How can she sound authoritative with a woman's voice? How is it possible that she can have any authority? She simply doesn't have the right tone of voice.'*

The audience is only part of the picture, however. While women are undoubtedly held to a different standard on-screen, they face skewed expectations off-air too. 'Famous broadcasters are famously diva-ish; temperamental,' Alison Mau says:

> *I know from direct experience the most diva-ish are the men, because women have to watch themselves, so you have to make sure that if you're going to chuck a hissy fit because something's gone dreadfully wrong, which I occasionally do – and when I say 'hissy', I shouldn't use that language, should I? – when you're going to speak strongly about something that's happened, or when you're going to complain about conditions or substandard work or whatever it might be, when you're a woman you have to make sure you don't do that too often. Or too strongly. Whereas there are male colleagues of mine, who I won't name, who appear to feel free to act like absolute toddlers. You can't do that as a woman. You need to be a bit careful.*

Another factor that may play a role in the lack of women sharing bold opinions both in broadcast and print media is the abuse they receive when they do so. Alexander has noticed that her female columnists are treated differently by the public than the men who write for her titles:

> *I do think that people are particularly nasty to women because it becomes an appearance thing, it becomes a sexism thing, and a lot of that has got to be [because] they must feel threatened entirely by a smart woman who wants to say something interesting and stand up for herself or have a debate about an interesting topic. The misogynist attitude comes through where people think they can just say whatever they want.*

Mau is no stranger to backlash. In news that should shock exactly no one, online abuse can be taken to a whole new level if you're a member of the LGBTQ+ community:

> *I've got pretty good mental health, which I'm very grateful for, but [reading the comments] can put me into a weekend long funk. I don't get rape or death threats, funnily enough, and I think that's because I tend to get the 'You'll burn in hell, you dyke' threats instead. I shouldn't say this, it does make me laugh though. I just find the extreme end of things perhaps easier to deal with sometimes than people who are deliberately misrepresenting what you were saying. That gets me more. And that's what will draw me into an argument online, not people who say 'burn in hell'. I say, 'Okay … waving emoji'.*

Mau and I sometimes commiserate over nasty social media comments, but she points out the differences between the insults that are lobbed at each of us:

> *I think because you are a young woman you are still seen by society as a sexual being, whereas I'm too old for that now. I'm invisible – well, I would be if I didn't have my column. They don't jump to that immediate gendered attack with me as they do with you. They're more angry that I can be happy in a same-sex relationship.*

Hilary Barry has also experienced her fair share of sexist feedback during her time. As a television broadcaster, she says that it comes with the territory:

> *You will as a woman, particularly in television, be critiqued on the way you look so much more than the men. The way your hair looks, what you're wearing, the lipstick you have on will always be a topic of conversation and feedback among audience members.*
>
> *Why are you [the audience] critiquing the way I look? Because that's important to you. Because I'm the woman on television, and that's what you require of a woman on television. That I'm pretty, I'm wearing nice clothes and you approve of my hairdo and the shade of my lipstick.*

And what if you happen to be pretty, wearing nice clothes, with a great hairdo and a lovely shade of lipstick, and insist on having opinions?

> *Then, oh my gosh! You'll probably be shrieking! And irrational, and you'll be stupid. All these sorts of things.*
>
> *Often when I do have to get strong and heavy-handed in an interview, I'll be accused of raising my voice, shrieking, being emotional; all those sorts of criticisms that are levelled at women who get annoyed or are forthright.*

Kamo echoes Barry's comments:

> *I'm often jealous of the men, they can just put on a suit, change their tie and maybe their shirt and get a little dash of makeup and they're done. [As a woman] the audience notices if you wear the same thing in a week. We are definitely held to a higher account in the appearance stakes. Without a shadow of a doubt.*

Prominent women are also often questioned by the media about their partners and children in interviews completely unrelated to their families. I remember being asked about boyfriends and future babies when I was still a teenager. One day I finally snapped, and retorted, 'Would you ask a young man that question?' after which the (female) journalist spluttered and apologised. I find reading interviews that ask powerful women with both careers and children how they 'balance it all' particularly maddening. For every one of those interviews a publication publishes, it should be mandated by law to publish five stories asking powerful professional men how they balance their work with raising their children, though I sadly suspect that the majority of their answers may have the effect of propelling us in a time warp back to the 1950s.

Hilary Barry has had her own experiences of gallingly sexist interviews:

> *When I first took on the news reading job with Mike McRoberts at TV3 I had a five and a three-year-old and I was asked during the course of a radio interview by this male interviewer, 'Oh you're going to be so busy, who's looking after the kids?' And you don't call it out because you're sort of shocked.*
>
> *Did he really just say that? We're live on air. It's supposed to be a really nice, fun radio interview and you ask me some dick sexist question like that? You're a moron.*

Barry has also been particularly vocal about sexist framing of stories about women:

> *It's always annoyed the hell out of me. I've always been a rabid feminist – a hysterical feminist – but I guess social media gave me an outlet to call out sexist crap. Also I think just because of my age and stage I've just got to the point where I go, 'You know what? That's bullshit and I'm calling it out.' And I will.*

Alison Mau agrees:

> *I think that we all come to that in the end, don't we? I feel like my journey has been probably quite similar to Hilary's in that we all*

> *come to that and we're not afraid to speak out. You get to a certain level of frustration where you think 'God!' and social media has helped us vent, which has been great. Probably you've heard me become more outspoken since Twitter was invented. There's probably a correlation.*

It's no surprise that both Barry and Mau point to social media as a factor in their willingness to speak out about sexism. Social media has flipped the script of the traditional media agenda, giving women the freedom to say what they like without it being censored or silenced. While both Barry and Mau have had access to highly visible public platforms for decades, on social media, there is no producer in their ear. They can set their own agenda, and speak about subjects that they personally feel passionate about.

For women without the enormous public profiles of Barry and Mau, social media has been a revolutionary tool that has given them a way to be heard. It has also allowed uncomfortable and subversive subjects to be raised, and for people who have not traditionally had access to media platforms to join in or even lead the conversation.

One such discussion, that started in the traditional media and then spread like wildfire on Twitter and Facebook, was a far-reaching conversation about sexual harassment. After a plethora of allegations against Hollywood titan of industry Harvey Weinstein dominated headlines late last year, many women, from all walks of life, came forward to speak about their experiences of sexual harassment. Some of those included women working in the New Zealand media. Sadly, sexual harassment is an experience that many of us share. As a young reporter, Barry says she was sexually harassed by a prominent New Zealander. It's an experience that has stayed with her for years:

> *As a far more confident woman at 47, I look back and I just go, 'I wish you'd stood up and said something.' He'd have no idea, because he's been doing it his whole life and probably doesn't even remember, but I cannot look him in the eye.*
>
> *I didn't shut him down at the time because I just thought, 'Oh my God I'm a young reporter and I feel so uncomfortable with what's just unfolded. You're a really well-known New Zealander, there's such a disparity of power here, I'm trying to do my job, I don't want to cause a fuss and then have you call my boss because you probably know him and you're mates.'*
>
> *[Sexual harassers] are relying on us needing them, or feeling like we need them in order to do our jobs and yet we don't. But you don't rationalise that in the right way at the time. I feel like [sexual harassment] is prevalent everywhere. Honestly, you look at that #MeToo campaign and you just go, 'Is there a woman in the country who hasn't been sexually harassed?' No, I doubt it.*

Alexander also points to power differentials as a big part of sexual harassment. Up until recently, power, or the lack thereof, likely prevented women from speaking out:

> *Weinstein has made [sexual harassment] a topic of discussion and many women have shared stories. [I've heard about] a lot of historic stuff. The power stuff. The stuff you couldn't, didn't want to talk to anyone about – bosses, basically, and feeling like you just couldn't tell anyone about it, and that stuff that goes on that makes you start to doubt your own judgment, which happens just so much.*
>
> *I've sadly, as a boss, had to deal with complaints against male staff from female colleagues. In all industries, everywhere, [sexual harassment] is real.*

For abusers and harassers, the media reporting of the dozens of allegations against Weinstein and the countless other men who were publicly accused of vile conduct after Weinstein's behaviour came to light must've been their worst nightmare. When the story gained momentum online under the #MeToo banner, a number of men from all different industries all around the world must've felt very uncomfortable. In a way, the Weinstein allegations represented perfectly the role that the media should play in changing the narrative of our society. It is important to note, too, however, that the slut-shaming narratives that had kept victims silent for so long had been (and in some cases still are) perpetuated and emphasised by the media for a very long time. Things may be changing, but as a society we still have a long way to go.

The media, as a reflection of society (though not an entirely representative one), deals with the same issues that plague the larger community. Like many other industries, it is taking gradual steps to try to address discrepancies and problems that have simply been 'normal' and accepted for generations. Unlike many other industries, it has an outsized impact on the way in which we understand and view the world. The way that the media tells stories, the viewpoints it chooses to broadcast, the faces it makes ubiquitous, and the news it doesn't cover all have an impact upon our society. In recent decades, the media has become increasingly aware of this, and has taken steps to alter itself. In my view, those changes have happened too slowly and too gradually.

A core function of the media is to speak truth to power. To comfort the afflicted and afflict the comfortable.

The media is an incredibly powerful voice. But perhaps it's time that it listened.

CHAPTER SEVEN

The crime of opining whilst female

My mother always told me to be good, and if I couldn't be good, to be good at it. At this point, she probably feels that I've followed her advice rather more literally than she'd intended. When I won two Canon Media Awards in 2017, and had a troll tweet that my victory represented the 'headstone on the grave of the New Zealand media', I thought to myself, 'Well, Mum, I couldn't be good, but I did my damnedest to be good at it.'

I've been outspoken for as long as I can remember. My mother tells a great story after a few glasses of wine about taking me to a Michael Houston piano recital when I was very young. I'd just started piano lessons, so I can almost see the logic of such an excursion, though expecting a wriggly four-year-old to sit still for an hour in an audience full of mainly elderly ladies while a man played sonatas up on stage was a bit ambitious. As Mum soon realised. I lasted through the first piece, then, when Houston rose for his third successive bow my patience ran out. 'Mummy!' I said, at the top of my lungs. 'Why does that man keep bowing? It's like he wants us to keep clapping for him!' If looks could kill, I'd have been slain on the spot. I actually met the lovely Houston years later, when we shared a stage. I didn't have the heart to ask him whether he remembered our first interaction. Neither did my mother.

Somewhere between the ages of four and 16, however, I became aware that being a young woman with heterodox views made you the schoolyard equivalent of a black sheep. I can't speak for other opinionated young women, but I found that my opinions came on like emotions – swiftly and strongly – and during my childhood I had little hope of controlling them. They got me into trouble, both with teachers and with my fellow students, and I eventually became very self-conscious about my views, worrying about the next time I'd be struck by a particularly robust opinion that I didn't yet have the filter to suppress. When you're known for your opinions, there's a certain wariness that can materialise in conversations with others. It can be accompanied by eye-rolling, belittling, dismissiveness and angry silences. As a teenager, I felt those reactions deeply, and by the end of my school years, I'd resolved to be less opinionated. I began to shut my mouth and bite my tongue, and although I couldn't see it then, I dislocated a part of myself.

During the early years of my music career, I largely suppressed my opinions. As a young female artist in a genre with a predominantly conservative audience, perhaps the most important part of my job was to be liked. Achieving that was a struggle from the outset, however, as I was marketed as a straight-A, over-achieving scholarship student, freshly graduated from one of the most elite private schools in the country. In a nation afflicted by tall poppy syndrome, there's nothing particularly endearing about being that kid people want to hate. So I shut up, opting to sit on the fence wherever possible. I became a kind of self-parody; a glittering character that appeared on stages in poufy dresses, sang pretty songs and was overwhelmingly inoffensive, if somewhat insipid. While my opinions did occasionally break free – like when I objected to Dame Kiri Te Kanawa's characterisation of musicians in my genre as 'the new fakes' – my identity as a 'popera princess' largely allowed me to hide all of my inconvenient thoughts behind a pretty voice and a winning smile. In hindsight, it's no great surprise that I felt trapped and unhappy.

I was 22 when I realised that I couldn't continue to play the role of the goody two shoes classical crossover singer and retain my sanity. My musical journey, during which I began to write and perform my own songs, was intrinsically tied to a personal journey of self-discovery, as I began to find my way back to myself. Around that time, I began sharing my views on social media, tentatively at first, and then with increasing frankness. Bizarrely, my opinions began to gain attention – I can only surmise because being a visible young woman sharing strong opinions publicly was an unusual phenomenon at the time – and within a few years, I began to be asked to share my views on television and radio.

Soon after, I launched Villainesse.com – an online media project for young women – then created #MyBodyMyTerms, an online campaign focusing on sexual violence, consent and revenge porn. Then, at the beginning of 2016, I began writing a weekly opinion column for the *Weekend Herald.*

When I began sharing my opinions publicly, the reactions to my views surprised even me. It seemed to occur in stages: first people were deeply surprised that I had an opinion that I was able to articulate with relative dexterity, then they either got used to it, or became outraged that a singer would take it into her pretty little head to think about such serious subjects as poverty, politics, racism and feminism and have the temerity to put forward her views as if they were worthy of the consideration of a large audience. The final stage for a hardcore handful was a kind of utter loathing that would motivate previous fans of my music to make contact to tell me that they hated my writing and now muted their television sets and turned their backs to the screen when I sang the national anthem at rugby tests.

Even among some of those who like my work, such appreciation can come with caveats. I am always amused by the mainly men who compliment me on my opinion writing but feel the need to temper any praise by first informing me that they don't always agree with me. I wonder whether they would feel the need to point out to a male writer that they admire that they don't agree with every word he writes. By this stage I'm acutely aware that the vast majority of people don't agree with every single opinion I hold, which, frankly, is a relief. If my work simply generated sycophantic accord I'm not sure I'd still have a job.

Taking a stand has never been easy. It's even harder if you're a woman. Throughout history, women who've dared to offer their views have been variously burnt at the stake, drowned, stoned, confined to asylums and the like. I count my lucky stars on a regular basis that we've moved from torture and death (for the most part) to online abuse. I'll take 'stfu stupid whore' over a witch trial any day, thank you very much. The stories of many of the women that have been punished throughout history for voicing their views have been lost to time, in no small part because the men writing history rarely thought to include them, but needless to say the persecution of women who dare to commit the crime of opining whilst female is certainly nothing new.

In a New Zealand context, the examples are plentiful. The one that stands out most vividly to me is the treatment Helen Clark received while she was Prime Minister. I was ten years old when Clark was elected after a ground-breaking election in which the leaders of the two largest parties in Parliament were women. A race in which the two options for Prime Minister – Helen Clark and Jenny Shipley – were female had never happened before, and, it's worth noting, hasn't happened again since. Throughout my teens, I watched Clark on the 6 o'clock news most nights. I came from a National-voting household, so the commentary from my father and grandfather was not especially favourable, but as I grew older I began to develop a deep respect for this formidable Prime Minister, the woman who was boldly demonstrating to me and my cohort of young women that girls really could do anything. As I began to pay attention to what she was saying, I also became aware of what was being said about her. Much of it was profoundly depressing. At school, the boys particularly would call her a 'man', or an 'it', ridiculing her looks and her voice. On a larger scale, looking back at old articles and news segments published and aired during the reign of the fifth Labour Government provides an interesting study into just how sexist (and homophobic) society was back then. I'd say it demonstrates how much society has evolved in the time since, but the treatment of Prime Minister Jacinda Ardern by some members of the press and the public suggests that we haven't come that far after all.

Well before her time as Prime Minister, Clark herself acknowledged the abuse she experienced during her 1981 campaign to win the seat of Mount Albert in the 1986 book *Head and Shoulders,* saying, 'As a single woman I was really hammered. I was accused of being a lesbian, of living in a commune, having friends who were Trotskyites and gays.'[1] When she entered Parliament and began her ascent to power, those narratives would continue to dog her. There were nasty low blows about her appearance and utterly idiotic beat-ups about the way she dressed[2] – during the Queen's visit to New Zealand in 2002, the BBC had a field day when Clark wore formal trousers instead of a gown to a state dinner – but perhaps the most underhand of all of the slights aimed at Clark were the persistent rumours about her sexuality and marriage. When Clark ousted Mike Moore to become the leader of the Labour party in 1993, he accused her of 'being part of a cabal of lesbians and barren women trying to take over the Labour Party'[3]. Moore would later pen an op-ed in the *New Zealand Herald* in 2007 in which he called then Minister for Auckland Judith Tizard a 'consort' of the then Prime Minister[4]. Even Prime Minister Jenny Shipley was not above the odd sexist remark during her tenure, famously (and obviously incorrectly) calling Clark 'the spinster of New Zealand politics'[5].

Later, Clark would be forced to deny that her husband of 25 years was gay, after newspapers and television stations picked up on a baseless rumour that Professor Peter Davis was having an affair with Ian Scott, an openly gay friend of Clark and Davis[6]. While prominent politicians can expect a certain amount of salaciousness, I suspect that Clark's identity as a formidable, ambitious woman who opted not to follow the path generally assigned to her gender (subservient wife and mother), who kept her own name upon marriage, valued and promoted the strong women around her and fought for women's rights played a role in the particularly unpleasant attacks she endured.

Some female journalists played their part, too, in forwarding tired gender stereotypes. The *New Zealand Herald's* Fran O'Sullivan variously called Clark, 'the political dominatrix' and, 'the blue-stockinged academic who shafted two former PMs on her way to the leadership'[7], playing into an image of Clark as an uncompromising, ball-busting, cunning shrew. Perhaps some of the most vile reportage came from conservative journalist Ian Wishart, who published, among many other hit-pieces, a scathing article entitled 'The Siege of Helengrad', in which he wrote about what he viewed to be her 'ruthless ambition', 'almost pathological dislike of men' and 'latent disdain for women with children'[8]. Wishart's acidic diatribe makes for exasperating reading. Among the many innocuous things he paints as significant is the number of powerful women who flourished during Clark's tenure. 'Prime Minister Clark has now assembled a network of very powerful women,' he wrote. 'Most of her key advisers – including long term aide

Heather Simpson are female. Many are lesbian.' This support of her colleagues seemed to be a sticking point for Wishart. Ironically, as a young Kiwi girl this stood out to me too, but in the opposite way to Wishart's view: Helen Clark was demonstrating through her support of women and LGBTQ+ people that it was possible to achieve great success regardless of your gender or sexuality.

Many of the portrayals of Clark and her policies were gendered, from the endless references to the 'nanny state' to bumper stickers trumpeting 'ditch the bitch'[9] to cartoons that portrayed her as a witch and even a pole-dancer[10].Former Mayor of Waitakere (and former Labour Party President) Sir Bob Harvey called her a 'diva' and described the 1999 election thusly: 'We're interested in a male country, which we are, in seeing two women battle it out – the two Xena princesses.'[11] An image that has always stuck in my mind that exemplifies the gendered nature of criticism hurled at Clark is that of then Leader of the Opposition (and now former Prime Minister) Bill English, sitting on a tractor outside Parliament during a protest against the so-called 'fart tax' with a big grin on his face holding a sign that read, 'The mad cow shouldn't have signed'[12]. Then there's this quote from Denis Welch, which further illustrates what powerful women like Clark were, and still are, up against:

> *Helen could get quite snarky. She didn't like it when they climbed into that speeding incident, or signing the painting that wasn't hers. She could get quite uppity, but I don't think any more than any politician when the tide was running against her. Even John Key can be quite dismissive when things are not going his way.*[13]

So John Key gets to be 'dismissive', but when Helen fights back she is described as 'snarky' and 'uppity'. Bear with me for a moment – I need to retrieve my eyeballs, as they appear to have rolled out of their sockets.

Helen Clark is far from the only female politician to have dealt with sexism, however. Across the ditch, former Australian Prime Minister Julia Gillard received just as much, if not more, of the chauvinistic claptrap that Clark did. To this day, one of my favourite videos of all time is one in which Gillard publicly lanced the great festering boil of Australian sexism in a speech in the House of Representatives. Goaded one too many times by then opposition leader Tony Abbott, who'd just (astonishingly) lectured Gillard on sexism, she reached a self-described 'crack point'[14], and launched into a speech that would later go viral. It began:

> *Thank you very much Deputy Speaker and I rise to oppose the motion moved by the Leader of the Opposition. And in so doing I say to the Leader of the Opposition I will not be lectured about sexism and misogyny by this man. I will not. And the Government will not be lectured about sexism and misogyny by this man. Not now, not ever.*
>
> *The Leader of the Opposition says that people who hold sexist views and who are misogynists are not appropriate for high office. Well I hope the Leader of the Opposition has got a piece of paper and he is writing out his resignation. Because if he wants to know what misogyny looks like in modern Australia,*

he doesn't need a motion in the House of Representatives, he needs a mirror.[15]

Every time I watch the video of Gillard's speech I find myself mesmerised by the splendid vision of a powerful woman publicly and expertly giving a man who has more than earned his comeuppance exactly what he deserves. Watching Tony Abbott – the man who once said, 'What if men are by physiology or temperament, more adapted to exercise authority or to issue command?'[16] – squirm in his seat is the soothing balm every exhausted feminist needs once and a while.

Back in New Zealand, discussion around gender has had something of a resurgence in the political sphere, most notably surrounding a different Labour Party MP for Mt Albert – and current Prime Minister – Jacinda Ardern. Ardern is no stranger to sexism. During her 2011 election campaign for the seat of Auckland Central, she campaigned against National Party candidate Nikki Kaye in a battle that was (maddeningly) dubbed the 'battle of the babes'[17]. I've heard the phrase more times than I can count, but it still astounds me that media commentators would cast the contest in such a sexist and patronising way as recently as 2011. If the election fight had featured two young men, the headlines would've been markedly different. Indeed, I doubt their gender would've been remarked upon at all. Around the same time, Ardern was condescendingly ordered to, 'Zip it, sweetie' by National Party MP Paula Bennett[18], and more recently, Ardern has been described variously as a 'pretty little thing'[19] (by former Kiwis coach Graham Lowe on the *Paul Henry Show*), 'pretty bloody stupid'[20] (by political commentator Matthew Hooton), a 'show pony' (by Fran O'Sullivan), a 'political celebrity'[21] (O'Sullivan again), 'stardust'[22] (by then Prime Minister Bill English), a 'chicky-babe'[23] (by NewsTalk ZB Radio Host Leighton Smith) and a 'pretty communist' (by Tauwhare farmer Craig Sinclair, whose cringe-worthy protest sign earned him the condemnation of former Prime Minister Helen Clark and most other Kiwis in possession of a brain)[24].

While some of these comments are not outwardly sexist, their various contexts betray their gendered nature. Hooton's insult was in response to Ardern's reaction to Lowe's 'pretty little thing' comment, insinuating that her reply to a tweet by Hilary Barry was foolish. In the tweet in question, Barry had said that she'd make sure that Lowe would not leave the studio without bruised shins[25]. Ardern responded by thanking Barry and saying that she hoped her shoes were pointy[26] (a response that, if you ask me, showed both great restraint and good humour). Ardern was stupid, according to Hooton, because Lowe was respected by rugby league fans, who may be likely to support Labour. Yes, that's right, a male political commentator mansplained to a female politician how she should handle a sexist and belittling comment made about her on national television, insinuated that female MPs shouldn't object to sexist comments made about them if there might be a risk of alienating voters *and* insulted the moral compasses of league fans in one fell swoop.

O'Sullivan's quotes appeared in the *New Zealand Herald* around the time when Ardern was elected as the Deputy Leader of the Labour Party, which, at age 36, was quite an achievement. Indeed, David Lange was 37 when he became the Deputy Leader in 1979. Instead of celebrating her impressive trajectory, O'Sullivan preferred to compare Ardern to a performing animal, while connotations of razzle dazzle with no credibility rang loudly between the lines. The question must be asked: if a young male politician had risen to become the Deputy Leader of the Opposition at age 36, what terms would've been used to describe him? I'd wager he would've been labelled, as Lange was, a rising star or a future Prime Minister, and his popularity would've worked in his favour. He'd be a 'good bloke', 'well-liked' and someone you'd 'want to have a beer with'.

When Ardern went on to become the Leader of the Labour Party, stepping up to replace chronically unpopular Andrew Little at the age of 37, some media commentators did their best to propel feminist progress in New Zealand back 50 years. 'A lot of women in New Zealand feel like they have to make a choice between having babies and having a career, or continuing with their career at a certain point in their lives – late thirties – so … is that a decision you feel that you have to make, or do you feel you've already made it?' *The Project*'s Jesse Mulligan asked, a mere seven hours after Ardern had been announced as leader. Again Hilary Barry came to her aid. 'I see @jacindaardern has already been asked about babies vs career. Please can every nob who asks that ask the same of Bill English?'[27] she tweeted.

Sadly, that wasn't the end of the baby talk. 'Is it ok to ask Jacinda Ardern about possible plans to have children?' *The AM Show* asked in a poll the next morning. The majority of respondents said no, although co-host of the Mediaworks show and former cricketer Mark Richardson was not among them. Richardson suggested that it should be the right of employers to know whether or not female employees planned to reproduce. 'If you are the employer of a company you need to know that type of thing from the woman you are employing … the question is, is it okay for a PM to take maternity leave while in office?'[28] he asked, referring to the said hypothetical employer exclusively with the pronoun 'he' throughout his rant, and repeatedly talking over Ardern and female co-host Amanda Gillies. Thankfully the sexism didn't go uncountered. Host Duncan Garner's final word on the subject was, 'I have never asked a male political leader, in 20 years of asking questions of politicians, that question.' Quite.

Mike Hosking appeared to agree with Mark Richardson, however (no surprises there), saying that, 'If you're going to be the Prime Minister of a country, you are an open book'[29], though, as no one asked then Leader of the Opposition Bill English how on earth he was going to juggle having 'six kids under 16' with being Prime Minister when he ran against Helen Clark in 2002, it seems likely that some would-be Prime Ministers are expected to be more of an open book than others – namely those who are female.

Unsurprisingly, Matthew Hooton was quick to shove in the boot. 'I think she'll fail. I think she's an absolute flake,'[30] he said.

ACT MP David Seymour also joined the chorus of detractors,

saying, 'I don't think it's credible to have a 39-year-old Prime Minister in coalition with Metiria Turei and Winston Peters. Good on her and good luck to her but what's she ever done?'[31] The fact that Ardern had arguably done more than Seymour ever had – which was especially apparent on the day when she became the Leader of the Opposition – also appeared to escape him.

Throughout the days that followed the announcement, Ardern was repeatedly described as 'inexperienced'. Many commentators seemed oblivious to the fact that at the time of her promotion to party leader, Ardern had more parliamentary experience than both John Key and David Lange did when they became Prime Ministers.

It is difficult to watch such a smart, capable and honourable woman be forced to endure narratives that seek to cast her as a pretty, inexperienced plaything with no substance, especially when I, as a friend, know that to be categorically untrue. I fear, however, that as long as Prime Minister Jacinda Ardern is in politics, she will have to deal with these kinds of exasperating comments, because she combines an unfortunate trifecta of female offences: being successful, intelligent and attractive. She takes it all in her stride with inexplicable – to me at least – restraint, and I'm confident that she will prove her detractors wrong, but my concern is that, as the old saying goes, children are listening. Just like I watched the way Prime Minister Helen Clark was treated by the media and the public as a child, children and young people are watching the way Prime Minister Jacinda Ardern is portrayed and spoken about. At times I wonder whether we've made progress at all in the decade since Clark left office.

The takeaway from all this? Whether you're warm, cold, young, old, attractive or unattractive, if you're also a woman who is bold enough to share her views, you'll be punished. Female politicians are up against an insurmountable paradox: be seen to be too stereotypically feminine and you'll be thought of as weak and flaky, but be seen to be too masculine and you'll be thought to be unnatural and untrustworthy.

Female politicians are far from the only ones to experience sexist abuse for sharing their opinions. Female writers are also visible targets, especially when they express views contrary to the dominant narratives of the time. The response to Booker Prize-winner Eleanor Catton's 2015 comments about her home country provides a particularly illuminating example. When Catton shared her opinion that New Zealand was run at the time by, 'neo-liberal, profit-obsessed, very shallow, very money-hungry politicians who do not care about culture,'[32] she was publicly vilified. Then Prime Minister John Key suggested that she'd shown a lack of 'respect', had 'no special political insight' and that it was 'a bit sad that [she was] mixing politics with some of the things she's good at.'[33] The undercurrent – that a successful young woman with an opinion on politics has no business sharing it, especially not if it would display 'disrespect' for the men running the show – was as galling as it was unsurprising. Similarly revealing was Pākehā shock jock radio host Sean Plunket's comment that Catton was an 'ungrateful hua'[34], an offensive Māori insult that a significant number of listeners misheard as 'ungrateful whore'. (Interestingly enough, Taika Waititi was also accused of being ungrateful when, years later, he made comments similar to Catton's, although the level of backlash Waititi received was nowhere near that inspired by Catton.)

In the aftermath of Catton's statements, the young author's face was splashed across the media in a national uproar that seemed largely disproportionate and tended to focus on Catton's right (or apparent lack thereof) to share her opinion rather than the merits of the opinion itself. While Key tried to walk back his comments, telling TVNZ's *Breakfast* programme that, 'it would be no different from Richie McCaw or the Mad Butcher or anybody else having a view on politics – they're absolutely entitled to do that – but her views on politics are no more authoritative than anybody else's,'[35] one has to ask whether McCaw or Sir Peter Leitch would've been accused of 'disrespect' or whether their right to have an opinion would've been questioned in the first place. I suspect not. Indeed, when Sir Peter Leitch shared a much more problematic opinion (telling a young Māori woman that Waiheke Island was a 'white man's island') a few years later, there were many who lined up to defend him. But Catton's ill-fated remarks broke several rules about how women – particularly young women – in the public eye should act.

Catton's story was one of the first I wrote about after launching Villainesse. It was featured in an article ironically entitled 'When did New Zealand become so sexist?'[36] It was stories like hers that encouraged me to start the site. The vilification of women who dared to have a view intrigued and disturbed me, so I decided to harness it, reclaim it, and use it for good. It has not been an easy journey, but it has been endlessly satisfying being able to create an alternative world in which a female lens is applied to every story we publish. Villainesse is a celebration of women's opinions, and I'm particularly proud of the way it has provided a platform for young female writers to express themselves. Villainesse is unashamedly feminist, and while we endeavour to uphold journalistic standards wherever possible, the site refutes the kind of false equivalence that results from a rigid journalistic imperative to apply a sometimes ill-fitting sense of 'balance' to each story. The very concept of 'balance' is subjective. As was demonstrated so devastatingly in the media coverage of the 2016 US presidential election, a quest for balance can result in overstating one story whilst understating another. In some ways, Villainesse provides a balance to a media landscape that has not always been accepting and encouraging to the stories and voices of women – by contrast, it celebrates the act of opining whilst female.

The idea for Villainesse came about in October of 2014. I'd just finished my degree and released my third album (a pop EP called *Collisions*) and after eight years in a music industry decimated both by new technology and the industry's embarrassing failure to realise the impact such technology would have, resulting in an inertia that was threatening and ending careers all around me, I was feeling well and truly jaded. I was sitting with a friend at a Parnell bar, talking in increasingly fatalistic terms about what I saw to be a bleak future. I loved music, and was lucky enough to have achieved a reasonable level of success, but I was tired of the continual struggle, bored intellectually and, at age 25, in desperate need of a change. In short, I was having your typical millennial quarter-life crisis. And yes, you have my permission to snigger.

My friend Dave, with the advantage of a few more years of life experience, took the time to listen to my dark prophesising, and reassured me that the future was bright. I gave him sceptical eyes over the rim of my wineglass as I polished off my third pinot noir.

Somewhere along the line, the conversation turned to my opinions, which at the time I was sharing mainly via social media. They were … *interesting*, Dave said (or words to that effect, accompanied by a raised eyebrow) and had I ever thought of starting something bigger that allowed other young women to share their opinions on a larger platform? I hadn't. Though over the next few weeks I found that I could think of little else. The idea of a platform created for the express purpose of prioritising women's opinions, increasing the number of young female voices heard in the media and providing a source of media for young women that wasn't there to tell them what to wear, what to think, how to diet or what products they should buy to transport them a little closer to the ever-moving, unattainable goal posts of being 'enough' was intoxicating.

With Villainesse I wanted to create something of an alternative reality, and indeed, I'd imagine that stumbling across the site when you're used to a mainstream media landscape that has often relegated women's opinions and stories to 'lifestyle' sections and 'tell all' exposés in women's magazines is something like arriving on a different planet. Villainesse's unwillingness to bow to demands from men for issues to be framed in a way that suits their worldview has led to a number of irate comments and messages over the years. Such comments almost always clang with irony, as the angry men clogging my inbox remain seemingly impervious to the fact that they're experiencing the very frustration that women have been dealing with for generations. My answer to men who can't bear to read a story that takes an unabashedly female point of view is to go elsewhere. It's hardly like the internet isn't teeming with places where men can go to find the male-dominated status quo.

Attention all man-babies, there's this site called 4chan. You're going to love it.

Villainesse could be accused of being an echo chamber, but as much as I want to support the notion that we should all read the writing of people that we disagree with to prevent us from existing in the kind of cyber bubbles that helped to deliver Donald Trump to the White House, I find that the philosophy falls down somewhat when readers then demand that the writer should re-shape their opinion to appease the status quo, cease to write at all, or die. This is the kind of quagmire that faces many female writers. If you follow the work of writers like Lindy West, Laurie Penny, Jessica Valenti, Lauren Duca, Roxane Gay, Clementine Ford, Van Badham, Jane Caro, Tara Moss, Rachel Stewart, Alison Mau, and basically any female writer who dares to share a bold view, you'll likely run into three main types of responses: 1. People telling them they're wrong and they should change their thinking; 2. People telling them to shut up; and 3. People telling them to go and kill themselves/that they should be raped/that they deserve to have some other kind of often graphically described violence perpetrated against them. Of course, the fourth response is the one that restores at least some faith in humanity: People supporting the work of these courageous women who continue to speak truth to power despite the vile abuse they endure.

When I began writing for the *New Zealand Herald*, I found myself encountering more and more of the first three responses described above. Within the first few months of my tenure at the *Herald* I quickly became one of the writers who generated the most letters to the editor. The ones that actually made the paper were the very tip of the frosty, furious iceberg of angry, stale male tears. The letters to the editor were the least of my concerns, however, filtered as they are in a manner that precludes the widespread dissemination of rape threats and suicide suggestions. The online environment has no such effective filter. When I stepped stridently into the pages of the country's most-read newspaper, I truly had no idea just how bad the backlash would be.

When I surfaced from the first few months of simply trying to keep my head above the water in a swirling sewer of revolting comments, I became aware that I'd simply joined the club. Other female columnists and journalists had been experiencing the same thing for years, and they became my friends. To this day, they are the sisterhood that keeps me sane. We share horror stories, laugh together at the plonkers who inadvertently prove our point, and support each other whenever the awfulness becomes especially hard to deal with.

I'll be slated for saying this, I'm sure, but being an opinion columnist whilst female is harder than being an opinion columnist whilst male. I'm sorry. It just is. I'm not saying for a second that male columnists do not experience abuse, especially if they are not Pākehā (and it is worth noting that there are very few non-Pākehā columnists of any gender in the New Zealand media), but the nature of the criticism they receive is far less likely to objectify, sexualise, belittle, or stretch to the level of suggesting sexual violence. It is not remarkable for a male columnist to share an opinion. There will be no debate about whether or not a man has the right to have an opinion. People may disagree vehemently with a man's opinion, but they will still grudgingly accept his right to possess and express it. They won't tell him to shut the fuck up, you stupid bitch, and get back in the kitchen before you get raped. Men are criticised for what they say. Women are criticised for daring to say something in the first place.

So where does this leave us? The reality is that committing the act of opining whilst female, whether in the halls of Parliament, on the page, on the internet, or in everyday life is no easy task. That doesn't mean that we should shy away from it. To my mind, the unfortunate reality we're faced with as strong women provides even more of an impetus for us to continue to share our opinions, loudly and unashamedly, whenever and wherever we want to. If we don't fight to change the culture, it will not evolve in our absence.

Opining whilst female will only become easier if more women speak out regularly; if we make a concerted effort to ensure that there is nothing remarkable about being a woman with a strongly held opinion. Victory will come when our opinions are met with thoughtful debate, strong (but respectful) opposition, unapologetic support and a complete, unspoken acceptance of our right to voice them. Until that day, we must continue to raise our voices, so that we drown out the echoes of sexism reverberating down the centuries.

CHAPTER EIGHT

'Someone please shoot this stupid bitch. NZ fucking hates her.'

There is an unwritten rule in our modern world: The more threatening thou art to men, the more online abuse thou shalt receive. The crime of opining whilst female is closely related to the crime of online abuse, only one is a real crime, punishable by law, while the other, though presented humorously, is actually a human right. Despite legislation prohibiting harmful digital communications, online bullying is still often minimised, with victims characterised as 'snowflakes' and offenders described, quaintly, as 'trolls' – as if the worst thing they're capable of is stomping out from the dank, grimy place they came from and yelling, 'Who's that walking over my bridge?!' Neither term does the online vitriol women receive for expressing their opinions online justice. Being a woman with an opinion and public social media accounts is a special kind of hell.

Sometimes, despite what apologists might say, our opinions don't even have to be particularly controversial in the first place. I could be posting a picture of shoes or asking for traffic directions and still find myself on the receiving end of venomous comments, and I'll never forget the response to a speech I gave in 2017 at a literacy week event for my alma mater, King's College. I spoke about fairy tales, delivering a seven-minute off-the-cuff talk that covered some of the ground tackled in chapter three of this book. While I often speak at schools about provocative topics like sex, women's rights and sexual violence, during this talk I didn't mention the word 'feminism' once, instead focussing on tropes in 'tales old and new' (the theme of the evening) and the importance of diverse voices telling different stories.

As I gave my talk, I felt warmth in the room. People were laughing. I had intended for my talk to be something of a play on the ridiculous conventions in traditional fairy tales and it went better than I'd hoped. I left the event at intermission to go home and finish my column in time for deadline the next morning, and was just opening my laptop when my phone screen flashed with a slew of Instagram notifications. I opened Instagram just as another notification popped up. That's strange, I thought. I hadn't posted anything on Instagram for days. As it transpired, a group of accounts were suddenly writing comments on an old photo – a screenshot of a particularly vile piece of online abuse. At first it was just a few, then new accounts joined in, clogging my notifications until I'd received hundreds of abusive comments across a handful of pictures over a period of approximately an hour and a half.

They called me a 'disgusting hoe', a 'thot', a 'stupid two hole', a 'petty bitch' and told me that I use feminism 'as justification for not getting any dick because [I've] past [my] used by date just like every other piece of meat that has been left on the shelf for too long' and that I 'should shove [my] stupid incorrect prejudice opinions up [my] gaping cunt'.

Their distaste for my opinions didn't preclude them from sexualising me, however, with a number of them commenting that they'd like to 'hit that' and making comments about my 'tits' and 'ass'. Their hatred wasn't reserved only for me, either. 'Life was good when women couldn't vote,' one said. 'You're the reason why I hit women,' said another. While the vast majority of the keyboard warriors had courageously decided to hide behind locked accounts with non-identifying names like the pitiful cowards they were, one hadn't been quite quick enough to obscure his identity. I tapped on his name, and found an account full of pictures of a teenaged boy wearing a King's College uniform. Surprise, surprise.

When I sent screenshots of the abuse I'd received to the school, they were horrified. While the senior staff leapt into action, the student body responded too. I received a handful of messages from both male and female students apologising for their peers' behaviour. 'I hope you understand that [the main student involved] doesn't represent all of us and to be honest he's a dick anyway,' one said. 'I just want to say that it's grossly appalling that the King's boys in my year are saying nasty things to you,' said another. I was later told that the investigation had revealed that 11 students had been involved, and that they'd used a private Facebook group to coordinate their attack. Two of the students were stood down, while the others received an assortment of punishments relative to the severity of their offences. Two of the accounts were never identified. It was suspected that they came from other Auckland private schools.

When I realised that the majority of my abusers were King's College students, I immediately knew that my fairy tale talk had simply upset an old wound. A year prior I'd given a lecture at the college about feminism, sexual violence, privilege theory, and gender issues. I'd been instructed to be deliberately provocative in that talk, to encourage the students to think about and debate contentious issues, and I'd been informed afterwards that I'd succeeded resoundingly in fulfilling my brief. It alarmed me, however, that my speech about gender equality had threatened some boys so profoundly that they would hold onto it and take it upon themselves to denigrate, sexualise, and abuse me a year later. Even when you're accustomed to online abuse, there are some levels of vitriol that are shocking regardless of how desensitised you become.

I receive nasty comments online on an almost daily basis. At times, my notifications will become flooded with bile faster than I can block and ban the perpetrators. There is a folder on my laptop called 'Haters'. If you imagine a Portaloo at the end of the last day of a music festival plagued by rain, a shortage of any food other than extra-spicy curry, and an outbreak of dysentery, it's a fairly equitable representation of the general look and feel of the thing. I'm not quite sure why I felt the urge to create it, and I'm quite certain that it's not healthy to maintain it, but it's become something of a pastime. Like collecting stamps. It's a good thing I don't do speed-dating.

You can just imagine the hobbies round. 'Hi, my name is Lizzie, and I collect the explosive digital diarrhoea of internet trolls.'

Inside my little Pandora's box of gore and grime are examples of almost every sub-category of online abuse imaginable, from the mundane to the rare. I've collected more misogyny than I know what to do with, a decent amount of condescension, nearly every possible variation of 'stick to singing' and a fair bit of racism. Every once in a while, however, I'll unearth a comment so rotten the stench of it takes my breath away. Though admittedly that happens less frequently these days – more because I've acquired an iron stomach after repeated exposure than anything else. Nowadays I tend to award points for originality. In a weird way, the odd utterly rancid pile of steaming cyber shit makes for a nice change to the usual, 'shut up, you man-hating feminazi'. The ones that surprise me even get their own sub-folder within the 'Haters' folder. It's called 'Truly Vile'.

I'm going to take you inside that awful place. Think of it as taking the plunge through the plastic toilet seat into the unholy mess below. I apologise in advance. There is a point, I promise, which will become apparent in due course. Before we start, however, I'm just going to put one giant, all-encompassing [sic] here, so we can get the strange correlation between being an asshole on the internet and having an abysmal grasp of basic spelling and grammar out of the way. I also need to point out (for legal reasons) that it is possible that the account names used below were used by someone other than their owners to make the comments included in this chapter. I know if I were behind one of these posts, I'd certainly say that I'd been 'hacked'.

There you go, gents. I've given you a get-out-of-jail-free card.

Everyone else ready? Hold your noses. Here we go.

First up, we have racism. All of the worst comments I receive on social media generally revolve around some form of discussion – for want of a better term – about my Māori heritage and fair skin. For example, this charming little Facebook conversation:

Len Walls: 'Bloody honky! Maybe we should roast her on the spit and give her a good old native welcome...... Bet she tastes like a Koni Koni with that pinky flesh! Mmmm bacon!'

Mark Rallison: 'My dog wouldn't even want to eat that.'

Len again: 'I dunno, a bit of garlic, some onions, add a little Asian with some soy sauce ... 8 hours in the hangi and shed turn out alright in the end! Lol. We could make a real native delicacy out of her!'

Welcome to the bowels of internet hell, where we will find a few repeat offenders. Mark, for example, was kind enough to bless me with another stroke of genius, in a separate thread, again about Māori people:

'We should've just made these people slaves back in the 1800s. Would've been better off for them.'

Then came Wayne, Trevor and Murray.

Wayne Walker: 'Typical trash from a pseudo moari. What a disgusting person. What about her predominant white blood. Does her single entitled brain cell not honour her white blood.'

Trevor Bryan: 'i'd of added tupperware european maori to that list.as in she has as much of the tar brush as a plastic chinese tiki sold at the airport'

Murray McKenzie: ‘LM, 5% maori, 100% Tangata F’wit.’

If it’s not racism, it’s almost certainly going to be rape, murder, the kind of misogyny that proves many of my points in one fell swoop, or a swipe at my father, because God knows a woman with an opinion must have daddy issues. Take, for example:

Lloyd Gretton: ‘Perfect set up yourself to be raped Your biography says you love wine and dating Lead besotted men on and then scream rape’ (This one is actually pretty funny. My biography says I love date scones. I can only surmise that Lloyd needs new reading glasses. And a shred of human decency. He later told me to ‘stick [my] ngati where it belongs’. Because, of course.)

James Jenkins: ‘Lizzie wishes she had tits worth an oggle… #enviousandbitter’

Mark Dash: ‘Lizzy marvelly’s face is enough of a contraceptive not sure what she is complaining about.’

NZ Men Fed up with the NZ Family Court: ‘Lizzie Marvelly is a singer who failed in her career and couldn’t attract the public attention. Now, she is a feminist trying to get more attention from the public and be more acknowledged. She is an anti-male because her dad didn’t give her enough attention during her childhood and now she thinks that all men are like her father.’ Honestly, you can just imagine the kind of conversations that take place on that rather revealingly named Facebook page.)

Geoff Booth: ‘OhHell no DumbLiberalSnowflakes like Lizzy wont wake up tothis till the Caliphate is half waythru removin her head.’

Bevnolz: ‘Go catch Ebola Lizzie.’

Lawrence Prasad: 'Seems like you have a tallpoppyitis affliction. Bungy jumping without the cord is known to help!'

Premsocial: 'You're the reason why I hit woman You stupid two hole.'

And of course, no discussion of online abuse would be complete without mention of this chapter's namesake: Whatyoutalkinabout Willis: 'Someone please shoot this stupid bitch. NZ fucking hates her.'

I could go on, but you get the general idea. Online abuse is a regular occurrence for me, whether I like it or not. It simply comes with the territory of being a young woman with a public presence on the internet, so I've learnt to deal with it. I'm not for a second saying that trolling behaviour is okay. Some of the comments that have been hurled my way have affected me deeply, but it's the volume and frequency of the online abuse hurled my way that has caused me the most anguish. While it's relatively easy to dismiss the odd awful comment, repeated waves of nastiness are harder to ignore. I'm not ashamed to admit that there have been times when particularly malicious threads of comments have made me cry. Vulnerability is not something we're conditioned to admit to, but when it comes to the effects of online abuse it's important for me to be honest. I've found that being at the receiving end of a particularly vicious and prolonged online attack can even trigger my fight or flight response. While I logically know that online comments carry no immediate physical danger, my brain still insists on flooding my body with adrenalin, sending my heart rate through the roof and preparing my body for evasive action as if a fairy tale troll had suddenly come to life, leapt through the screen, club held high above its head, and threatened to clobber me to death. When I'm attacked online, there is little I can do to control how I feel about it. I can mitigate the impact, but I can't stop myself from feeling the initial hurt. Reactions to online abuse have nothing to do with strength or weakness, they are often due to brain chemistry.

Thankfully, over time any anger and hurt I've felt has become dulled almost to the point of numbness, but in the early days I sometimes wondered how on earth I was going to handle the next week's wave of vitriol.

When women online refuse to give in to their detractors and continue to share their opinions despite fierce and sometimes violent opposition, angry, threatened people hiding behind a screen become even more incensed. To these people, women are supposed to know their place. When we step out of line persistently, and refuse to be cowed, we need to be taught a lesson. In our culture, women have consistently been represented as pliable creatures who will eventually give in. In my interactions online, and in the media, I've deliberately chosen to attempt to subvert this narrative wherever possible. And in doing so, I've affixed a target to my back.

Traditional wisdom, most likely intent on protecting the so-called 'weaker' sex (and I'd like to see whoever called us that give birth) tells us to de-escalate any conflict. I have no doubt that during an aggressive encounter in the real world, where the threat of violence may be frighteningly valid, de-escalation would usually be the safest option. Online, however, where we generally trade words rather than punches, the official advice not to 'feed the trolls' feels completely inadequate, and frankly patronising to me. Telling someone that they're 'feeding the trolls' is just another way of blaming the victim, especially when the act of 'feeding' the internet monsters is, in actual fact, standing up for oneself. Telling someone not to 'feed the trolls' is basically telling them to allow the bullies to mock, demean and abuse with abandon. Which they will, ruthlessly, especially when the purpose of many groups of abusers is really to gang up and engage in a masculinity-building ritual that doesn't actually require the victim's involvement. 'Don't feed the trolls' is about as effective a piece of advice as 'Don't pat the angry lion that's about to rip your head off'. It is the trolls – or, as they should be called, the perpetrators – who should be the focus of any discussion around internet abuse. What the victim does – whether she 'feeds' the shitheads or not – is irrelevant.

What is missing in the online equation is any real consequences for the creatures who trawl the internet spewing abuse and harassment. The Harmful Digital Communications Act[1], for all the fanfare it received in the press, is largely toothless; rendered impotent by a lack of case law, a civil pathway through the courts and a Government-endorsed organisation, Netsafe, that's main function is to 'offer advice and support on how people can mitigate harm caused to them digitally'. When I'm being attacked by an angry horde of misogynists, I don't want advice and support, I want some kind of deterrent that will stop them once and for all. I want an easily understandable course of action that will allow me to report revolting comments and repeat offenders with some confidence that they will be appropriately dealt to. One of the major flaws of the HDCA is that even after reporting the vilest comments imaginable, the victim is still required to go through what's called a 'harm assessment' procedure, during which they must prove that the harmful digital communication in question caused them 'serious emotional distress'. If a victim is unable to prove that a particular disgusting comment caused them serious pain, the complaint will not reach the threshold required by the law. Which is about the most idiotic and flawed system I can think of. When the law penalises the victim for showing resilience, what is the point of suggesting that we don't 'feed the trolls'? We'd be better off serving them a delicious banquet of vulnerability and misery. At least that way the law would take us seriously.

In the real world, repeated exposure to abuse often results in desensitisation. My experience suggests that when you've faced incessant harassment online, and survived, you can develop a kind of acquired immunity. As strange as it may sound, inoculation seemingly provides a barrier of protection. Like a condom protecting you from a tiny flaccid penis. There are only so many times someone can call me a rude name before it begins to lose its sting. After a while, even the best efforts of disgusting and no doubt devastatingly threatened social media users begin to manifest as a low hum, like the drone of a particularly dozy blowfly. More annoying than distressing. With this resistance running through my veins, I find I'm more inclined to roll my eyes or tell online abusers exactly where to go.

On some rare days I find that I actually have a taste for the fight. There is something deeply satisfying about taking the implicit victimhood that has been thrust upon you and shoving it right back in the faces of the (usually) men who are determined to make your life miserable. Is my willingness to tell idiots where to go in exacting detail likely to be advantageous to my mental health in the long run? Probably not. Do I give a fuck? At this point, no.

My anger, however, is taboo. To be an angry woman is to swim against the tide of femininity. I am supposed to be endlessly tolerant and sweet, acting decorously and continually turning the other cheek. I am supposed to allow men to have their 'jokes'. I'm supposed to accept their rudeness as 'banter'. I'm supposed to have the patience of a saint, explaining myself over and over again until I come to see the error of my ways. Under no conditions am I supposed to retaliate, to stand staunchly in support of my views, to go into battle for other women, or to utter an unladylike word. To react to threatening, abusive, condescending, disgusting or bullying behaviour with anything other than a laugh or a sob is the height of offensiveness.

Fuck that.

In the discussion around online abuse and bullying, there is a key point that is missing. Trolls, bullies, perpetrators – whatever you want to call them – overwhelmingly target women. Regardless of a troll's gender identity, the recipient of their hatred is most likely to be young and female. A 2016 study by Norton found that 72 per cent of Kiwi women under the age of 30 experience online harassment[2], while the New Zealand Attitudes and Values Study found that women aged 18–19 reported the highest levels of online bullying, with approximately three in five experiencing some form of cyber-abuse[3]. Whatever the motivations behind the abuse, young women are overwhelmingly likely to be targets.

While discussions about online dehumanisation as a contributing factor of online abuse have merit, and it is likely that a lack of face-to-face contact with correspondents and an accompanying lack of consequences, social or legal, for bad behaviour makes it easier to abuse someone online, women experience a compounding of circumstances in the digital world when anonymity, access, distance and misogyny combine to create the perfect environment for abuse. If those women happen to be women of colour, LGBTQ+, people with disabilities or belonging to another group that experiences discrimination, those factors often lead to even worse experiences. It's no surprise that the worst abuse I receive online usually attempts to belittle and denigrate me on the grounds of race, either through negating my identity as a person of Māori descent, or through insinuating that I'm somehow inferior because of my cultural background. It is at the intersections of oppressions that the worst abuse is found. Ironically, my privileges – my affluent upbringing, my white face, being cisgender, etc. – protect me from even worse abuse. As unpleasant as many of my online experiences have been, they are nothing to what some other women are forced to endure.

When we know that women are more likely than men to be targeted on social media, advice telling us to block, ban, mute and report our abusers misses the mark. How is it that in every arena in which women are disproportionately victimised conventional wisdom always lands on the side of making such abuse a woman's responsibility? Where is the accountability? You can't tell me, in our age of algorithms, when Facebook scans our private messages for days and dates and automatically provides an option to 'make a plan', that digital media companies couldn't work together to solve online abuse. When comments about rape fail to violate community standards, it becomes clear that online abuse is a systemic problem that persists simply because those at the head of the system have chosen not to prioritise its eradication. Which is not to say that it is an easy (or cheap) problem to solve. It's not. A serious attempt to address online bullying would involve significant engineering innovations and investment in specialised teams of staff at all of the major digital networks. It would involve significant expenditure, but when the biggest digital companies are posting enormous profits as some of the most successful organisations in the world, it becomes difficult to argue that they can't afford to address the problem. Online abuse exists because some people are damaged, cruel, and deeply insecure human beings, but it continues to be such a large-scale and devastating problem because the corporations that have the power to address it properly choose not to. There is no law in the world that could have as much of an impact upon online abuse as the digital media companies could, other than a law that forced the digital media companies to act. Until such a time, the responsibility for dealing with online abuse will continue to fall to victims, some of whom will develop coping mechanisms to deal with it, and some of whom who will literally die because of it.

The abuse that I receive causes me much less distress than the knowledge that children and teens are suffering profoundly as a result of online bullying. When teen boys abuse me online, I am most concerned about the kind of online interactions that they're having with girls their own age. While as a nearly 30-year-old woman I find their taunts immature and idiotic, as a teenager I'm quite sure I would've found them deeply upsetting. How do they treat their peers who express feminist views? What do they say to and about girls who refuse to see themselves as objects for male enjoyment? How do they react when their sense of entitlement over women's bodies is rejected? God forbid they might actually have real, flesh-and-blood girlfriends to mistreat. And it's not just the boys who are engaging in cyber-bullying. While sexualisation of female victims is largely the domain of male perpetrators, time-honoured schoolyard nastiness flourishes in an online environment. Technologically savvy kids of all genders will use everything from private groups to messaging services to Apple's AirDrop to abuse their targets. In many ways we've created the perfect storm. A system that enables rapid and widespread communication; legislation that is lagging behind, inept, ill-fitting, toothless, or a combination of all four; a society that encourages bitchiness among women and misogyny against women; and enormous tech companies that profit from user engagement, whether that engagement is positive or negative.

Minimising or eliminating online abuse will require the best combined efforts of tech companies, governments, schools and communities, but until such a time as it impacts upon the bottom lines of tech companies, I suspect that the situation will remain much the same. At this stage, all I can offer are some thoughts on how to deal with it on an individual level. I'm no expert, and I can't promise that my coping mechanisms will work for everyone, but as a young woman who knows just how destructive social media abuse can be, I feel that I would be remiss not to at least share a few tips with my sisters in arms. Thus, I present my Six Commandments for Surviving Social Media:

1. Thou shalt not feel guilty for blocking, banning or muting internet philistines. I think of my social media accounts as my digital lounge. Being the opinionated rabble-rouser I am, I feel quite comfortable having heated debates in my lounge, but if someone barged into my home to tell me that I was a stupid bitch who should stick to her singing, that person would find themselves turfed out on their ear with a firm request to never come back. If someone came into my house to tell me that I should go and kill myself, or that someone should shoot me, I'd insist they left before I called the police. Your online spaces are yours. You get to set the tone, just as you would in your own home. Guests are more than welcome, but if a guest forgets their manners – or turns out to be a psychopathic fuckwit – you are well within your rights to ask them to leave.

2. Thou shalt surround thyself with wonderful, warm-hearted friends, family and colleagues both online and IRL. I firmly believe that support networks are the key to surviving online

abuse. If you know, without a doubt, that you are liked, loved and respected by people that actually know you, it's very difficult for a nasty stranger to make you believe that you are worthless, inadequate, or unlovable. Having people to reach out to who will refute without blinking all of the horrible things that an online bully might say means that you have an antidote that will protect you from even the most toxic bile. Never suffer online abuse alone. Always reach out.

3. Thou shalt tailor thy response to online bullies according to thy inner state of mind at the time on a case-by-case basis. Sometimes it is truly best not to 'feed the trolls', not because it's the official advice given, but because you don't need the strife that comes with engaging with nasty people. If you are feeling vulnerable, down or upset, the last thing you need is a race to the bottom of the barrel with someone whose sole purpose is to make you feel miserable. If you're feeling strong, however, there is no reason why you shouldn't respond as I was taught to at kindy – to say, loudly, 'stop it, I don't like it, go away,' – only feel free to substitute the pre-school vocabulary with stronger, age-appropriate synonyms.

4. Thou shalt not stoop to their level. While telling a bully exactly what you think of their opinion and offering them a suggestion of where they should get off is perfectly acceptable, bullying them in return is not. Bullies, after all,

are people too. They are most often pitiable people who are preying on others in a misguided and pathological attempt to assuage their own inferiority complex and make themselves feel better. Standing up for yourself or a friend is fine, but there is a delicate balance that must be upheld. If we stoop to their level, we become part of the problem.

5. Thou shalt remember that online bullying is not thy fault. As women, victim-blaming can be almost hard-wired into our brains. No, he wouldn't have been nice to you if you'd written that tweet differently. He came after you for a reason; he didn't threaten to rape you because you expressed your view a certain way, he attacked you because you expressed a view he didn't like and he didn't know how to deal with it like a civilised grown-up. You can rest assured that he was a shithead long before you and your tweet came along.

6. Thou shalt find refuge in the real world. When your social media accounts resemble the aforementioned Portaloo, sometimes the best thing to do is to turn off your devices and take a blissful holiday in the world around you. Going for a run, calling a friend, having a bath, reading a book, watching a movie, or even doing the vacuuming can provide a much-needed break from the horror that is unfolding online. It can take immense self-control to disengage from an incident of cyber-bullying, but during my worst moments

> online, I’ve found that logging out of the digital world has been the best option. You don’t have to read the nasty things people write to or about you. You are allowed to switch off.

The last thought I have to offer is that there are far too many bystanders online. While I absolutely understand the reluctance to get involved in an abusive conversation, I’ve also witnessed and experienced the effects of positive intervention. It is very hard for a bully to gain any traction when the friends, colleagues, and online comrades of the victim come to their defence. When we sit back and watch online abuse being perpetrated against others, we are complicit. Until corporations and governments around the globe step up, it is up to us to create the kind of environment we want online. We need to be the kind and supportive citizens who we’d like to come to our own rescue. Online abuse is a lonely affliction that thrives in isolation. The best way to treat its symptoms is to expose it to a warm and protective crowd. Whenever we’re online, we need to keep an eye out for each other. We need to be the light that banishes the creatures of darkness back to the slimy cesspit from whence they came.

CHAPTER NINE

Pornication

There is something about heterosexual porn that reminds me of trained animals in a zoo exhibit. The actors make noises I've never heard in the wild as the women teeter around like gazelles and the men, grunting like gorillas, lumber toward their prey in wide strides, as if they have bowling balls between their legs rather than a shaved and extremely veiny penis. The first time I saw it I found it perplexing, a bit disturbing and above all, I found myself fighting the urge to laugh. It was more mystifying than arousing. I'd been more titillated by one scene of *The Fast and the Furious* than a whole 13 minutes of skin-to-skin thwacking. Frankly, *The Fast and the Furious* was more realistic.

Now, before the porn connoisseurs jump down my throat (pun not intended, but acknowledged), I know that there is a porn video for every proclivity and fetish, and that many people feel very strongly about their favourite varieties of porn. People have been creating and viewing sexual images since they figured out how to scratch on cave walls. I do not advocate for banning porn. I do, however, have some pretty profound concerns about the pornification (to use a highly scientific term) of our society and particularly our young people. In our modern world you can barely walk round a corner or watch television without having your eyes assaulted by sexual content. Sex is now so ubiquitous, especially in the online environment, that children are being exposed to it at younger and younger ages. I would unintentionally run into a pornographic image online – mostly soft-core, but sometimes explicit – at least once a month, and I'm a fairly savvy internet user. Sometimes it can feel like it is our modern destiny to be chased around the internet by a pair of enormous breasts until we die.

Today's teenagers have grown up in that same highly sexualised environment. No matter how hard their parents may have tried to shelter them, if they have a smartphone, an internet-enabled device or friends, it's highly likely that they will have been exposed to X-rated content, particularly if they are boys. At this stage, none of this is news. There have been more newspaper articles trumpeting the moral calamity of teens and porn than I can count – I've even written a few myself. What should be news, however, is that porn is just the tip of the iceberg. Porn is not a problem in and of itself, but a symptom of a much larger issue that threatens to drag humanity backwards. As much as we don't want to think about teenagers watching pornography, it's an essential starting point in this discussion. And so we must follow them down the fucking rabbit hole, quite literally, to Pornhub.

Honestly. The lengths I go to for research.

The most-viewed video on Pornhub at the time of writing was called 'Best Friends Fuck Together'[1]. It features three young women clad only in their underwear (at most) and begins with a persistent man trying to enter their room with a camera while they twerk in front of each other. As you do? They tell him to stop and go away, but he's not easily deterred. 'Are you serious? Stop messing with my friends. This isn't cool, okay?' is one of the first lines uttered, but to no avail. Dudebro with the camera will not be dissuaded. Porn: 1; Consent training: 0.

Scene change. The persistent man finally leaves the women alone and goes to set up a camera below a presumably imaginary television set in a lounge room. He engages in a little chat directly to the camera, in which he reminded me of the serial killer in *The Fall.*

Scene change. The three young women lie on their stomachs facing the camera, apparently watching a zombie movie on the television above. Mr Persistent begins his 'seduction' by 'surprising' one of the three young women, telling her to 'Shhh' while her two friends watch the movie right beside her and well within both earshot and the line of vision, should they turn their heads slightly to the right, of what is so 'discreetly' going on (let's just say it involves his mouth and her, ahem, derriere).

Scene change. Persistent has now finished with Woman One's behind, and we're suddenly confronted with a close-up of Woman Two giving Persistent oral sex. Woman One and Woman Three are suddenly in on the act, affected oblivion abandoned, whispering and laughing to each other as they look on.

Scene change. We are now abruptly thrust into full penetration of Woman Three.

Scene change. They change position.

Scene change. They change position again. Woman One and Woman Two join in.

And so on, and so forth.

I should mention that there is not a single condom in sight. Clearly chlamydia doesn't exist in porn fantasyland.

The rest of the video consists of the man telling the three women what to do to him, and each other, which they obey without question. They are passive objects, while he is the subject. There is a lot of high-pitched squeaking. There is almost zero physical contact with any of the three clitorises. One woman in particular gets spanked a lot. Then, the grand finale: Persistent ejaculates all over Woman Three's face and hair while the whole cast looks totally thrilled about it. 'Oh yeah,' one of the other women says sycophantically. 'Do you like it?'

I don't, actually. I spend the last few moments, knowing full well what is about to happen, with my face screwed up, yelling 'Ew!' at the screen. Afterwards I feel slightly queasy, and feel an irrational urge to go and shampoo my hair. Nevertheless, the video has been viewed 61,977,811 times. What's one unhappy customer when many millions have already gone home satisfied?

The great modern masterpiece 'Best Friends Fuck Together' is an extremely tame (and yet still problematic) version of the kind of porn that is easily accessible to any teen (or pre-teen) with an internet-enabled device. One of the main problems with our modern teen porn affliction is that the porn parents remember was largely that found in *Playboy, Maxim* and *FHM*. Sure, adult content was available in video form too, and now I come to think of it, I do remember there being a sad, seedy little R-18 room off the side of my local video hire shop, which lonely-looking men skulked into after a quick glance to check whether anyone was looking, but it was nowhere near as prolific and easily accessible as it is now. When we talk about teens watching porn, we are not talking about boys having a glance at Dad's hidden stash of dirty magazines, we're talking about anal sex, choking, smacking, punching, urination and pretty much everything else you can think of (and a number of things that you would likely never otherwise dream of in a million years – *2 Girls 1 Cup* anyone?). We're talking about the kinds of sex that many adults wouldn't have, all served up on a platter to young minds with no context, no guidance and no reality check. I call it pornication.

When I think back to my own teen years, I feel so incredibly lucky that our smartphones were crappy plastic bricks with tiny screens, and mobile data cost an arm and a non-essential organ. I had sex for the first time quite late at 19, and, unusually, managed to make it to that age without having watched a full porn video. I'd seen still images, of course, and snippets of videos after unintentionally stumbling across them online, but when I had sex for the first time, I had no porn film to refer to in my mind. In hindsight, I cannot put into words how grateful I am for that. When I started having sex I had no explicit pre-conceived notions of what my role in the encounter was expected to be. I was never tempted to stagger around like a doe-eyed damsel, make overly feminine and performative high-pitched moaning noises or speak in a baby voice. I had no knowledge of the ridiculous conventions of porn, and therefore no desire to fulfil them in my own relationships. Thank God. Had I been born even two or three years later, my experience would've been very different. I was just lucky to grow up in a time when smartphone sophistication was being able to play Snake in colour.

How I wish that were the case today. Instead, I hear about 13-year-old girls who despair because they believe their boyfriends will dump them if they refuse to give them a blowjob. Fifteen-year-old girls whose boyfriends demand that they have anal sex, because they think it's a normal, non-negotiable part of sexual intercourse. Girls who are bullied mercilessly because a naked picture they sent to a crush was then forwarded around the whole school. Young men who can't get an erection with a flesh-and-blood young woman because after so many years of watching and masturbating to porn, real women (who might – gasp – have *pubic hair*) just don't arouse them. The many enlightening – and terrifying – lessons I have learnt during the last few years of speaking in schools have proven to me without a doubt that easily accessible online porn has radically changed the landscape of teen sex.

Studies support this. While there is currently very little New Zealand-specific research around teens and porn, a recent Australian study found that the average age when teens were first exposed to pornography was 13 for boys and 16 for girls[2]. All of the boys in the study of more than 940 young people told researchers that they had watched porn, and over 80 per cent of them watched it on a weekly or daily basis. The study also found that there was a link between watching porn and poor mental health outcomes.

In another recent study, researchers found correlations between men viewing porn and holding misogynistic attitudes. The effects differed depending on how old men were when they first started watching porn. 'We found that the younger a man was when he first viewed pornography, the more likely he was to want power over women,' researcher Alyssa Bischmann said. 'The older a man was when he first viewed pornography, the more likely he would want to engage in [promiscuous] playboy behaviour.'[3] Another study found that exposing men who had a particular personality trait – low agreeableness (which can manifest as hostility, coldness, antagonism, etc.; basically, asshole tendencies) – to pornography in a laboratory had the effect of modestly increasing their hostile sexist attitudes (i.e. turning them into even bigger assholes). The same study surveyed participants before exposing them to porn and found that 'among men increased past pornography consumption was ... found to be associated with more negative attitudes toward women including more hostility, negative prejudices, and stereotypes.'[4]

It doesn't exactly paint a pretty picture. While much more research is needed, especially studies that specifically focus on how to mitigate the impact that pornography has upon teens, what is abundantly clear is that young people today are growing up in a vastly different sexual environment to that of their parents and grandparents. To pretend otherwise is both foolhardy and dangerous. When the majority of teen boys are watching online porn on a daily or weekly basis, we need to be realistic about the potential such repeated exposure has to influence their ideas, beliefs and behaviour. Simply raising sons to 'act like gentlemen' doesn't really cut it when they're watching videos like 'Best Friends Fuck Together' (and, let's be honest, likely much worse) on the regular.

And we shouldn't forget about the impact that porn has upon girls and women. In the aforementioned Australian study, researchers found that of the girls who said that they'd watched porn, nearly two thirds watched it monthly. They too are seeing pornographic media and absorbing the messages it sends about sexual relationships. And even if they don't watch it themselves, they may still end up inadvertently playing out porn narratives in early sexual experiences, as the boys in their lives seek to experience what they've watched online. A British study of over 1000 children and young people found that 39 per cent of 13- to 14-year-old boys and 21 per cent of the 11- to 12-year-old boys surveyed wanted to try out the behaviour they had seen in pornography[5].

In a study conducted by researchers at the London School of Hygiene and Tropical Medicine[6], pornography was implicated in the reasons why young men are seeking anal sex (if only 'partially'). In the study, 130 young men and women aged between 16 and 18 were asked about the sexual activities they engaged in. Researchers found that coercion of female heterosexual partners was common in anal-sex practices among young people:

> *Some men … described taking a 'try it and see' approach, where they anally penetrated a woman with their fingers or penis and hoped that she would not stop them.*
>
> *Shane told us if a woman said 'no' when he started 'putting [his] finger in', he might keep trying: 'I can be very persuasive […]. Like sometimes you just keep going, just keep going till they just get fed up and let you do it anyway'.*

Even in cases where young women's refusal was taken seriously, the study found that 'Women seemed to take for granted that they would either acquiesce to or resist their partners' repeated requests, rather than being equal partners in sexual decision-making.' It was at this point in the study when I was suddenly reminded of 'Best Friends Fuck Together'. Would it have received so many views, I wondered, if the women in the video had been treated as equal sexual partners with equally important sexual desires?

Perhaps the most enraging part of the study, however, was this:

> *Men in a group discussion said anal sex was 'something we do for a competition', and 'every hole's a goal'. By contrast, men and women said women risked their reputation for the same act, a sexual double standard familiar from previous literature.*

Every hole's a goal. Every hole. Is a goal.

Christ on a cracker.

While the researchers went to great lengths to point out that they believed that the access to pornography was only one element of young men's desire to engage in anal sex, the attitudes displayed by the young men in the study, such as Shane with his persistent finger, are prevalent in porn. Far be it from me to confuse correlation with causation, but when porn scenes are starting to be enacted in the bedrooms (cars, basements, and God knows where else) of teenagers, questions need to be asked not only about where boys are getting the idea to determinedly shove a finger up some poor girl's ass (perhaps from a friend who heard it from a friend who heard it from a friend who heard it from a friend who saw it in a porn video?) but also about why girls think that it's okay for a boy to either ignore their refusal to engage in a particular sexual behaviour (a phenomenon known as rape) or to exclusively determine the course of a sexual encounter.

The main bone I have to pick with porn is that it largely reinforces a paradigm where men have power in heterosexual relationships and women don't. As a fantasyland, it has the potential to be revolutionary, presenting female sexuality in ways that have previously been marginalised and taboo, but the fantasies it caters to are overwhelmingly the heteronormative and male-dominant fantasies of men. Which are generally pretty fucking depressing for the female of the species. While feminist porn does exist, and some producers have begun exploring different narratives and gender identities and finding new ways of making porn (one notable example is Cindy Gallop's project Make Love Not Porn), the overall landscape is a minefield for gender relations – one that is particularly difficult to navigate when you're young and inexperienced.

* * *

I firmly believe that porn is just a part of a larger problem. While I didn't grow up watching porn, I did grow up thinking that men would take the lead in sexual experiences. I spent much of my teens and twenties in relationships with men, in which I waited to *be* kissed, and to *be* asked out. I worried that any forwardness on my part would make men think that I was a slut. I cast myself in the role of 'girlfriend' and spent my time auditioning for a supporting role in someone else's story. It wasn't until an older friend sat me down at about age 24 to share some hard-won wisdom that I even realised what I was doing. Her advice sent a lightning bolt through my perceptions, and with the power of hindsight it is mind-blowing that I'd managed to get to my mid-twenties without having ever heard it before. 'You choose them,' she said. 'Don't let them choose you.' It seems astoundingly obvious, but until that point I'd coasted through a number of unsatisfying relationships feeling that I should have some sense of gratitude for a man finding me attractive and wanting to date me. What I wanted out of a relationship wasn't even a conscious thought in my head. If an attractive man found me attractive and asked me out, I said yes. He led, I followed – without much thought about how I actually felt about him. The same thing happened in the bedroom, as I played the role of the object, catering to my male partner's desires. Which led to a lot of really, really bad sex.

It's worth noting that, in my experience at least, sex between women has totally different dynamics. I've never had really, really bad sex with a woman.

The thing is, male-dominant, misogynistic heterosexual porn is really only the visual manifestation of a shitty sexual environment on every level. If our real-life sexual expectations were ones in which equality was the norm and had been so for millennia, I have no doubt that our pornography would reflect that on some level. Porn is just the one part of the problem that you can easily see, and it truthfully doesn't deserve the magnitude of bad press that it receives. There is a lot of porn out there that is unequivocally fucked up, but that is because there are a number of attitudes out there that are equally fucked up. We can't blame porn for our problems when it is merely a reflection of society.

A similarly concerning reflection of society that I've seen written about in increasingly anxious terms is the rise of sex robots. While the idea of a robot that caters to the sexual desires of a human owner may sound like a plot line from *Futurama*, it is a rapidly growing industry. One story from late last year stands out to me as being especially illustrative of the problems that sex robots bring to the fore; not because the issues are created by the robots, but because the robots magnify extremely ugly parts of our culture. In late 2017, a sex robot named 'Samantha' was so badly molested and abused at the Linz Ars Electronica Festival that she had to be sent for repairs. A pack of men mounted and manhandled her so violently that she was left 'badly soiled' and with two broken fingers[7]. Now of course, Samantha was not a human woman. Her abusers will not be investigated for their crimes, but the fact that they thought it was acceptable to treat a robot resembling a human woman with such contempt raises a number of questions about the state of misogyny in our society. Indeed, the very idea of a sex robot hinges on the fact that it will be a willing participant in any act its owner decides to subject it to. Female sex robots, although they look like human women, have no right to say no. They have no thoughts, desires, needs or objections of their own; they exist solely for the purpose of being the conduit for a man's pleasure, fantasies and proclivities. That they are sold as an ultimate male fantasy is a deeply problematic reflection of a misogynistic society.

What is needed is an enormous balancing of the scales. In porn, in sex robotics, and even in real life, female sexuality is often missing in action. I phrase it that way because women are actively having sex, watching and participating in porn (and pornication), but many of us are missing out on what should be our due: pleasure.

Society's mainstream ideas about sex don't exactly benefit women. For a start, the immense focus on heterosexual penetrative sexual intercourse discounts the fact that many women just don't find it all that pleasurable. As Elisabeth A. Lloyd found after reviewing nearly 80 years of research for her book *The Case of the Female Orgasm: Bias in the Science of Evolution*, only a quarter of women experience orgasm 'often' or 'very often' through 'unassisted' sexual intercourse (that is, sexual intercourse that is not accompanied by additional clitoral stimulation). That's only one in four of us who reliably gets off from vaginal penetration, but what do we see over and over again in porn videos? You got it. Vaginal penetration. Men often struggle to believe that so few of us come through penetration. I once dated a young man who told me quite defensively that every woman he'd slept with had orgasmed through penetration alone. He didn't take too kindly to my suggestion that he'd witnessed a lot of fake orgasms. On the other hand (or tongue, or vibrator), around 90 per cent of women experience orgasm through direct clitoral stimulation. While there are sub-categories on some porn sites called 'clit stimulation' and the like, it is common for mainstream heterosexual porn videos to include little or no clitoral stimulation whatsoever. It is also rare to hear the clitoris discussed outside of health class, feminist groups or among groups of very, very close female friends. It's little wonder that the majority of female porn viewers – heterosexual and otherwise – prefer watching lesbian porn[8].

Also telling is the false equivalence between male and female sex organs. We often think of heterosexual sex as involving penises and vaginas as matching counterparts, when arguably we're only describing one version of events that results in male pleasure a lot more often than it results in female pleasure. In pleasure stakes, the female equivalent of the penis is not the vagina; it's the clitoris. It's the one part of the human body that is entirely dedicated to pleasure-giving, and yet it is marginalised in importance compared to the part of the female body that is designed to accommodate a penis. Big surprise there.

While this may all sound like biological conjecture, it demonstrates the way in which our thinking around sexuality has consistently set the pleasure of men above that of women in heterosexual contexts. The same double standard exists around masturbation. While male masturbation is so normalised that it has inspired a slew of jokes, gags, and iconic movie scenes, female masturbation is still taboo. A study by researchers at the University of Chicago[9] found that women were much less likely than men to masturbate, with only 38 per cent of female respondents admitting to masturbating during the last 12 months, compared to 61 per cent of men. It utterly astounds me that over 60 per cent of women in the study reported not having masturbated during the year prior, although I'd theorise that the study's results owed more than a little bit to truth-bending due to embarrassment. Which, when you think about it, is nonsensical. Why should anyone be ashamed of indulging in the neurochemically explosive experience of self-love? Masturbation is literally one of the most foolproof ways of giving yourself a potent dose of feel-good neurotransmitters. It's good for us. Do we feel ashamed when we eat vegetables or go for a run? Do we lie about going for a massage or soaking in a hot bath? Feeling ashamed of self-pleasure is similarly illogical.

Shame around masturbation was dispelled rather forcefully early on in my life. When I was in Year 9, my class had the kind of health teacher I wish every girl had. Let's just call her Mrs D. Mrs D was a very matter-of-fact lady with a warm smile and a rather short fuse. She was kind, she was straight up, and she didn't take any bullshit. One particular day in Mrs D's class, we were studying female anatomy. We'd learnt about the labia minora and majora, vulva, vagina, etc., then we began to talk about the clitoris. As you can imagine, a room full of 13-year-old girls found the clitoris rather funny. To be fair, the (mortifying) height of humour that year was to be asked by a classmate whether you'd found your G-spot yet. Anyway. Mrs D had just finished explaining the role and function of the clitoris when she turned to the class to drop a bomb. 'Now, girls,' she said breezily. 'When you're in the shower tonight, make sure to have a feel around down there to see what feels good.' The effect was immediate. The 30 of us collectively snorted, giggled and hooted. To this day, the memory still makes me smile. Mrs D made an embarrassing subject normal at a crucial time in our lives. In the context of our current sexual education system, her little pearl of wisdom was revolutionary. While a number of schools, parents and educators are terrified of teenaged sexuality, Mrs D made sure that a group of 13-year-old girls not only knew that their bodies were made to give them pleasure, but encouraged them to seek that pleasure themselves. Mrs D's words are as applicable today as they were 15 years ago. Indeed, if you haven't already, when *you're* in the shower tonight, make sure you have a feel around to see what feels good.

As women, we deserve to enjoy sex, whether we're engaging in sexual behaviour by ourselves or with others. We deserve to have our desires catered to and our needs met. We deserve to be listened to, respected, adored and satisfied on our own terms. We deserve great, earth-shattering orgasms. Many of them. And we deserve to grow up in a society that acknowledges that our pleasurable experiences are just as important as our partners'. We deserve to grow up knowing that we have a right to pleasure too.

Whenever I see a porn video that treats a clitoris as an ornament we wear on our vulvas for shits and giggles I want to scream. Whenever I see a porn video in which a man directs a passive woman to perform sexual acts on him without bothering to return the favour I lose any hypothetical hard-on I might've otherwise mustered. There is nothing less sexy than watching a woman be bossed around by a lazy, ungrateful, entitled lover so that he can come all over her face while the best chance she has of an orgasm is if she closes her eyes and fantasises about her vibrator. As angry as portrayals of sex in porn make me as a feminist, the rather more enormous problem with a generation of young men growing up watching this crap is that they grow up thinking that all they have to do in bed is a bit of jack-hammering here, a bit of spanking there and they will be rewarded by the shuddering screams of female rapture. Porn is setting men up to fail, and it's setting women up for unsatisfying sex lives.

Bad sex is seemingly contagious: it has leapt off the screen and infected the vulnerable. When I was younger I would occasionally find myself in situations where I would realise that faking an orgasm was the best option after it became abundantly clear that my sexual partner had no idea either where the clitoris was located or what it was used for. At the time I wouldn't have dreamed of taking matters into my own hands as I would've been worried that I would've hurt my lover's feelings. Now I'm neither so stupid nor so concerned. I've since adopted a hard and fast rule that I wholeheartedly encourage every woman everywhere to take for her own. Repeat after me: Never will I ever fake an orgasm. I will not reward bad behaviour.

The simple truth is that we deserve better.

* * *

The other major concern that emerges in conversations about porn is consent. As can be quite clearly seen in 'Best Friends Fuck Together', consent can be hazy in pornographic encounters. Funnily enough, in scenes where the only goal is a man's orgasm, it's not unusual for the equation to be problematically one-sided. Consent has become something of a buzzword in recent times, and yet it's still rare in porn to hear an actor ask their screen partner for consent before a particular sexual behaviour is initiated. It's not surprising that young people using porn as a guide for real sex would be confused about consent, given the clear lack of airtime given to the idea that both partners need to be on the same page and enthused about whatever (or whoever) is about to come next. Perhaps relatedly, it's not uncommon to hear people complain about how asking for consent is supposedly 'unsexy'. Which is both ridiculous and troubling. For one, I can think of plenty of very sexy ways that I'd like to be asked whether or not I'd like to partake in certain sexual activities, but bearing in mind that my mother is very likely to read this book, I'll leave them to the imagination. Two, the idea that it's more important to act sexily than to make sure that you're not sexually assaulting someone is 50 shades of fucked up. It should go without saying that consent should be the number one consideration in any sexual encounter.

This haziness around consent was one of the things that led me to make #MyBodyMyTerms, a social media campaign that focussed on consent, sexual violence, victim-blaming, slut-shaming and revenge porn. #MyBodyMyTerms was created in mid-2015, after I became aware of an incident of revenge porn in which someone I knew was victimised. For the uninitiated, revenge porn occurs when intimate photographs are taken and/or shared without their subject's consent. I was appalled and angry that a woman was being smeared and shamed for daring to be a sexual being, and I vowed to do something about it.

I began reaching out to likeminded people, and started talking about the idea of creating a campaign, but it wasn't until I met with television producer Jo Raj that I began to think that my blurry, unformed idea could actually become a reality. Jo understood immediately the essence of what I was trying to achieve, and together we set our minds to bringing it to life. I could not have made #MyBodyMyTerms without her. Indeed, one of the essential truths I've learnt in this life is that when women work together, shit gets done.

With #MyBodyMyTerms, Jo and I set about dispelling and disputing many of the myths we'd had hurled at us during our combined then 68 years of walking the planet as female human beings. We created a manifesto, and enlisted an army of well-known New Zealanders to deliver it to the masses in a video that would eventually receive over half a million views and land on the front page of Buzzfeed. Our manifesto read:

It's my body. My terms.

I respect myself and I deserve to be respected.

Make decisions that are right for you.

You don't have to have sex if you don't want to.

It's your body, your terms.
Don't do it just to fit in.
Having safe, consensual sex doesn't make me a 'slut'.
Taking, or posing for naked photos doesn't make me a 'whore'.
Having a naked picture or video of myself with a partner
does not give anyone else the right to view it.
When you share private pictures of someone without their
consent, you violate them.
When you view private videos of me without my consent, you
violate me.
I'm a human being. Not some stranger on a screen.
Just because I express my sexuality, that doesn't mean
I'm asking for it.
My choice of clothing isn't an invitation to assault or rape me.
Dressing a certain way doesn't mean she's asking for it.
If she chooses to drink alcohol it doesn't make her responsible
for the criminal actions of others.
Pressuring someone to have sex is not okay.
When I say 'no', I mean it.
Sex without consent is rape.
It's my body. My terms.[10]

#MyBodyMyTerms was an attempt to push back against a rising tide of misogyny in an unapologetically frank way, subverting the conventions of pornography by using semi-pornographic images to fight back against the shame that has been foisted on women who dare to portray themselves as sexual beings. Our cast took a considerable risk in joining our mission, and in revealing so much of themselves to an international audience of hundreds of thousands. Many of our cast chose to strip to their bare skin, with the words #MyBodyMyTerms emblazoned on them like defiant tattoos. In fact, one of our cast members found the experience so powerful that she refused to have her #MyBodyMyTerms war paint wiped off after the shoot, and wore it home that night. The campaign aimed to hit back against sexual violence and revenge porn, all framed through a lens that put consent at the centre of the discussion. Its success exceeded our wildest dreams.

When I look back at the #MyBodyMyTerms manifesto now, however, I can't help but still feel angry. Every statement contained therein should not need to be highlighted. Everything that #MyBodyMyTerms stands for should be registered as unwritten rules that society abides by instinctually. The fact that there was (and still is) a need for #MyBodyMyTerms says a lot about the society that we live in.

Any number of campaigns and videos have tried to teach people about consent. We are at the stage where one of the most famous – the Cup of Tea video – has to use the idea that you wouldn't force a cup of tea down someone's throat if they were unconscious as an allegory for how to not be a sexual predator. Because clearly the idea that one shouldn't force one's body parts into another person's body parts if that person is asleep or passed out is such a complicated one. Creating content that fights back against the pornification of youth culture is an ongoing challenge, one that Jo and I took on again with the sexuality education webseries *The REAL Sex Talk* (which can be found at therealsextalk.com). The fact that the series generated hundreds of thousands of views seems to suggest that there is a hunger for decent information about sex and sexuality, and if the content that we make helps even one young woman to feel empowered about her sexuality, or prevents her from being victimised, then we'll keep rabbiting on until we're blue in the face.

Why? Because as human beings, as much as we have a right to pleasure, we also have a right to be safe. The two are not, and never should be, mutually exclusive. Consent shouldn't be a difficult concept to understand. In practice, it simply means making sure that all parties in a sexual encounter are enthusiastically on board with and happy to participate in whatever is happening. The simple fact is that respecting someone's boundaries and ensuring that they feel safe should be the absolute bare minimum condition for engaging in any sexual experience. That some people find it hard to rise above that very low bar is deeply concerning.

The influence of porn can also be seen in the ugly phenomenon of revenge porn. It should be a no brainer that you shouldn't share intimate pictures without making sure the people in them are okay with it. Something seems to happen, however, particularly when a woman poses for a naked photograph or video – namely, it is used as ammunition against her. Using a woman's sexuality as a weapon to terrorise her with is nothing new; it is part of an age-old misogyny that strikes with ferocity particularly when a woman spurns a man's affection. The public narrative surrounding revenge porn is similarly depressing. I can't tell you how many times I've heard some variation of 'Well, what did she expect when she took her clothes off and sent him a naked picture?' Although people may not say it aloud, the thought that follows that statement goes like this: 'SLUT!' Comparatively, the question of 'What kind of asshole does such a heinous thing as violate the trust that an intimate partner has bestowed upon them in such a nasty, humiliating way?' is asked infrequently, if ever. Of course, when a man poses for a naked picture that is then shared without his consent the reaction is usually that it's all a bit of a joke, which is also not okay, but it is a far cry from the utter vilification many women experience. Unsurprisingly, the time-honoured slut vs stud dichotomy has been easily updated to continue its dominance in the digital age.

Over the past decade, coincidentally in the time when online porn has become more and more prevalent, naked bodies have quickly become a kind of sexual currency that is expected to be invested early on in a romantic encounter. It is common particularly in relationships between young people for naked pictures to be either sent or requested, sometimes even before the first date. Anyone older than 40 will likely find this idea baffling. Why would you send a naked picture of yourself to someone who you've yet to see naked in the flesh? I have no answer other than to say that when you've grown up taking pictures of yourself, your food, your pets and everything else in your life for the purpose of sharing it online, perhaps the concept of sharing naked pictures doesn't seem like such a stretch. When you've grown up seeing nearly naked selfies of celebrities like Kim Kardashian published publicly on Instagram, maybe it doesn't seem like such a big deal.

I've personally always been too scared to share intimate pictures with others, but I can understand the idea. It can be an empowering experience. It can be a joyful expression of self-love. It can be a mutually enjoyed celebration of sexuality and sexual chemistry. It can also very quickly become a nightmare from which there is no escape. If you haven't heard the horror stories about revenge porn – of intimate photos circulating around the internet for years, sometimes attached to names, addresses, workplaces and even phone numbers, and showing up in a simple Google search routinely conducted these days by any prospective employer – count yourself lucky. This criminal action has made life miserable for millions of people around the globe. A 2016 study[11] found that one in 25 Americans had been a victim of revenge porn. That equates to almost 10 million people. The study further found that one in ten young women had been threatened with the possibility of having intimate images of them shared without their consent.

Revenge porn is illegal in New Zealand, though that hasn't stopped it from occurring here. Revenge porn crimes can be prosecuted under the Harmful Digital Communications Act 2015, and by the end of April 2017, the Act had resulted in 50 convictions and sentences[12]. If the prevalence of revenge porn in New Zealand is anything like that in the United States, however, 50 convictions seems rather light. Time will tell, I guess, whether the HDCA is acting as any useful kind of deterrent against this sickening crime.

A related phenomenon (which may also be illegal under the HDCA if a particular incident met its high thresholds) is the way in which messaging services have created an environment where random men go around sending unsolicited dick pics (photos of their naked penises). In the old days, we called these men (clad, in our collective imagination, in trench coats and little else) perverted exhibitionists, flashers and creeps; now they're called things like '@bigboy696969'. These are not the sad elderly men of old who were most probably in need of psychiatric help; these are often young men who seem to think that it's no big deal to force women they've never met or spoken with to look at pictures of their junk. I've encountered a few of these men in my time. They've slid into my Instagram messages unannounced and uninvited, determined to shove the images of their penises into my brain, whether I like it or not. Instagram has since wised up to this trend, and now blurs images sent by direct message pre-emptively, but before that happened, I devised a system that also seemed to work quite well and that I sometimes still use as a fall-back. I find that sending a picture of a sausage being sliced by an enormous butcher's knife in response to an unsolicited dick pic is a fairly effective deterrent. You're more than welcome to give it a try.

The men who send pictures of their naked genitals unbidden are also part of our pornified society. In sending those images to me – sometimes without even saying hello first – they are sending me a message that to them I am just a receptacle for their sexual urges. Why should they waste their time trying to strike up a conversation when I am merely a means to their sexual gratification? Whether or not I want to engage in their sexual exchange is irrelevant to them. They don't need my consent, they're telling me. They can do whatever they want, just as the men in porn do. When a random man searches for my name in order to send me a photo of his penis, I am simply the visual manifestation of his fantasy; a kind of digital sex robot.

Whichever way you skin it, our modern sexual landscape leaves much to be desired. The impact of online pornography is often blamed for everything that is concerning about our sexual culture, but such a judgment represents an oversimplification. Porn is not the great singular evil that threatens life as we know it; it is a symptom of life as we know it. Until we're ready to have a discussion about the unbalanced, dangerous and misogynistic sexual narratives that have underpinned our society for generations, attributing blame to pornography is like blaming a child for its own difficult upbringing.

Pornography is not the root of the problem. We are.

CHAPTER TEN

The possessed body

When I was 13, I was fingered without my consent. It happened at a social – an informal high school dance in the school hall that was held once or twice a term, hosted alternatively by Rotorua Girls' High School and Rotorua Boys' High School. Think of a nightclub with no drugs or alcohol – on the premises, at least – and teenagers disappearing in pairs behind the thick velvet curtains (at RBHS) to do things that need no further explanation here. Needless to say, those curtains were avoided by students year-round, so notorious was their reputation. It was my first social, and I was dancing with one of the popular boys – a boy I'd been at intermediate school with, but who was far too cool for me to have called him a friend – and desperately trying to hide the fact that I was stunned that he'd taken any notice of me, a renowned teacher's pet. One minute I was happily dancing away, trying excruciatingly hard to play it cool, then we were kissing, then he reached his hand up underneath my short skirt and penetrated me.

I was more surprised than anything else. I didn't quite know how it had happened. I'd never been fingered, and I certainly hadn't planned for the first time to be in the middle of the school hall. I felt confused as I whispered what had happened to my friends as we huddled outside in the cool night air, taking a break from dancing in the hot, crowded hall. I had been very keen to pash my dodgy new love interest, but therein lay the full extent of my intentions for the evening. I can't remember how my friends reacted, but I know that I eventually shrugged it off. It was just one of those things that happened at socials, I reasoned. I should've known better than to dance with a boy like that. And I was wearing a really short skirt.

The next time a similar thing happened, I was 15, wearing another short skirt, at another social, and dancing with a friend I'd known for years. I was dancing with him for fun, and felt fairly sure that there was nothing between us, until he pulled me close, reached his arm around me and began touching me between my legs from behind, which – when you think about it – is quite a feat. He didn't quite manage to penetrate me, if that was his aim, and I pulled back, putting some distance between us. This time I knew it wasn't right. I told my on-again, off-again boyfriend a few days later (we'd been in an 'off' phase when this happened), who was a close friend of Mr Long Arms. I wasn't there for the confrontation, but it marked the end of their friendship, at least during our teen years. If I'm honest, I'm not sure whether that was more down to valour or territory-marking.

Throughout the rest of my teens and into my twenties, there would be other non-consensual encounters. Kisses that I'd feel pressured into, and more incidents of groping than I can count. One of the reasons that I only very rarely go out to clubs is that almost every time I'm on a dance floor I'll end up with some douchebag behind me grabbing my arse. Or worse. One of the last times I went to a club – for a friend's birthday – there were two separate incidents within an hour when men waltzed up behind me, started touching me and, when I told them to get their hands off me, refused to leave me alone. On the first occasion, the birthday girl, who is a very fierce woman who I adore, pushed me out of the way and threatened the two jackasses with all sorts of retribution. On the second, when a creepy, very drunk young man wouldn't leave me alone despite my moving left, then right, then across the circle ('No?' he said, when I'd uttered the word for what felt like the 50th time. 'What do you mean, "no"?'), a group of decent men saw what was happening, had forceful words with him, then physically dragged him away from me.

Other events were more serious. I've written before about my experiences of sexual harassment and abuse in the music industry, ranging from unwanted attention from much older men to molestation. I've fielded more inappropriate comments than I can count, endured having three male colleagues non-consensually force their tongues into my mouth, and been told to 'Come to bed' by a much older and much more powerful man as he gripped my wrists, among many other incidents. Indeed, it was a supposed friend from the music industry who 'stealthed' me in my early twenties. Stealthing is a relatively new term in the vernacular of shitty, horrible things that can happen to women. Its most common definition is the duplicitous failure to wear a condom during sex, either by removing it or leading a partner to falsely believe that a condom is being worn. When it happened to me, I remember feeling intensely angry, but he acted like it was no big deal. I swallowed my outrage and went to sleep, but the next morning when I told the pharmacist that 'the condom broke' as she went through the mandatory interview that is required in order to dispense the emergency contraceptive pill, I felt an extreme sense of injustice. But I didn't yet have the words to explain my fury. It wasn't until I was 27 that I realised that what had happened to me was a crime. Stealthing has been described by the legal fraternity as 'rape adjacent'.

As a woman, the ownership of my body has often been contested. My personal boundaries have been pushed and violated more times than I can count, and I've often blamed myself. Each early violation began to chip away at my sense of agency, kick-starting a macabre trend. From 13 onwards, my body was not truly my own, or at least not in the eyes of the people who wanted something from me. As much as it frustrates me to say it, that baffled 13-year-old still lives somewhere inside me, and there have been times even in recent years when I've felt just as confused as she did.

The most bewildering experience of all was one I've never spoken about publicly. When I was 22, a much older female friend (and colleague) touched me inappropriately, sliding her hand down the front of my tights as we lay side by side, surrounded by other friends sprawled sleeping on an enormous couch after a night out. I assume that she thought I was asleep, and I froze, eyes closed and transfixed in horror, unable to either move or say anything. Nothing even vaguely sexual had passed between us before that moment, and I was caught totally unaware. My saving grace that night was the lucky fact that, as anyone who has ever worn thick, opaque stockings can attest, the form-fitting tights were too snug and unwieldy to allow her to reach further than a couple of inches below the top band of my underwear. She fumbled around for what seemed like an eternity, trying to stretch the tights enough to gain easier access, but eventually gave up. Though I never opened my mouth, I can vividly remember, as she glided her fingers over my belly button and stroked the sensitive skin below, a voice screaming over and over in my head: 'Please make it stop.'

Over the years, I became increasingly desensitised to sexual violence. The last time I was abused was by a friend and music industry colleague, at one of the after-parties of the New Zealand Music Awards in 2014. I was sitting in a booth with a group of high-powered industry insiders when he suddenly started sliding his hand up my leg under the table. He tried to touch my arse, which was fairly futile, given I was sitting on it, then returned to my leg, moving his hand higher and higher. I turned to the female acquaintance sitting next to me and told her what was happening, hoping she would help me. 'Oh, you need to learn to laugh it off,' she said in response. While people often assume that the fight or flight instinct kicks in during situations of sexual harassment or abuse, my infuriatingly useless reaction has often been to freeze. It's something I've since gone to great lengths to understand and overcome. In any case, on the evening in question, I was trapped in the booth. I couldn't flee, so I remained frozen in immense discomfort as he manhandled me until a colleague standing a few metres away from the booth caught my eye and saw what was happening. 'Are you okay?' he mouthed. I shook my head. He quickly moved to extract me, and stayed with me for the rest of the night, while my friend repeatedly requested that I sit in his lap. When it was clear that he wasn't going to leave me alone, my rescuer walked me out of the club and put me into a taxi. I remember walking away from the scene of the crime (quite literally) feeling angry, disgusted, exasperated and completely resigned to the fact that I would do nothing about it and that it would likely happen again to another young woman who just happened to be in the wrong place at the wrong time. I still carry that guilt to this day, but to name predators – especially famous and/or powerful ones – is to risk being hauled into court and sued for defamation. It requires victims to gamble their careers, livelihoods and sanity with full knowledge that the system was not built to support them. In the end, in sharing my stories without naming the perpetrators, I've made an uncomfortable decision that is nonetheless best for my mental health at this stage.

In the years after the last time I was groped, I began to wonder whether sexual violence is just part of the experience of womanhood. This was before the allegations of sexual harassment and assault against Harvey Weinstein emerged. After that, and the hundreds of thousands of #MeToo posts that were published on social media during the weeks following, I knew that my suspicions were correct. Overwhelmingly, experiencing sexual harassment and/or violence simply comes with the territory of being female.

Consent and sexual violence are complicated subjects that many people struggle to understand. There are a number of myths that surround sexual violence, which many of us have fallen prey to at one time or another. For example, my own assumption when I was 13 that because I was wearing a short skirt I was somehow responsible for unwanted digital penetration. Or that I was to blame for my female friend violating me, because she and I kissed consensually in a phase of utter emotional disorientation while I was trying to make sense of what had happened to me a number of months after that awful night on the couch. Or the notion that boys and men are somehow incapable of resisting their sexual urges, and so women must take every possible precaution to make sure that they won't 'get raped'. As if 'getting raped' were something victims should be held responsible for. In our attempt to live in a world of clearly defined categories of black and white, we've overlooked the fact that sexual violence often occurs in unexpected ways at unexpected times, and can be perpetrated by people you'd never think were capable of such a thing. Like friends, and even family members. So-called 'rape myths' are so deeply embedded in our society that it can be difficult to identify them. Here's an incomplete list of offensive, yet common assumptions that are all utter bullshit:

- Getting drunk means you're asking for it
- Wearing revealing clothing means you're asking for it
- Expressing your sexuality in any way means that you're asking for it

- Consenting to one form of sexual behaviour means you're giving your consent for other sexual behaviour to happen
- Consenting to sexual behaviour once means that you've given consent for it to happen again
- If you're a woman accusing a man of rape, you just regret having consensual sex with him and you're a nasty slut trying to ruin his life
- Flirting or 'leading someone on' means you're asking for it
- Even if a woman says 'no', we can't be sure it really means 'no'; especially if she has been drinking
- It's normal and even 'sexy' for men to pursue women doggedly, even when they've refused their advances on multiple occasions
- Women who have lots of sexual partners are sluts
- Men who have lots of sexual partners are studs
- Transgender people are dangerous and shouldn't be allowed into female bathrooms
- Rape victims must react in an appropriate manner, determined by other people's idea of how a rape victim should react, otherwise they're probably lying
- Men can never be raped by women, because they must've 'wanted it'
- Women don't perpetrate sexual violence
- If a victim/survivor has any consensual sexual contact with their abuser after their assault, the assault must also have been consensual
- Women who dress provocatively shouldn't be taken seriously; they are liars.

All of these assumptions are false, but you don't have to look far to find prominent examples of myths seeping into society. Take the case of Margaret Comer for example, at the time a corporate services executive at Gallagher Group Limited – a major sponsor of the Chiefs rugby team – who was asked in an interview with Fairfax about the Chiefs players' alleged inappropriate touching of Scarlette, the dancer they had hired to perform at that infamous end-of-season function. Her summation of the alleged assault? 'If a woman takes her clothes off and walks around in a group of men, what are we supposed to do if one of them tries to touch her?' What are we supposed to do if a man non-consensually touches a woman, Margaret? I can think of lots of things that don't include throwing up our hands and absolving perpetrators of responsibility.

Margaret is far from alone, however. In my opinion, the 2016 rape trial of then Northern Districts cricketer (and Black Cap) Scott Kuggeleijn also deserves special mention. During his cross-examining of the complainant in court, prominent defence counsel Philip Morgan QC asked her, 'Were you saying no but not meaning no?'[2] Which is apparently very important to clarify. I mean, imaging saying 'no' and actually intending to convey the very simple and almost universally accepted meaning of a word that the vast majority of us learn to use with precision around age two.

Morgan also described a conversation that had allegedly taken place between the complainant and Kuggeleijn, in which she told him that she was on the pill. One of the esteemed lawyer's follow-up questions was this: 'Did you not recognise that telling him you were on the pill in those circumstances was you telling him you wanted to have sex with him?'

No Philip, she didn't recognise that because saying 'I'm on the pill' DOESN'T FUCKING MEAN 'Yes, I want to have sex with you'.

Philip Morgan is an experienced and respected lawyer who was doing his job within the bounds of the rules our justice system gets, but the kinds of questions defence counsels are permitted to put to complainants make my stomach churn. In the end, the defence tactics worked. Kuggeleijn was acquitted in his second trial. He has since been played for our national cricket team. So much for the idea that being accused of rape 'ruins' men's lives.

The idea that allegations of sexually problematic behaviour are used as a ruse by women with the intention of getting back at men and destroying their lives/families/reputations/careers is an old and enduring one, but it is extremely unrealistic. If the man in question is powerful, more often than not any allegation of misconduct reverberates powerfully against the woman who made it. Case in point: our ponytail-pulling former Prime Minister. I happen to know and like Sir John Key, which may come as a surprise, given our differing views on many things. We have a personal acquaintance that began when we met at a concert I performed at back in early 2008. My personal admiration for John, however, does not prevent me from seeing the ponytailgate saga as weird, wrong and a particularly instructive example of what happens when a woman speaks out against a powerful man.

Whichever way you want to spin it – and at this stage it's been spun in every which way – being the Prime Minister of a country (or any sentient adult man, for that matter) and pulling the ponytail of a woman you don't know extremely well without her consent, or worse, a waitress who is essentially bound by the terms of her employment to serve customers with politeness and deference, is not okay. It's extremely odd and creepy, and irregardless of it being meant in a daggy 'dad-joke' kind of way, it involved repeatedly trespassing upon the personal boundaries of a woman who was largely powerless to fight back. I don't think that the former Prime Minister was intending to be a creep, but in a way that is also part of the problem. Sir John Key, like all of us, lives in a society where women's personal space and boundaries are not respected on the regular. His behaviour was bizarre and inappropriate, but the fact that he didn't stop to think about that before he yanked on Amanda Bailey's hair is in itself a reflection of the culture we all grow up in.

The repercussions for Bailey were severe. When she decided to go public with the story, she was accused of carrying out a politically motivated attack. *Seven Sharp* presenter Mike Hosking took particular umbrage, calling her 'selfish' and describing the saga as 'a puffed-up self-involved pile of political bollocks' in an editorial segment delivered at the end of the television show[3]. The Broadcasting Standards Authority later upheld complaints about his comments[4], but Hosking was far from alone. Controversial gossip hack Rachel Glucina called her a 'piece of work' with a 'massive political agenda' in a text to the Prime Minister sent just after she'd interviewed her[5]. Blogger Cameron Slater called her a 'very politically motivated woman'[6] and suggested that by considering her legal options she was 'throw[ing] her employers under the bus' and had gone 'a bridge too far'[7]. The irony of Slater later considering his own legal options, and opting to have his name suppressed after he'd railed against suppression practices, speaks rather loudly for itself.

Another prominent case that was remarkable not only for its staggering sexism but for how little impact it had upon a powerful man's career was Paul Henry's 'perfect titties' tirade. The thing has to be seen to be believed. This is what Paul Henry said to *New Zealand Herald* journalist Greg Bruce at lunchtime on a Tuesday:

> *We were nearly finished lunch when his attention was drawn to the breasts of the woman at the next table: 'The girl with the perfect titties,' he said. 'Am I right or am I right? No, I'm right – perfect titties. Talking to a girl with entirely adequate titties but she's decided to have lunch with someone with perfect titties.'*
>
> *'That's perception, eh?' the publicist said.*
>
> *'Oh, it's just my perception,' Henry said. 'I could be wrong, but I'm not.'*
>
> *'How do you know the other one hasn't got perfect titties?' the publicist said. 'She's just covered them up.'*
>
> *'Okay, I'll tell you why: because she's covered them up.'*
>
> *'No, that's not true,' the publicist said.*
>
> *'No, if you've got perfect titties, you know you've got perfect titties, because you see them all the time and you let them come out and play.'*

'This is a subjective thing isn't it?' I said, 'Your impression?'

'No, oh no, you might like different titties to me, right, but there's titties you like, titties you don't like, then there's perfect titties. The titties you like might be different to the ones I like but the perfect ones are the same.'

'What are they?' I asked.

'You can see them now, if you care to glance.'

I said I didn't feel comfortable doing that.

'Well what can I do?' he said. 'They are there in front of you. All you need to do is look.'

'Is it the geometry of them?' I asked.

'It's a whole collection of things, isn't it?' he said.

'Wait until she has children,' the publicist said. 'They won't be perfect then.'

'No they won't,' Henry said. 'No they won't. Oh, absolutely! And it won't be her fault – it will be part of the transition through life, which I fully understand, but right at the moment, this moment in time, it's like, at the moment she's Palm Springs. She will be Rancho Mirage, but at the moment she's Palm Springs. And you know, at the end of the day you want to spend the rest of your life with Rancho Mirage, but you want to dream about Palm Springs.'

'Do you?' I asked.

'Oh, yeah,' he said, his voice low and sultry. 'And you know what? When you're fondling Rancho Mirage, in here,' – he tapped the side of his head – 'it's Palm Springs.'

Around this point, the woman put on and zipped up a tight leather jacket.

> *'Do you know what she's done?' Henry said.*
>
> *'Covered them up,' the publicist said.*
>
> *'Yeah. She has not only covered them up – she has hermetically f***ing sealed them, in leather! By crikey, they're going to be ripe for a while. She's caring for them.'*
>
> *'Who could blame her?' I said. 'Hermetically sealing them after listening to that onslaught.'*
>
> *'Well,' he said, 'I don't know that she could have heard that, but if she did, you know what? She's going to walk away 1) outraged, which is a feeling people love, and 2), very f***in' proud.*
>
> *'Outraged and Proud, of Remuera.'*[8]

If you feel like you need to take a scalding hot shower, and/or scrub your skin with hospital grade bleach, you're not alone.

The interview, published in the *Herald*'s flagship weekend magazine *Canvas*, understandably created a sensational scandal. In a strange twist of fate, I was scheduled to be on Henry's show the first morning after the story broke. Paul Henry is another man that I know and, somewhat against the odds, like. At his best, he is whip-smart, hilarious, warm-hearted and kind. At his worst … well, let's just say he was clearly not at his best the day he went to lunch with Greg Bruce. I decided to cancel my appearance that Monday, as I knew I realistically had two options: 1) go on the show and pretend nothing had happened, which would have been both what was expected of me as a professional and completely morally untenable or 2) go on the show and have a blazing row on live national television. So I chose option 3. Upon advice from my management I posted a brief note on social media explaining my absence, which was then picked up by the major media organisations, leading to lots of comments like this one, from @clingwrapkiller: 'The question I'm left with is "I wonder if @PaulHenryShow would pull out of Lizzie Marvelly?"'

Charming.

The impact on Henry's career, however, was minimal. The interview didn't even dent his ratings. He soldiered on, undeterred, after offering a half-apology: 'I meant no harm or offence by what I said ... There is absolutely no way the woman could have heard the conversation that took place. I would never want to make anyone feel uncomfortable.'[9] And that was that. He eventually bowed out in his own time, leaving behind a network that had been desperate to keep hold of him. Meanwhile, scores of New Zealand women – myself included – have never felt the same about the word 'titties' again.

In New Zealand there is a tacit acceptance that talking about women's bodies is just a normal thing that blokes do. The framing goes something like this: any red-blooded male would [insert sexist/demeaning/objectifying behaviour here] women because that's just what guys do. Men can't fight their biology. It's just not realistic to expect [insert dignified/respectful behaviour here] of them. Given how much men supposedly struggle to control themselves, it's astonishing that they've been allowed anywhere near positions of power. I mean, how can we expect men to run companies and countries when they can't even get their brains to override their penises? The biological argument – that it's somehow okay for men to treat women as sexual objects that exist for their gratification because it proves that a man is a 'real man' – is insulting to men and women. And yet, it continues to this day. It is just part of the landscape in a country that regularly collects trophies in developed-world rankings for its terrible treatment of women.

Of course, no discussion of inappropriate sexual behaviour in New Zealand would be complete without mentioning the case of the Roast Busters. If you were lucky enough to miss this particularly revolting news story, it involved a group of young men in Auckland whose goal was to intoxicate underage girls and rape them. I don't quite have the words to explain how utterly repugnant and unjust it is that a group of young men were able to ply underage women with alcohol, coerce them into non-consensual sexual activity, share videos boasting about their crimes, name and shame their victims by posting images of them online … and (inexplicably) get away with it. It is even harder to understand the actions of the New Zealand police, including an officer who allegedly asked a 13-year-old victim what she was wearing when her sexual assault took place, and Detective Bruce Scott, who told the public that there was nothing the police could do until one of the victims was 'brave enough' to make a formal complaint. It later emerged that one of the victims had indeed been 'brave enough' to make a complaint two years before, but hadn't been taken seriously by the police[10].

In New Zealand, it is estimated that only nine per cent of sexual assault incidents are reported to the police[11]. Given the attitudes sexual assault victims are up against, I'd suggest that it's not difficult to figure out why.

Perhaps the most insulting of all of society's narratives surrounding sexual violence is the deafening roar of implication that lies just beneath the surface of 'innocent until proven guilty'. There are many very good reasons why our justice system is built upon the presumption of innocence, but when crimes of sexual violence are tried before the court (whether of law or public opinion), the assumption that the accused is innocent somehow seems to suggest that the alleged victim is lying. As far as I'm aware, this doesn't happen to victims of any other crime. Complainants accusing defendants of theft, fraud, or assault are not automatically assumed to be liars. Complainants accusing defendants of sexual assault are.

As famous American criminologist Freda Adler famously said, 'Rape is the only crime in which the victim becomes the accused.' For many female victims, the presumption of innocence can quickly become the presumption of whorish guilt, fanciful falsehood, or a scorned woman's revenge, all with the eventual goal of ruining some poor upstanding man's life (unless, of course, the man in question is poor and brown – then there's a possibility that he might be a 'bad bugger' who deserves what he has coming to him).

The binary of not guilty or guilty is a fundamental cornerstone of our justice system, but in cases that often boil down to 'he said, she said' scenarios being tried in a culture that already mistrusts and harshly judges women, it is problematic to say the least. When what he says holds more weight than what she says, the scales of justice seem decidedly off balance.

Having such cases tried by a jury is equally troublesome. Although it comforts us to believe that we've evolved somewhat over the past few centuries, rape myths still permeate our society. In criminal cases, all it takes is for two jurors to believe that a woman was a stupid slut who was asking for it, and a mistrial will be declared, requiring the victim to go through the entire arduous trial process again, if they can face it. Figures from the Ministry of Justice suggest that sexual assault trials result in hung juries at a much higher rate than other trials. An investigation by the Law Commission found that during 2014/2015, eight per cent of sexual violence cases heard in the District Court were retrials, compared to just 0.8 per cent of the total number of criminal cases heard by the District Court that were retrials during that year[12]. There has to be a better way to see justice done.

The legal profession is well aware of these problems, and has begun to take steps to try to combat them. A new scheme has been piloted in recent years, aiming to improve the experiences of sexual assault complainants by speeding up the process, restricting the scope of admissible questions that can be put to complainants, and providing judges and lawyers with expert training[13]. It is an important first step, but arguably what really needs to happen is legislative change.

Even if legislative change were to occur, however, we can't expect the justice system to fix a problem that infects each and every one of us: New Zealand has a rape culture. Even if you hate the term, you can likely agree that when 13-year-old boys are non-consensually fingering their peers, 17- and 18-year-old boys are plying young girls with alcohol in order to sexually violate them, and lawyers are questioning the meaning of the word 'no' in open court, there's something going wrong. A report published by the Ministry of Justice in 2014 found that 24 per cent of women and six per cent of men have experienced sexual violence[14]. Whether we want to acknowledge it or not, we're living in a society that is ridden with sexual violation, where high school-age boys are saying things like, 'Fuck women. Not even drunk, pass her out then fuck her job done,' and 'If you don't take advantage of a drunk girl then you're not a true WC [Wellington College] boy,'[15] as if it were no big deal. This is the part that concerns me the most. We've reached the point where teen boys think that joking about raping comatose women is the height of comedy. But boys will be boys. Shrug.

Rape culture is something that should make us profoundly uncomfortable, but it's important to clarify that rape culture is not just about rape. It is about behaviour that normalises or trivialises sexual violence (like making rape jokes, or suggesting that it's okay to rape someone while they're unconscious, for example); attitudes that demean groups of people due to their gender or sexuality (like suggesting that men can't be raped, that trans women are perverts or that lesbians could be 'cured' by having sex with – or being raped by – a man); and environments that shield perpetrators and blame victims (like private Facebook groups, fraternities, sports teams, or even court rooms). Rape culture involves a disconcerting spectrum of behaviours and circumstances that should inspire national soul-searching, rather than knee-jerk denials.

The only way to address it is head on, and the work begins in our own communities. Fighting back against rape culture starts with small and consistent action: calling a friend out for their sexist joke, standing up for a woman being attacked online, educating the children and young people in our lives about their inalienable right to make decisions about their own bodies, and teaching them to respect the bodies and decisions of others. It means being brave enough to examine our own behaviour and stand up to our peers.

Individual action alone won't solve the problem, however. Not when rape culture relies on systems of oppression in order to survive. It is clear, for example, that the justice system is currently failing the majority of victims. When less than one in ten victims reports their experience to the police[16], we can conclude both that the number of sexual assaults taking place in New Zealand each year is much higher than official statistics reflect and that there is a terrifyingly large group of uncharged rapists living free in our communities while their neighbours, co-workers, classmates and families are often none the wiser.

It's also apparent that schools are either ill-equipped or in some cases unwilling to deal with the effects of pornography, a sexualised media landscape, harmful, discriminative myths and rampant online misogyny. They're certainly not bound by legislation to take any meaningful action to address issues like consent and sexual violence. While decisions about sexuality education remain in the hands of individual schools and their boards, with only a set of toothless 'guidelines' being provided by the Government, a large number of Kiwi teens are left to navigate an increasingly porn-soaked culture with little reliable information and even less reputable guidance. Unbelievably, New Zealand schools are not required by law to teach their students about consent. In a country with such horrific sexual violence statistics, surely it should be a no-brainer to update the curriculum to include a comprehensive and compulsory programme delivering the same high standard of evidence-based and well-designed sexuality education to every Kiwi student. Instead, it's a political hot potato that no Government has yet had the fortitude to address.

There are any number of other systems that contribute to the health and perpetuation of rape culture. Reporting rape jokes and sexually demeaning content on social media, for example, provides no guarantee that the content will be taken down. The Advertising Standards Authority states that:

> *Advertisements should not employ sexual appeal in a manner which is exploitative and degrading of any individual or group of people in society to promote the sale of products or services. In particular people should not be portrayed in a manner which uses sexual appeal simply to draw attention to an unrelated product. Children must not be portrayed in a manner which treats them as objects of sexual appeal.*[17]

Yet ads depicting naked women and women wearing swimwear or other form-fitting clothing are still regularly used to sell unrelated products, and the media still prints headlines like, 'Northern Districts cricketer's rape trial: "She was dressed provocatively"'[18].

While systems and structures allow rape culture to flourish, individual action looks to me a bit like a (thankfully growing) horde of feminists at the bottom of a mountain, all trying to push an enormous dung boulder up a steep incline while the Government, the justice system, the education system, the media, advertisers, social networks, and other powerful forces are sitting on top of it having a nice picnic (and yes, I know: #NotAllJournos, #NotAllSchools, #NotAllLawyers, etc.). Which is why our efforts as individuals must focus not only on speaking out against rape culture, but on forcing the people running the powerful structures that enable it to take notice, helping them to realise that they're currently part of the problem, and encouraging them to join the fight. We may be fierce, dedicated and willing to get our hands dirty, but unless the powerful put down their sandwiches and join us, we'll be stuck pushing shit uphill for a long time.

It's not just rape culture that threatens women's possession of and agency over their bodies. The right to make our own reproductive choices is also hotly contested. In fact, legislatively speaking, in New Zealand we don't have that right, as abortion is technically illegal. Instead, if we choose to terminate a pregnancy we are forced to lie to two 'certifying consultants' (who, in order to be certified, cannot believe that 'the question of whether an abortion should or should not be performed in any case is entirely a matter for the woman and a doctor to decide'[19] – yes, strictly pro-choice doctors need not apply) by telling them that continuing a pregnancy would result in 'serious danger' to our mental health.

I don't want to waste time going over the same tired debate, but what I will say is this: I cannot wait for scientists to figure out a way to make it possible for men to gestate and give birth to human babies. On the blessed day when that new technology becomes available, I'd like to hereby propose that every man who decides that he's going to wade into a conversation about abortion to 'speak up against the murdering of the unborn' has an embryo forcibly implanted inside him. He may also need to have his penis cut off in order to give birth, but that shouldn't be a problem, of course, given that he had no issue whatsoever with forcing women to undergo a medical event that would likely result in irreversible bodily changes. What's one little penis when some poor cluster of foetal cells is at stake?

Until that day, I humbly suggest that all people who are not in possession of a uterus shut their mouths. I'd also suggest that anyone who happens to be in possession of a uterus keeps their nose out of anyone else's uterus. Just because you have a uterus doesn't mean that you get to make decisions for all uteri. If you don't like abortion, don't have one.

The legal framework is quite bad enough without anyone interjecting their opinions into the argument. The idea that a woman making an informed decision about her own body should be classified under the Crimes Act in 2017 is an insult to every Kiwi woman. As it currently stands, the law says quite clearly to women that they cannot be trusted to make a decision about whether or not they should continue a pregnancy. They must instead defer to the expert knowledge of two certifying consultants who will decide whether they will be forced to become walking incubators for the next several months. Which actually does happen. It's important to note that in 2016, 252 'not justified abortion' certificates were issued, meaning that hundreds of Kiwi women were denied an abortion[20].

In practice, the medical and legal systems have chosen to look the other way (for the most part – I'm sure the women who have been denied abortions would feel differently) for almost as long as the law has been in place, using the mental health criterion in the legislation as a loophole. Which surely lends even more weight to the idea that abortion should simply be legalised and dealt with under health legislation. But no. Instead we soldier on with a 41-year-old framework that serves absolutely no one, costs millions[21], causes ridiculous delays, stigmatises women, forces them to jump through unnecessary hoops and infantilises them to the point where they cannot legally make a perfectly reasonable decision about their own bodies and futures without the permission of two doctors. All because it would be a 'controversial' conversation to have. Let's be honest, it's just one of the many. Are you noticing a pattern here? Rape culture? There's no such thing. Sexual violence? #NotAllMen. Abortion? Let's not talk about it.

When the topic of abortion does come up, we rarely continue the discussion long enough to allow for any kind of critical analysis. For example, if anti-abortion advocates really wanted to prevent abortion and 'save children' they'd advocate for free contraception, comprehensive sexuality education and decent incomes for families with children, all things that have been proven to either prevent unwanted pregnancies or produce better outcomes for children.

Instead, many of them campaign for abstinence education, balk at taxpayer money being used to fund contraceptive options and engage in beneficiary bashing. Why? Because the anti-abortion movement is far more concerned about women's sexual choices than it is about the wellbeing of children. The qualification by some anti-abortion advocates that abortion should be allowed in cases of rape supports this. A number of abortion advocates are not concerned about foetuses when they're begotten by rapists, but when they're the result of a woman having sex on her own terms (slut!), that woman must not be allowed to have an abortion. As utterly repulsive and reprehensible as the standpoint is, at least anti-abortion activists who are completely against abortion in any and all circumstances stick to their principles. For the vast majority, however, the abortion discussion is not truly about 'saving the innocent' (which necessarily requires women to not be innocent), but instead about punishing women for being sexual beings.

And if you need further convincing, consider author Patrick Tomlinson's Burning Building dilemma.

> *You're in a fertility clinic. Why isn't important. The fire alarm goes off. You run for the exit. As you run down this hallway, you hear a child screaming from behind a door. You throw open the door and find a five-year-old child crying for help. They're in one corner of the room. In the other corner, you spot a frozen container labelled '1000 Viable Human Embryos.' The smoke is rising. You start to choke. You know you can grab one or the other, but not both before you succumb to smoke inhalation and die,*

> *saving no one. Do you A) save the child, or B) save the thousand embryos? There is no 'C'. 'C' means you all die.*

Tomlinson has been posing the question to anti-abortion campaigners for a decade, but has never received a simple answer. As he explains:

> *They will never answer honestly, because we all instinctively understand the right answer is 'A'. A human child is worth more than a thousand embryos. Or ten thousand. Or a million. Because they are not the same, not morally, not ethically, not biologically.*[22]

If anti-abortion activists really want to save children, they should devote their efforts to the many millions of children all around the world who are currently standing in metaphorical burning buildings with no hope of escape. Children suffering from preventable diseases, children who are malnourished, children dying in armed conflicts, children drowning while trying to escape warzones, children living in poverty in their own communities; there is sadly no shortage of children in desperate need of help.

Actions speak louder than words, and as happy as these people are to picket outside hospitals and abortion clinics, hoping to guilt vulnerable women into doubting their decisions (in the name of protecting them, of course), you'll be unlikely to find them doing anything that will make a real, tangible difference to the lives of women and children. Funny that.

* * *

Have you ever wondered why society is obsessed with 'protecting' women? If you haven't, you should. Women are advised not to walk home alone at night, not to drink alcohol, not to wear clothing that may show off our bodies, not to openly acknowledge that we are sexual beings, all in the name of protecting us from the unspeakable horror delivered by the crazed sexual sadist hiding in the shadows. We're cautioned against getting pregnant, which, especially when we're young and unwed, could bring about ruination, and somewhat counter-intuitively warned against the (largely fabricated) 'dangers' of abortion. We've been warned about the pressures of work environments, the 'cut and thrust' of politics, the rigours of professional sport and the high stress of academia by a society that is seemingly so concerned for our wellbeing that it sees danger for the female of the species at every turn.

How very convenient.

It's a pretty sleight of hand; a preponderance of concern that is closely related to another word that starts with c: control. I've come to think of it as malignant benevolence. It's the perfect decoy, reminding us of all the ways in which the world is dangerous for us and distracting attention away from all the ways in which the world needs to change. Malignant benevolence tells us that our bodies are not our own. It tells girls that if they step outside of any of the restrictive barriers that society has built around them, they will be responsible for their precarious fate. It tells women that their precious sense of selfhood, volition and agency is an illusion that will be shattered should they mistakenly fall pregnant. It lets men off the hook, reasoning that if it's a woman's fault that she 'got raped' there is no need for men to address the fact that they are overwhelmingly the ones doing the raping. It has been designed to remind us that we're spending our lives walking around in a man's world that was not built to accommodate us as equals, but instead to subjugate and exploit us as baby-makers, helpmeets, housekeepers and whores. It does us no favours, and it certainly does not have our best interests at heart. It wants to hold us in its big strong arms, and strangle us if we ever try to break the embrace.

And even when you've disavowed it, thrown it off and washed it off your skin, it lingers. I smell it in the guilt I still sometimes feel for the sexual violence that has been perpetrated against me. I taste it in the rush of fear that floods my body when I'm alone in the dark and a strange man starts following me. I fight it on a regular basis, when the voice inside my head tells me that I should be afraid.

I am afraid.

But I am also brave. And angry. We deserve better. Our protection has become our possession, and it's done a terrible job of keeping us safe.

Some days I find myself dreaming about what would've happened if I hadn't been violated, if I'd grown up without knowing bodily invasion, without realising that even friends couldn't be trusted with the boundaries of my selfhood. I wonder what that woman would've been like. I wonder what that world would be like for her.

I grieve for the fact that I'll never know.

CHAPTER ELEVEN

The possessed mind

Rock bottom comes in many different guises. For me it was the corner of my wardrobe, where I had rolled myself into a ball to rock and cry and hide away from the overwhelming realness of the world outside. Curled up in there, wearing the same pyjamas I'd had on for days and shaking with silent, suppressed sobs, I realised that I had a problem. I was breaking apart, watching the tiny specks of my sanity falling through my fingers like sand. I had, I feared, gone crazy. Nuts. Mental. In that moment, however, I was finally lucid enough to realise that the desperate unhappiness that had plagued me for so long had finally taken over. I was shackled, tethered to its downward spiral, fully aware, but powerless to do anything about it.

Before it happened to me, I thought of the word 'breakdown' as some kind of strange Hollywood term. It was bandied about in tabloid magazines with gleeful, gossipy relish. So-and-so was having a breakdown because her husband had been caught cheating with the nanny. Such-and-such was having a breakdown because he'd been arrested for punching a paparazzo while drunk and/or high. That kind of thing. There was almost a macabre kind of glamour to it. When I found myself in the midst of one, however, I realised that it was a private hell that no amount of salaciousness could ever truly capture. And there was nothing glamorous about it.

I was diagnosed with depression and anxiety in August of 2009. I'd just turned 20, and I was about to embark on my second European tour, a 40-date run as the guest artist for the original *Britain's Got Talent* winner Paul Potts that would culminate in a performance at the Royal Albert Hall in London. I'd just recorded my second record, *Home*, and was in the middle of negotiating a licensing deal with EMI Australia. Outwardly, I had everything going for me. Inwardly, I was a bubbling cauldron of misery.

As most mental health professionals will tell you, there is rarely just one cause of depression, or major depressive disorder, as it's known clinically. In my case, a cluster of ill-fated stars aligned. I'd spent my childhood as a chronic overachiever, highly driven and terrified of failure. I was the child of two highly successful, self-employed workaholics, and while there was no shortage of love in my home, work life often won out over family life. I'd grown up travelling close to the edge emotionally, holding myself to unattainable standards of thinness and perfection, and often finding myself crippled with guilt when I fell short of my impossible vision of who I thought I should be. I'd started secretly cutting myself at age 11, and I would continue to self-harm as a coping mechanism until I was in my early twenties. I had very little true self-knowledge, and while I'd been living in an adult world since my mid-teens, I was fairly naïve, partly because I hadn't had the chance to experience what it was like to be a 'normal' teenager. I often felt overwhelmed, but coped by busying myself so that I wouldn't have to address my feelings. As a result, I became so good at running away from them that I would later struggle to identify emotions correctly. Excitement felt like fear, and frustration quickly turned into anxiety.

When I look back on the events leading up to 2009, it was a miracle I'd held it together until then. In late 2008, I'd lost my first record deal. As a casualty of the global recession, a rushed and premature first album and the departure of the president of the label who had signed me, I found myself cast adrift, with the thing I'd sacrificed my childhood for taken from me. The dream started to shatter around me, and there was nothing I could do to piece it back together. Around the same time I embarked on an ill-advised fling with a man twice my age while on tour on the other side of the world, which would have a lasting emotional impact on me as I struggled to make sense of what had happened. On top of that, my family relationships began to fracture, both as a result of the normal adjustment that takes place when a teenager becomes a young adult and the fact that my father was acting as my manager. I don't envy any parent who manages their artist child, nor any child that is managed by their parent. When a parent is required to see their child as a product it is generally a recipe for disaster. To be clear, I don't blame my father, but it was certainly an impossible situation. Then, on my 20th birthday, I fell ill with swine flu. It may well have been the final straw, but for a while at least it was a relief. When I was so sick that I could do nothing but lie on the couch all day, I didn't have to make any excuses. I gave in to the tiredness not only in my bones, but in my soul. No one could ask anything of me.

Somehow, in the middle of carnage, illness and emotional chaos I managed to fly to the UK to record an album in July. When I touched back down on New Zealand soil, however, my borrowed time was up. I imploded.

Much of the time that followed remains a blur, both as a result of the anti-depressants I took for 14 months, and the strange suspicion I still have that depression somehow prevents the correct encoding of some memories. One memory that stands out as perhaps the lowest point of my life remains crystal clear, however. It was the night of 4 November 2009, and I was standing in the dark in my hotel room in Canary Wharf. Earlier that night I'd performed at the Royal Albert Hall, fulfilling a dream I'd had since childhood. It was one of the most astounding nights of my career, but as soon as I walked off the stage the adrenalin stopped, and despair overwhelmed me. In my broken mind, I'd achieved a life goal, and now, finally, I could put an end to the pain and suffering. Standing in the dark hotel room, looking out the window at the cold London sky, I was done with this earth. I'm not quite sure what happened next, whether I found the resolve to make the call, or whether I merely answered the phone, but I was infinitely lucky either way to speak to a friend who talked me down from the cliff I'd built inside my head. I can't remember the conversation we had, but when I got off the phone, I resolved to hang on a little longer.

Remembering that there were people who cared about me gave me the moment of pause that I desperately needed that night. There would be other brushes with suicidal thoughts over the next couple of years, but that night was the closest I came. I had the means, I had the despair, but I also had a friend. And once I'd climbed out of that particular abyss I'd slowly discover that the only way to go from there was up.

I was fortunate to work with a brilliant psychologist during that time, who slowly helped me to put my life back together. I had weekly therapy for nearly three years, during which time I learnt more about myself than I'd figured out in the 20 years prior. Strange though it may sound, I almost feel like she reorganised my mind. It was certainly a disorganised mess when I showed up on her doorstep. She used a combination of different therapies, from cognitive behavioural therapy, which helped me to adjust my catastrophising thought patterns, to snippets of psychoanalytic therapy, which helped me to deal with the vivid and sometimes terrifying dreams that accompanied the high dose of citalopram I was taking. It's been nearly a decade now since I started working with her, but occasionally I'll go searching for a way to cope with a challenge and I'll locate the answer almost as if she'd left it there for me to find it. She has since retired from practice, but I still hear her voice in my head when I need it. Mental health professionals don't receive anywhere near the glory and respect they deserve. They are lifesavers. Literally.

While depression affects people of all genders, it affects women disproportionately. It's something of a cliché, but the idea that depression is anger turned inwards resonates with me, and seems particularly fitting when we consider that female anger is still taboo. When women aren't permitted to be outwardly angry, those negative feelings don't simply disappear. To this day I find it difficult to really rage; in my emotional landscape, anger quickly slides into sadness. On the rare occasions when I'm moved to yell, it will often be with a painful lump in my throat and involuntary tears running down my face, which completely undermines my fury and turns it into a kind of melodramatic comedy. It's very annoying. To make a broad generalisation that is entirely anecdotal, it seems to me that women are far better equipped and more willing to inflict pain upon themselves than they are on others.

The female mind is rarely its own. Just as the female body has been controlled, co-opted and exploited, the female brain has faced similar challenges, the first of which being the struggle to be thought of as equal to the male brain. It wasn't that long ago that women were thought to be intellectually inferior to men. Such an idea still exists in some enclaves. While many of the people who believe in male superiority belong to extremist groups, there are researchers today who still posit that women are not as intelligent as men, which is unsurprising really, given the field of psychology's chequered history with women. The historically male-dominated field has used everything from IQ tests – which, it should be noted, have been slammed by researchers and educators alike, and largely discredited as a standalone measure of intelligence – to comparisons between the weight of male and female brains, to suggest that men are superior to women. While brain weight and IQ scores remain operational definitions of intelligence, there is no proof that just because someone's brain is heavier or they perform better on a test of entirely arbitrary questions, they are more 'intelligent'. Intelligence is a manmade construct that is impossible to truly measure. Truth is in the eye of the interpreter, but categorisation and authority have long been in the hands of men. In an age when girls and women regularly perform better at school[1] and university[2] than their male counterparts, the claim that men are more intelligent than women deserves to be relegated to the history books in the 'disproved sexist bullshit' chapter. But here we are.

The fact that some psychologists continue the quest to place men above women says a lot about the staying power of misogyny. For centuries, women have been cast as 'mad, sad or bad' if they've dared to step outside of the rigid constraints of femininity. Diagnoses of hysteria or puerperal madness (post-birth psychosis) were given to women for any number of reasons[3], malleable so as to account for all of the many symptoms that may inadvertently come of being born female. I can't help but wonder, however, whether there is more at play when it comes to women and mental illness. As the World Health Organisation notes, 'Overall rates of psychiatric disorder are almost identical for men and women but striking gender differences are found in the patterns of mental illness'[4]. Gender differences are particularly prominent in rates of major depressive disorder, the most common mental illness. Twice as many women are affected by depression than men[5]. Why? Science still doesn't have the answer. Historically, women were simply thought to be biologically weaker and inherently unstable, and much research has focussed on possible hormonal causes that could explain the gender discrepancy in rates of depression – the results of which have been mixed[6]. It seems more likely that social factors are to blame. Researchers have found, for example, that gender differences in depression are more pronounced in societies that adhere to traditional gender roles[7], resulting in higher numbers of women suffering from depression than men. Other factors that seem to suggest the social determinants of depression in women include an increased exposure to childhood sexual abuse[8], increased likelihood of exposure to poverty and the stresses of caretaking[9], and higher levels of concern about body image[10]. While of course the causes of depression are multi-faceted, and often a number of factors compound with genetic pre-disposition to trigger mental illness, it's hardly surprising that women are more likely to feel sad than men. Basically, to dramatically oversimplify for the sake of scorching clarity, it seems that a system that exposes more women than men to sexual abuse and stress, ensures we are less likely to have economic power, and tells us that we have to look a certain way fucks with our heads. Who knew?

Eating disorders provide another frightening example of what happens when malignant external forces take up residence in women's minds. In disorders like anorexia and bulimia, we see the frightening outcome of patriarchal beauty standards becoming internalised to the extent where dangerously underweight girls look in the mirror and are tortured by a fictional body that doesn't belong to them[11]. While the causes of eating disorders are also often multifactorial, when women have grown up acutely aware of the importance of fitting within the boundaries of heterosexual desirability, it's difficult to really determine which thought processes are organic, and which have been transmitted via the media and societal conditioning straight into our minds. When we're malignantly sad and/or skinny, it's hard to say whether we're truly in control of our own minds, or whether we've been possessed, taken over and turned against ourselves.

And it's not just diagnosable illness that screws us over. A fascinating (and horrifying) study even found that women perform worse in maths tests when they'd recently tried on swimsuits[12]. Women who'd tried jerseys on instead performed significantly better on a maths test than those who'd been instructed to strip down to their togs. The theory posited by the researchers was that women unconsciously self-objectify themselves – a phenomenon that negatively affects intellectual performance. Which makes sense. No matter how feminist we are, we're not immune to stereotypes that pit beauty and brains against each other. Being bootylicious *and* good at algebra hasn't exactly been held up as a common societal trope.

Another female mental fallacy that deserves urgent attention is the idea that we're not enough. When we believe that we're inadequate, we are basically gaslighting ourselves, buying into a self-defeating internal monologue whilst forgetting that our masochistic thoughts didn't simply drop from the sky into our consciousness. They were largely implanted there against our will, spread by means of shitty societal messages. I'm not sure whether there are enough words in the English language to account for all of the things that women are 'not enough' of. We're not thin enough. We're not smart enough. We're not kind enough. We're not generous enough. We're not fit enough. We're not tolerant enough. You name it, and you'll find an article or advertisement that tells women that we're not meeting the arbitrary standard we should.

A fun new take on this age-old torture tactic is to implicitly make women responsible for not feeling [insert virtue here] enough. A recent illustration of this was provided by Kellogg's 2016 #OwnIt campaign. Kellogg's, the company that had been marketing Special K cereal to women for decades as a product to help them lose weight (implication: you're not thin enough), decided to get in on the 'femvertising' trend, and created a hashtag campaign encouraging women to 'just own' their bodies. Had I been eating cereal when I came across the campaign on social media I would've choked. Here was a company that had profited handsomely from telling women that they should buy its cereal in order to lose weight telling those same women to own those same bodies that it had been implying were in need of improvement for decades. As if it were a simple case of deciding to just get over years of self-scrutiny and insecurity implicitly promoted by companies selling diet foods. If anyone in this situation needed to 'just own' something, it certainly wasn't the female consumers who had been fat-shamed for years.

The real trick lies, however, in the combination of being made to believe that we're not [whatever] enough and being expected to be perfect. It's both a set-up and a mind-fuck. From an early age, we become aware that we will be held to a different standard than boys and men. Little girls are expected to be pretty, tidy, and caring; to play in ways that are 'nice' and gentle. Little boys, by contrast, are allowed to get dirty and play rough. No one ever says, 'girls will be girls' unless they're referring to so-called 'bitchy' behaviour. Perfectionism affects people of all genders, but studies have shown that it can affect women disproportionately[13]. It certainly affected me. I spent the entirety of my childhood consumed by perfectionism. I was the kind of child that sought approval and praise, and the best way to have those particular needs met was to be good at things. That was fine when I excelled, which I did, often; but my track record of successes made failure that much harder. I still remember being the only kid in my class at primary school who didn't go up a spelling level during one very routine and unimportant test. I would've been nine. At high school, receiving a merit grade instead of an excellence made me feel ashamed. Later, when I was at King's, and studying under the Cambridge International Examinations system, we would receive 'orders' every term, in which we were graded A–E for both effort and achievement. I received one solitary B grade in my whole two years at the school, for effort in my favourite class. I was so devastated that I cried. My housemaster and my form class teacher both tried to intervene on my behalf to get the grade changed, but the bestower of the B grade refused to budge. In a later report he would write that he thought the cracks were beginning to show. He observed that I was starting to buckle under the pressure of trying to be perfect at everything. Perhaps that B grade was his way of delivering tough love. If so, it wasn't a message I was ready to hear.

Throughout my childhood, I believed that my self-worth lay in the things I achieved. I can remember feeling down when I was a teenager and writing a list of all of the things I'd achieved that year. Funnily enough, that list never made me feel happy, it just steadied me enough to continue my weary trudge. While I was likely an extreme case, my experiences, both as a teenager and later as an advocate for young women, have shown me that perfectionism seems to be particularly rampant among teen girls at private schools. Well-intentioned parents and teachers are forgetting to let kids be kids, while teen girls in particular are setting punishingly high standards for themselves. Too often, the result is stress and misery, with teens caught between a desperate fear of failure and expectations that they will excel.

And it doesn't just go away with age. Even now I still battle with perfectionism. To borrow from addiction vocabulary – because I believe that perfectionism can easily become an addiction – I'm a recovering perfectionist. In 2017, when my in-ear monitors cut out and I lost my place during an anthem for the Māori All Blacks in front of my home crowd in Rotorua, I was gutted, disappointed in myself and wracked with a surge of guilt and self-loathing that continued for months. Though I logically knew that the error wasn't something I could have prevented, I beat myself up regardless, holding myself to some kind of superhuman standard. It took time and soul-searching to remember that I was human, and that I wasn't defined by either my successes or my mistakes, but by the sum of my humanity. By that measure, I was doing just fine. Yet perfectionism is one of those problems that lingers quietly long after you think you've fixed it. Particularly in New Zealand, where tall poppy syndrome ensures that high fliers will be punished resoundingly at any given opportunity.

The ludicrous thing about the typically female combination of perfectionism and not being enough is that it traps people into a paradigm where they can't win. The paradox required of women – that they be perfect, but also never perfect enough, so that they continue to seek unattainable perfection – is so mind-boggling that it's easy to see why it has had such a malevolent impact upon our collective sanity. In the face of such a discombobulating reality, coping mechanisms such as self-harm become more understandable. Indeed, you could argue that an insane reaction to an insane situation is in some senses an entirely sane response. When you've never had any experience with self-harm, it can seem like an alarming and extreme sign of calamity, but for me, it seemed perfectly reasonable. When I harmed myself, I could turn my mental pain into physical pain, which was easier to deal with. Physiologically, every time I cut myself I also received a dose of endorphins – one of the body's natural painkilling hormones – which paradoxically made me feel somewhat better. Harming myself in secret also enabled me to maintain the illusion of perfection, allowing me to hide how much I was struggling.

People are often terrified when they discover that a loved one is harming themselves, often not realising that the self-harming can be a maladaptive coping mechanism and/or a cry for help. Ironically, self-harming never put me in any danger, as the objective was always to purge myself of overwhelming emotion and anxiety so that I could keep going. I became very good at basic first aid, and made sure that I never harmed myself in a place where it could be seen. Don't get me wrong, self-harming is a terrible way to deal with problems, but truthfully, the pain in my head was infinitely more dangerous than my physical wounds.

Self-harming was a habit that I kicked when I was 21. By the time I eventually sought treatment, self-harm had developed into a compulsion that had become second nature over nearly ten years. Cognitive behavioural therapy, mindfulness and a shift to relying on other coping mechanisms such as exercise and journal-writing helped me to finally vanquish it, although it took a year or two to fully extinguish. I eventually found that if I could simply sit with my thoughts and emotions and greet them as friends rather than enemies, I could regard them as interesting clues to what was going on in my mind. When I viewed them as clues, I achieved a level of detachment from them – I was the island around which my thoughts and emotions were swirling, rather than feeling like I *was* my thoughts and emotions – and I was able to talk myself out of harming myself. I also learnt that what appears utterly insurmountable, unbearable and excruciating in the darkness of the night will almost always improve in the morning. I will still on very rare occasion feel the urge to harm myself, when I am completely emotionally overwhelmed, but I've thankfully learnt other ways of coping. With the benefit of having beaten the impulse to hurt myself, I can look back and see just how destructive it was, though it kept me going at the time. In some ways, it was a kind of internalised misogyny that I perpetrated against myself. When I inevitably failed to live up to the unrealistic standards that women are held to, I turned my anger inward, instead of railing against a system that was designed to disempower women. Now I do everything in my power to direct my anger to its rightful target, and to fight against the all too common impulse to use myself as a punching bag.

As a woman, the battle for possession of my own mind is one I'm likely to fight for my entire life. It is waged on the streets, when I look through the windows of shops to see stick-thin mannequins. It's fought online, when men like Cameron Slater insult my intelligence[14] and keyboard warriors insinuate that I'm a 'dumb mowrie'. It continues when I consider whether to go on a crash diet in springtime and when I berate myself for making a mistake. The enemy may have an outpost in my head, but I've spent my twenties strengthening my defences. Now when that ugly voice in my head tells me that I'm fat, stupid or a failure, I retort that I'm human, I do my best, and that's enough. As women, taking control of our inner monologues and choosing to be kind to ourselves is perhaps the most important political act we can commit to. We need to remember that billion dollar industries selling diet products, cosmetic surgery, beauty products and procedures have been largely built on women's insecurities. If the women of the world woke up tomorrow and suddenly believed that we are enough just as we are, some of the most profitable international corporations would go bankrupt. I know it's not that easy, that it takes hard work and healing to undo years of narratives telling us that we're not enough, and that it's not fair to ask people to take a personal stand against a systemic problem, but at this stage what choice do we have but to reject the lies that have been implanted in our minds? It's awfully difficult to fight the many systems of oppression while we have their propaganda playing inside our heads.

Which is not to say that mental illness can be cured by simply willing yourself not to listen to a negative internal narrative. If you are currently living with a mental illness, I just want to take a moment to send love, strength and peace your way. I wouldn't presume to know what you're going through, as everyone's experience is different, but I do know that the world would be a much darker place without you in it. If you haven't already, please reach out to someone who can help you. I would wholeheartedly recommend speaking to a psychologist, but the important thing is that you just tell someone you trust how you're feeling. I know it may not seem like it at this point in time, but you absolutely can get through this. I believe in you. You deserve to feel better.

You are enough. I am enough. We are all enough.

CHAPTER TWELVE

That F word

I wasn't always a feminist. I did not emerge from the womb crying, 'Screw the patriarchy!' In fact, I vividly remember, at age 11, proclaiming to my speech and drama class, 'Oh, I'm not a *feminist*,' as if being a feminist were akin to being an enormous pus-filled pimple. 'You don't believe that men and women are equal?' my teacher countered, leaving me momentarily dumb-founded. In that rare moment of speechlessness, something finally clicked.

The equality angle was news to me. The meaning I'd ascribed to the term 'feminism' was somewhat different. Feminists, so I'd been told, were ugly, man-hating, stuck-up bitches that no one wanted to be friends with and no boys ever wanted to pash. At that point, I was both eager to be liked and quite keen on pashing boys, so the label didn't exactly seem like something I wanted to embrace.

But this equality thing … Of course I believed that men and women were equal. My parents were equals at work and at home – something I wouldn't realise was uncommon until adulthood. I'd been told that girls could do anything since I first marched out the door to primary school. In fact, I'd beaten plenty of boys over the years in various tests and competitions, and the maturity of 11-year-old boys (or rather, the lack thereof) made me wonder whether this whole idea of being equal with boys sold girls a bit short.

Admittedly, the fact that so many grown men struggle to grasp the meaning of a word that I figured out as a tween has done little to dispel my concerns in that area, but I digress.

In that moment in the drama studio, a ray of light may as well have shone through the window as the goddess reached out to claim me. I had been called to service, and I accepted my summons with vigour. Despite the fact that when I was at school, feminism was deeply unpopular.

When I was a teenager, declaring yourself a feminist was something that would conjure sniggers from the boys while the girls hastily avoided your gaze. Which is hardly surprising. To be a feminist was to stand out, which to this day is about the worst thing a teenager can do. It doesn't get much easier with age. Feminism is still a scary word for a lot of people. Calling yourself a feminist means admitting that you are dissatisfied with 'the way things are', and as I learnt during my time at King's College, people can be very resistant to the idea that 'the way things are' isn't the way things should be.

Feminism, as a movement unapologetically framed through a female lens, has never been particularly palatable to the mainstream. It is one of the most misunderstood ideas of modern times, mischaracterised early on in the piece by those to whose egos and positions of economic comfort it posed an existential threat, and still dependably misconstrued today. I've always been amused by the resistance to feminism by men due to its origin as a female-created and led movement. It becomes increasingly ridiculous when you consider that most movements, from the socialist revolution to the civil rights movement, have been male dominated for generations and have simply expected women to fall into line, fight for the cause and make the cups of tea at the meetings. When you flip the paradigm and suggest putting women in positions of leadership, it doesn't take long for the self-proclaimed 'good guys' to start feeling threatened.

Feminism, by its very nature, challenges a status quo that has put boys and men at the centre of the universe for pretty much ever. When you're used to occupying a position where everything revolves around you, whether you're conscious of it or not, I can imagine that it would be fairly difficult to give it up. Feminism sticks its beak into the little things that society simply accepts as 'normal', and asks prickly questions. For example: Why does the term 'first XV' always refer to boys' rugby teams, with no need for gender identification, while the girls' team is referred to as 'the girls' first XV'? Why do ads for household products almost always feature women doing the cleaning, or apparently useless men failing to do what should be a 'women's job'? Why are female honorifics so bloody nosy? Why should women have to identify whether they're married (Mrs), young (Miss) or it's-none-of-your-business (Ms) when men can just be men (Mr)? Feminism draws attention to the fact that women have never been the default human – men have.

The world we live in has been largely created by men in their image (while women stayed home, cooked, cleaned and raised families, freeing men from domestic responsibilities). Women may have been the engines that kept the whole world running, but men were the ones steering the ship. The *Titanic* springs to mind, but with women shovelling the coal into the furnaces and men giving the orders to go faster no matter what. Perhaps in that haphazard analogy feminism is the iceberg.

We've certainly crashed into something. I suspect it was the realisation that the 'girl power' we'd been inhaling since birth had done little to change the fact that dudes are still in control of almost everything in the entire universe. Feminism is undoubtedly in the midst of a renaissance, and while to those unfamiliar with feminist history it may seem to have exploded out of nowhere, it's been a while coming. I would argue that feminism is now in its Fourth Wave, following a pattern that has broadly held since feminism's inception, by which periods of furious organisation and activity have been followed by years of marginalisation as feminism has fallen out of the mainstream. The way in which feminism has burst back into the public conversation seems to suggest that a new feminist cycle has begun, and this one is quite different to those that have come before.

While the first 'waves' of feminism focussed largely on definable goals like suffrage (First Wave), access to abortion, freedom from violence and discrimination, and the right to work outside of the home for equal pay (Second Wave), diversity and the right of women to make individual choices (Third Wave) the current mood of feminism is less distinctly organised – or it was until 2017, when the Women's March and the #MeToo movement provided rallying points around which new structures began to form. The fight against sexual harassment and sexual violence has quickly become a key Fourth Wave battle, as has the push for gender equality in positions of power. Many of the feminists I know feel both invigorated by the potential of a feminist future, and frustrated that progress has been so slow. If I had to mark out another distinguishing feature of this wave I'd say that a sense of disbelief that we're still fighting battles we hoped had been long won is a common thread among many of us. Our elder sisters in earlier waves raised and fought for many of the issues we're still campaigning on today decades ago. As the famous protest sign says, 'We can't believe we still have to protest this shit'. It may well be that we've now reached a level of frustration that will ensure that real change is in the offing. I live in hope.

This new wave has been forming for a while. When I was at high school (between 2003 and 2007), I think we were likely between waves of feminism. While feminist women of my generation may have grown up looking up to the Riot Grrrls and the punks of the Third Wave, we belong to a distinct wave of our own. The Third Wave feminists – our immediately elder siblings – were raised by Second Wave feminists to become the coven responsible for the tide of girl power I grew up with, raising a collective middle finger to restrictive stereotypes, white feminism, and arbitrary binaries while championing intersectionality. While I never made zines or listened to Bikini Kill or Hole (I was much more interested in Britney Spears and Christina Aguilera), I certainly benefitted from the wave of feminism that empowered women to do whatever they goddamn wanted to do and be whoever they chose to be. As such I am much in their debt. The world the Third Wave grew up in, however, was very different to the world in which we took our first steps.

Third wave feminism had been co-opted and commoditised and girl power had hit the mainstream. It was subsequently packaged and sold to us from early childhood. From Spice Girls merchandise, to Dove's 'real beauty'-inspired products, to Kellogg's' #OwnIt campaign, and H&M's 'She's a Lady' advertisements, female empowerment has since become so prosaic that large multinationals are now lining up to profit from it. Which is an exponential improvement to the time-honoured tradition of making women feel that they're not thin enough pretty enough, young enough, sexy enough, fashionable enough, or, well, anything enough – without [insert unnecessary product here], but it is still, at its heart, a phenomenon driven by profit in markets where men continue to hold the lion's share of the power and resources. In short, ironically, girl power has largely lined the pockets of men. While that remains the case, the commercial adoption of girl power may be projecting an empowering image but its feminist credentials are seriously questionable.

When the rebellious and revolutionary becomes mundane, you can almost always be sure that there has been some watering down somewhere along the line – baby pink 'lady tool boxes' stand out as an apt illustration. Third Wave feminists may have told the system to go and fuck itself, but the system took their message, rebranded it, and published it on a billboard. For example, during my teens and early twenties, discussions about pay equality were drowned out by arguments about whether it was feminist or not to get a Brazilian wax. If there's anyone still in doubt, let me clear that up. You will be as much a feminist with a full bush as you will be plucked and pube-less. But do take a moment to question why women are presented with the option to torture themselves as if it's some kind of gift. 'Pay us fifty dollars and we'll rip the hair from the most sensitive part of your body! But wait, there's more! Sign up for ten tearing-the-top-layer-of-skin-off-your-vulva sessions and we'll give you a discount!'

What lucky girls we are.

Beneath the commercialisation of feminism, there's an intrinsic tie with neoliberalism. If we're all busy defending our rights as consumers, buying empowerment in the form of the newest 'fierce' lipstick or athleisure wear, then who is going to raze the patriarchy to the ground? I mean, sure, the revolutionaries can take their axes to the structures that oppress us in the latest Ivy Park collection if they want, but the decision to buy clothes from Beyoncé, the renowned queen of the universe who is nonetheless profiting mightily from the neoliberal status quo in partnering with Topshop, a company that regularly receives low grades from watchdogs monitoring workers' rights[1], is not a feminist statement. It's a decision feminists are perfectly entitled to make, but, to be frank, it's pretty fucking irrelevant in the big scheme of things. Apart from the bit about the terrible conditions that people making clothes for companies like Topshop are forced to work in. That part is extremely relevant.

* * *

The challenge of the new wave of feminism – the Fourth Wave – is to build on the work of our elder sisters while resisting the temptation to give in to a commercialised version of individualism that is simply masquerading as feminism. The focus on individual choice has led feminism through the looking glass into a kind of alternative reality that was likely cooked up in a marketing department somewhere. While it benefits brands and companies for feminism to represent individual choices (especially the choice to buy their products) it does little to liberate women from their status as the second sex. It's unsurprising that the two are often conflated, however, as for most of history women have had little or no right to make their own individual choices. That we do now is a success story of feminism in its quest to ensure women have equal human rights, but if the crux of the feminist movement is for women to be able to make their own individual choices while women as a group remain disadvantaged and discriminated against, then we have set the bar far too low.

Millennials can't claim to be naïve about the power of branding and commercialism. We've been bombarded with media and advertising since childhood – in our homes, on the streets and in our pockets. Brands have been trying to get us to buy stuff almost since we emerged from the womb. Frankly, we should be too smart, too jaded, and too wise to be suckered into believing that feminism is simply a fancy codename for personal choice, especially when our choices have been manipulated and influenced by media – overtly and subliminally – for our entire lives. We have more choice than we know what to do with, yet women are still disadvantaged. We can buy what we want, say what we want, wear what we want … but we still have to fight to be paid what we deserve. The Emperor is not only naked; he's twerking before our very eyes.

Discussion about feminist 'choices' has, however, often dominated the conversation. In the late 2000s and early 2010s particularly, think pieces about whether you could wear stilettos and be a feminist and the like often dominated feminist discourse – and I'm guilty of having written a few myself – while core feminist concerns were often ignored by the mainstream. Important issues like access to abortion, freedom from sexual violence and the right to equal pay were buried in the public discourse while we were encouraged to instead muse upon whether or not we could wear makeup without losing our feminist licences. Individual choice became the new front woman of feminism, and equality was pushed into the shadows. 'Feminism is all about choices!' became a common defence whenever a woman was questioned about a decision she'd made, which obscured the nuance that the idea that women should have the equal human right to make choices is only one of the many parts of feminism, and that questioning women's personal choices, which happens a great deal more often to women than it does to men, is in itself sexist.

Have you ever, for example, heard a man be asked why he chose to keep his name upon marriage? To my mind, there's no better illustration of the battle between choice and equality than the tradition of a woman taking her husband's name. While it is commonly held that it is a woman's right to choose to take her husband's name, the word 'equality' is seldom uttered by those supporting husband-wife identity sharing. No one can argue against an individual's right to choose, but if you believe that feminism is fundamentally about the equality of the genders, you can't tell me that deciding to take your husband's surname is a feminist decision – unless you can point me to the 50 per cent of the world's heterosexual grooms-to-be ditching their surnames in favour of their betrotheds'. For the record, I support a woman's right to choose to take her husband's name because, as a supporter of human rights, I support the notion that people should be able to make their own decisions – and also because it is none of my bloody business. But I also believe that the decision has absolutely nothing to do with feminism and would never personally relinquish any part of my identity to take on that of a spouse. As unpopular as it may be to contest any aspect of the 'choice' argument, feminism is much more than a justification for making individual choices, whether it be the choice to get a Brazilian or to give up a part of your identity. We should not need to evoke feminism to defend our decisions.

Where this appears to fall down is in the argument about abortion. When it comes to the termination of pregnancy, feminism is proudly 'pro-choice'. Beneath the 'choice' moniker, however, is an argument that at its heart rails against the structural oppression of women. While the front-facing, more palatable message is that women should have the right to choose what to do with their bodies – which you'd think most reasonable people could agree with whether they were feminists or not – the more salient point is that the state should not have the power to penalise and oppress women by forcing them to endure a serious, nine-month-long, life-changing medical event and then have to decide what to do with a child that they never wanted in the first place. Or to force women to endure the tragedy of carrying a pregnancy that will result in the death or suffering of the foetus against her will. If the state decides that it is within its purview to legislate that pregnant women must be forced to give birth and have their own personal right to agency over their own body voided, surely there should be some kind of equivalent punishment for unwilling fathers. Nine months imprisonment, many hours or possibly days of severe, orifice-tearing pain with lasting after effects, an 18-year curfew and tens of thousands of dollars in yearly fines for the rest of the unwilling father's life, perhaps?

I can't see that one gaining any traction in Parliament, can you?

When you boil it down, having the freedom of choice (within reasonable restrictions) is, or should be, simply part of being a human being living in a democracy. Do men have to explain their choice to not have children? No. Do they have to defend their choice to drink alcohol when they go out at night? No. Do they have to justify their choice to go back to work after their children are born? No. They may be ridiculed for choosing to stay at home to look after their children – yet another injustice that feminism seeks to dismantle – but by and large, men's choices are simply seen as their own personal prerogative. Women's should be too. Men don't need 'meninism' to justify having the right to make their own choices. That women need to use feminism as justification for theirs proves just how far we have to go in the battle for women's rights.

When I think about feminism today, I'm acutely aware that while more people than ever before now walk underneath our banner, we still need to reclaim a feminism that has been forced to contort itself into a sellable, sanitised, knock-off imitation of the radical and confronting movement that actually got shit like winning the vote for half the population done. We need to remember that while the personal is political, the political is also personal. Feminism is not a get-out-of-jail-free card for a dubious decision. It is not a slogan on a T-shirt that you can take on and off at will. If we view feminism through the lens of individualism, or worse 'equal rights for consumers' rather than 'equal rights for human beings who identify as women', then we need to think about who the new version of feminism is really benefitting.

Feminism fought for women to have the right to have a voice by demanding the radical alteration of a structure that had been hostile to women for millennia. Our foremothers didn't buy empowerment. They demanded it.

We must too.

The days of politely asking for permission to request a small improvement to our position in the world are over. It's time to reclaim the 'angry feminist' slur and embrace it. Hell hath no fury like a woman undervalued, underrepresented, underestimated, patronised, abused, and disrespected by a system that was built on the premise that she would always put others' interests above her own. As women standing up for the equality of the genders, we're going to be called all kinds of things anyway. Why not live up to them?

CHAPTER THIRTEEN

Hashtag feminism

When you are a woman with an internet connection, it is very difficult to pretend that sexism doesn't exist. The internet presents us with millions of examples of sexist and/or misogynistic comments, images, advertisements, videos, threads, forums, etc. on a daily basis. When you see the same misogynistic shit day in day out all it takes is a moment of realisation and it starts to stand out a mile away. Once you've seen it, it cannot be unseen.

The hyper-connectivity of the modern world has allowed such moments of awakening to spread like wildfire. Hashtags like #EverydaySexism, and, most notably, #MeToo have reached millions of people, changing the way that we see the world and creating momentum towards a very different future. So-called 'hashtag activism' gets a bad rap, but it's hard to deny the powerful role that social media plays in global awareness raising.

While popular hashtags are propelled into the mainstream when they strike a chord and the mass media begins to cover them, social media's power begins at a much more grassroots level. The modern digital world allows millions of women worldwide to communicate with each other, making it easier to raise consciousness of oppressive structures and sexist bullshit. The Fourth Wave of feminism, though it is mocked for its hashtags and online activism, has spearheaded the emergence of a global network of feminists who are using social media masterfully to forge connections and drive change.

Though it may sound counter-intuitive when you think in terms of Instagram filters and Snapchat animations, in a way the digital age has provided a more truthful reflection of the world we live in. It has revealed a level of misogyny that has previously been largely hidden. Once you've spent time in the comments section under an opinion piece written by a woman on almost any major website, for example, you develop a pretty good understanding of the need for feminist action. Which may account for the number of young women – so called digital natives – who are currently flocking to the movement. The Fourth Wave has a comprehensive understanding of the fact that society still holds some pretty fucked-up attitudes about women.

Online, if there's a conversation to be had about women, particularly if that conversation involves #feminism, there's a misogynist just waiting to inject themselves into the discussion. They remind me somewhat of blast-ended skrewts from the *Harry Potter* books. They start off as slimy, malformed crabs, blindly bumping into each other and giving off a stench of rotting fish, and end up as explosive, armoured arachnids, vulnerable only to jabs to their soft, fleshy undersides[1]. I'm not sure what the point of their existence is, or why they take it upon themselves to ram their negativity down the throats of anyone who is unfortunate enough to be in the vicinity of them, but the digital skrewts seem to adapt (in a kind of reverse evolution) in stages. First comes the whining about chivalry and debates about whether a man opening a door for a woman is sexist, quickly followed by arguments about who should pay for dinner on a hypothetical (heterosexual, of course) date. Eventually, when you've had enough of these arguments to last several lifetimes, you realise that common sense (opening a door for someone, regardless of gender, is just courteous, and splitting the bill or having the most economically stable person pay for dinner won't bring about the extinction of the species) is generally the first thing to go flying out the window when the status quo is threatened. It swan dives from the windowsill into oncoming traffic before you can say, 'male fragility'.

During the next stage (when the skrewts have started to form shells and it becomes apparent that there's no way to tell their backsides from heads), you'll meet men who insist that they put the women in their lives 'on a pedestal', and women who disavow feminism in favour of being 'treated like a princess'. These types of people are clearly made for each other. I sometimes think that I should start a match-making service for idealistic, traditionalist, anti-feminist romantics, I have that many of them in my social media notifications. The problem with being put on a pedestal or treated like a princess is that it requires women to play a very specific role, and God help those princesses if they one day decide to hang up their glass slippers and start having opinions of their own. It also does nothing to ensure that women in low-paid industries receive a fair wage, to get more women on boards, or to combat New Zealand's horrific domestic violence statistics – in fact, it implies that while you're perched up there being worshipped, there's no need to worry your pretty head about those things, sweetheart, because you've got a big strong man to look after you. It also reinforces the idea that there are 'good' women – the princesses who are put on pedestals by the men in their lives – and 'other' women who those men have no relation to, who are thus free to be judged against some kind of arbitrary standard and penalised if they don't meet it. In my entirely unscientific, anecdotal, and yet extensive experience, I've found a strong correlation between men who loudly announce that they treat 'their' women like queens and men who go around the internet calling women 'bitches' and 'whores' at every opportunity. Namely, they're often one and the same.

If you're a feminist who dares to express her sexuality in some visual way, you'll meet lots of these princess-worshipping men ('If you want to be treated like a princess then don't dress like a slut!'), and a significant number of what I've come to term 'the double standard police'. These crusaders for the public good will jump on any picture of you wearing anything vaguely revealing for the express purpose of pointing out the magnitude of your hypocrisy for having the gall to display agency over your body publicly when you've argued against a hypersexualised culture in which brands exploit female sexuality to make squillions of dollars. Never mind body positivity, swimming, or self-determination. If you listen closely as you post a bikini photo, you can almost hear them orgasm.

None of this compares, however, to the final stage (powerful armoured shells, lethal fire power, and still no way to tell arse from face), in which you'll learn an absolute truth of contemporary feministing: if you speak up against Islamophobia you will be deemed a sham and a fraud, because how could you possibly be a feminist if you support the idea that it's not right to discriminate against all of the 1.6 billion people who belong to a religion that has been interpreted by a comparatively small number of believers in extreme ways that have resulted in the oppression or harm of women? Easily. That's how. The funny thing about othering and persecution is that a number of women instinctively understand how shitty it is. Maybe after centuries of being treated like chattels, burned as witches, raped by soldiers, confined to asylums for divorcing husbands or masturbating, sexually assaulted on dates, cat-called in the street or sexually harassed at work – all of which, I might add, have occurred (and some still occur) in the West – it's in our DNA. Whether or not I believe that women should be able to play sport in Saudi Arabia (and the answer to that should be obvious), I find it suspicious that a certain group of men suddenly become 'feminists' when supporting these women's rights. Especially when their 'feministing' is done from a distance in a way that could never result in any meaningful change for the women they purport to care about, and when it handily gives them an excuse to say disgusting things about people who happen to worship Allah. The kind of 'feminism' that those particular people hide behind is a ruse; an illusory cover that they use to attempt to justify their bigotry. If they were suddenly required to take action over and above impotently pontificating on the internet, their 'feminism' would quickly be shown for what it was. If they were called upon to speak out in support of the rights of women in their own communities, their 'feminism' would likely evaporate faster than a summer puddle in the middle of a heat wave.

Feminism and Islamophobia are incompatible ideas. Abuse – such as female genital mutilation – will always be abuse, and feminists will always be opposed to violence against women, but as a Western feminist, it is not, nor will it ever be, my place to offer an opinion on the burqa or the hijab. My place is to support Muslim women in their own choices, whether they tally with my own worldview or not. Furthermore, as a Māori woman, the idea that Muslim women are in need of some kind of salvation, brought by white Western saviours (or rather, white, Islamophobic, anti-feminist keyboard warriors) sends a chill down my spine. The last thing the Muslim world needs is an army of modern missionaries spreading the Good Word of Western Cultural Colonisation.

As you can see, there is basically no safe subject for a feminist to talk about online. The proliferation of social media has undoubtedly brought a rise in the incidence of day-to-day sexism but it has also given women the technology to speak up on a scale that we've never been able to access before. Social media has also allowed women to thwart the agenda of the media and forced feminist issues into the public conversation. Social media and blogging have launched the careers of a number of women now writing in the mainstream media (indeed, without social and digital media, I wouldn't have become a columnist) and have ensured that story angles that would previously have been buried in a male-dominated media landscape have been broadcast far and wide.

Social and digital media have given women power. Can you imagine a global women's march taking place simultaneously in 673 places around the world and involving approximately 5 million participants before the advent of social media? While there have been other global marches that have involved millions of people, they have generally been to protest specific events, such as the American invasion of Iraq. That a group of feminist activists were able to take over the global news media and the main streets of cities all around the world to protest about women's issues provides an astounding example of the way that social media is a force to be reckoned with and proves its immense value to feminism.

Social media has given women a microphone, a soapbox and a public square. It has provided a digital lounge in which to congregate, drink wine together, commiserate and organise. It has introduced likeminded women to each other and given them an easy way to keep in touch. It has its challenges and its dark corners, but it is infinitely more valuable to feminism than it is damaging.

In the digital age, women's voices have rung out despite the many attempts to silence them. We won't be shutting up any time soon.

CHAPTER FOURTEEN

The non-feminist

I was once asked by Mike Hosking whether I was worried about being seen as an 'angry feminist'. I was being interviewed on his NewsTalk ZB show and conversation had turned to my then new site, Villainesse. I found the question hilarious, given that he rants and raves in the New Zealand media on a daily basis. There are some things worth getting angry about, I responded. In truth, being labelled an 'angry feminist' is the least of my worries in a world where women are disadvantaged every day, but the question potently illustrates the negative connotations that feminism has had foisted upon it.

No one ever said being a feminist was easy. Or, if they did, they likely had no personal experience of being a feminist. It is sad that being an advocate for gender equality – AKA a feminist – should be such a controversial thing to be, but while the status quo is one of inequality that benefits one gender at the expense of others, feminism will continue to represent a dangerous threat to those who fear they have much to lose in a gender-equal future. Feminism consciously rejects the way things are, not only in its aims but also in its methods. People who call themselves feminists signal to whoever is listening that they want change. Female feminists who speak up about feminist issues violate social codes that suggest that women should be quiet, compliant and agreeable. Male feminists who advocate for women in male-dominated spaces challenge men to be better. Feminism rocks a boat that has been tilting dangerously to one side for the last few thousand years, and people have become so used to seeing things from a slanted angle that they misinterpret an attempt to right the ship as an attempt to capsize the thing instead. Perhaps understandably, their protestations quickly become panicked and hysterical.

It is under the weight of all this that feminists labour. I'm not here to provide some rose-tinted view of why all women should be feminists. Don't get me wrong, women should be feminists, but there is no way that I can make that proposition sound like a lovely walk in the park, because I understand just how difficult it is to be one. My being a feminist has raised more eyebrows than I've had cups of tea, and I drink tea from the moment I wake till the moment I go to sleep. My being a feminist has earned me more derision than anything else I've ever done, and my nearly-naked #MyBodyMyTerms image has circulated around the globe and ended up on *The Daily Mail* website. So I get that it's hard. I also, however, understand that unless more people make demands for equality, the status quo will win, and women will remain at the bottom of the heap. Feminism is the vehicle that wants to drive women to their rightful place on an even playing field, smashing through the boundaries of gender, class, race, ability, sexuality, and all of the other walls that constrain us. People of all genders should be feminists, if they believe in justice, fairness and basic human decency.

With the exception of women who identify with womanism (which Alice Walker described best when she said, 'Womanist is to feminist as purple is to lavender;'[1] my understanding of the term womanism is that it denotes an intersectional women's rights movement led by women of colour that acknowledges other markers of identity – particularly race – as being central to oppression and liberation, alongside gender) and other movements founded by non-Western women, indigenous women or women of colour, the idea of being a woman and not being a feminist makes little logical sense to me. As Gloria Steinem famously said, 'Women have two choices: either she's a feminist or a masochist'. For every proud feminist, however, there is a passionate non-feminist just waiting for an opportunity to diagnose everything that is wrong with feminism. They come in all different shapes and sizes, so I've prepared a handy guide, should you happen to meet one in the wild:

The humanist

The humanist usually has an issue with the fact that the word 'feminist' has a feminine prefix. If feminism is a movement for equality, they argue, shouldn't it have a more inclusive name? The humanist, in this context, is not known for the depth of their research, and is usually oblivious to the fact that humanism was a movement of its own with a long history of standing for something else. Humanism is originally a rationalist movement that (and I am oversimplifying here) essentially refutes supernatural beliefs and advocates for personal liberty. It is not a gender-neutral version of feminism. Sorry.

The equalist

The equalist has similar issues with feminism being a female-sounding term, but, to their credit, has at least done a Google search of the term 'humanist' and realised that the word has already been taken. Beneath the equalists' 'we want everyone to be treated equally!' veneer is the unfortunate truth that a movement that sounds like it advocates for women's rights makes them uncomfortable. Equalists can sometimes be passive aggressive mansplainers, no matter what gender they identify with. They might, for example, be Bob at the staff meeting who rephrases what Aroha has just said and gets slapped on the back by John, Michael, Dave, Steve and Phil for coming up with such a great idea about how to support women in the workplace. Basically, they've taken the hard work and beliefs of a group of mainly women who have been working tirelessly in the pursuit of equality for generations, slapped a new name on it, mansplained it to anyone who will listen, then, when feminists rightly pointed out that there's already a name for this shiny new thing and that they in fact invented it, told them that they'd been doing it wrong. Sometimes they also call themselves 'egalitarians', and at all times they are ready to inject themselves into a conversation with a well-placed, 'Well, actually …'

The I'm-not-a-feminist-but

The I'm-not-a-feminist-but really is a feminist, but they're too scared to acknowledge their true identity. They've generally grown up surrounded by negative narratives about feminism, whether from their parents, their siblings, their peers or the media. If you sat down with them one evening in a quiet, safe place, and had a deep and meaningful with them about the sisterhood over a few bottles of wine, there's a good chance that they'd eventually confess that deep down they *are*, in fact, a feminist, but they don't want to deal with the backlash that comes with being a feminist. They believe in the equality of the genders, and they've likely even spoken up in support of women's rights. They usually don't realise that their constant refrain of, 'I'm not a feminist but I think that [insert shitty, unequal thing here] is discriminative and I don't like it,' actually makes it harder for feminism to fix said shitty, unequal things. The I'm-not-a-feminist-but is fundamentally a good person, but they need to decide what's more important: not having ill-informed people say a few nasty things about you whilst reinforcing the idea that feminism is inherently bad, or standing up for your beliefs.

The guy who is petrified of offending feminists

The guy who is petrified of offending feminists would quite like to call himself a feminist, he thinks, but he's probably had one too many run-ins with feminists on Twitter to know whether it's okay to do so or not. He may identify as a male ally, and has probably royally fucked up a few times in his quest to be a feminist, for which he has likely been called out on social media. He believes in equality and wants to do what he can to fight for the cause, but he can't find anyone to sign his feminist permission slip.

The man-lover

The man-lover is usually a woman who thinks that feminism equates to man-hating. 'I'm not a feminist because I love men,' is her battle cry, and she's willing to go to great lengths to prove her love for the guys. The man-lover usually takes great pride in her femininity, and she is often very traditional. She might believe that feminism threatens her position as a woman who is taken care of by men, especially if she is in a breadwinner-homemaker relationship. She also might be a young woman who cares deeply about what men think of her. Ironically, her refutation of feminism may occur because of a system that holds her in a position of little or no power; the exact kind of system that feminism is trying to change.

The faux feminist (female)

The female faux feminist is a woman who calls herself a feminist in order to co-opt, distort and invert everything feminism stands for to further an anti-feminist agenda. She says things like, 'If you're pro-choice, you should respect my choice to be pro-life.' She often bangs on about something she calls 'classical feminism', and angrily tells random men on the internet that the kinds of feminists she disdains (i.e. the kinds of feminists who she believes are radical baby-murdering communists) do not represent her.

The faux feminist (male)

The male faux feminist is the kind of guy who thinks that he deserves a very special good-boy lolly every time he does anything to advocate for women. He loves to speak for and over the top of women, and is a big fan of telling women how to be better feminists. He talks about his advocacy to anyone who will listen and expects applause and adulation. He pushes himself forward and occupies spaces that should be filled by women, then plays the victim when he's called out. He accuses any feminist who points out his problematic behaviour of being part of the reason why men are alienated by feminism.

The anti-feminist (female)

The female anti-feminist is, to put it kindly, shooting herself in the foot. She's the kind of non-feminist that I find the most challenging to deal with. Sometimes, when I'm particularly tired and/or grumpy, I find myself finishing anti-feminists' mind-bending explanations in my head. Like this: 'I'm anti-feminism because … I'm completely and utterly ignorant of the ways in which feminism has ensured that I am not a chattel of my husband, that I am legally able to own property, that I won't be sent to an asylum for disagreeing with a man, and that the law supports my right not to be raped in my marital bed. I've conveniently forgotten that women once didn't have the right to vote or to stand for Parliament, that my foremothers were paid exponentially less than the men they worked with – if they were allowed to work at all – that universities refused to admit women, that the police treated domestic assaults as marital problems to be resolved, and that feminism was what addressed these problems. I'm so ensconced in my own worldview that I have not taken the time to educate myself about the relatively recent acquisition of the many privileges that I enjoy as a direct result of feminism and I am so insecure about myself that I couldn't bear it if someone, particularly a man, thought of me as a woman who would stand up for my rights and speak out against injustice. My own life is comfortable, and I am incapable of looking beyond the boundaries of my own existence to see that other women are struggling, suffering and being denied basic rights. I take for granted the hard work of the generations of women who delivered to me many of the human rights I have today, and I spit in their faces. I'm anti-feminism because I'm ignorant, ungrateful, masochistic and self-absorbed.' And then I reprimand myself and go and make myself a snack, because if I'm that grumpy it usually means that I'm hangry.

The anti-feminist (male) AKA the meninist, men's rights activist, neo-masculinist, pick-up artist, man-baby

The male anti-feminist is a misogynist. He runs around the internet screaming 'FEMINAZI!' at any given opportunity in a vain attempt to distract himself from the yawning abyss of desperate insecurity that he knows lies deep inside him. He sees empowered women as an existential threat to his fragile masculinity, and may advocate for things like the legalisation of rape on private property. No, I'm not exaggerating. He sees almost every single feminist victory as a rallying point for men who, to his mind, should be the rightful leaders of the world, lording over the feeble damsels of their imaginations and the 'cucks' and 'betas' they see to be gender traitors. While most of the time he impotently squawks in the bowels of reddit and 4chan, occasionally venturing into the mainstream to yell at people for wanting safe spaces before retreating to his own safe space, sometimes he turns into a fully fledged homicidal sociopath, maiming and murdering innocent people in an attempt to get the attention and respect he thinks is his birth entitlement.

And so concludes an encyclopaedia of the kinds of people who seem to be magnetically drawn to my social media accounts.

The way I see it, there are broadly two groups who oppose feminism on different grounds (both of which then break off into many subgroups). There are those who oppose women's equality – many of whom are frankly beyond help – and there are those who oppose the word 'feminism'. And you know what? I get that. Feminism has got a bit of a branding problem, through no fault of its own. If there's one thing that a patriarchal, hierarchical system is very good at (other than screwing over vast swathes of people) it's smearing the good name of any of its opponents. Feminism, as one such opponent, has been dragged through the mud over the course of decades. Some opponents of the word simply suggest that we ditch it and come up with a new one. Arguably, it worked for the Nazis when they rebranded themselves the 'alt-right' – which should be no great source of comfort. To toss feminism out, however, like some out-of-fashion dress, would be to disrespect the women who have fought, sacrificed and died for it. It would also be to hand a symbolic victory to the patriarchy, relegating feminism's proudly women-centric 'fem' prefix to the trash-heap of history. The truth of gender equality is that women are the ones who have borne, and continue to bear, the brunt of the most crushing oppression, especially those who are not straight, not cisgender and not white. Achieving equality will require the advancement not only of women's rights but of their realities. As such, it is entirely appropriate that feminism should carry a name that acknowledges the long and painful struggle of women.

Which is not to say that feminism doesn't give a toss about men. Indeed, feminism's deconstruction of rigid gender ideals seeks to liberate men too. But the idea that we should have to get rid of the word 'feminism' just so that men can feel more comfortable is frankly maddening. We live in a world where terms like 'mankind', 'sportsmanship', 'workmanlike', 'right-hand man', 'forefathers', 'chairman', 'ombudsman' 'gentleman's agreement', 'man made', 'manpower', 'man hours' and the like have been the default for centuries, regardless of the gender of the person or people they've described. As such, I propose a trade. Men can keep one of the many, many male-centric terms used to describe people of any gender while getting rid of all the rest, and we'll keep feminism. There. And they say feminists are unreasonable.

Jokes aside, however, we need to stop arguing over the word. Conjecture around whether or not the name 'feminism' should be updated or replaced, and what then could replace it are all distractions that amount to little more than time-wasting while the actual inequalities and injustices that feminism is concerned with persist. To be honest, you could call yourself a 'human person equality-worshipping justice-ist' but unless you actually did something to support or assist the cause it would mean sweet fuck all. Indeed, if you're worried about the name, you've resoundingly missed the point.

So my message to anyone out there who believes in gender equality but feels squeamish about the word 'feminism' is to call yourself whatever you want, but don't waste time trying to explain why your name is better, why 'feminism' is fatally flawed, or why everyone else should adopt your word – just start doing the mahi. And if you find yourself beside someone like me doing the work in the trenches, don't be offended if we praise your feminism.

We mean it as a compliment.

CHAPTER FIFTEEN

Bitchiness is a patriarchal construct

When I was 11, I got into a catfight. It was exactly as you would imagine, if you pictured two feisty tweens clad in green tartan culottes and Roman sandals engaged in a kind of ludicrous competitive hissy fit. We stood on the steps in front of our classroom at lunchtime and slapped each other, arms flailing like two cats striking out at an imaginary clawing post, panting and squealing as our classmates watched in fascination, some dumbstruck, and some roaring with laughter. The cause of our quarrel? A boy. Obviously.

The idea of two women fighting over a man is so ubiquitous that it is almost a female rite of passage. I am ashamed to say that almost all of the worst fall-outs I've had with women have been over men; the last of which, thankfully, was many years ago. The historical origins of such conflicts likely lie in a society that forced women to depend on men for material survival, ensuring fierce competition between women to find the most suitable husbands. Clearly, old habits die hard. In an age when women are no longer viewed as chattels – for the most part – the catfight, however, remains a prominent feature of female relationships. Why? Largely because women are conditioned to view each other as competition. Jealousy, insecurity, and fear all play a role in the catfight, and are introduced early in life. Little girls see female characters pitted against each other in fairy tales, tweens see media that tricks women into thinking that they're inadequate in order to sell them products they don't need, and teens quickly become aware that having a boyfriend affords you a certain social status that is not available to single girls, while having an attractive and popular boyfriend is like winning the schoolyard lottery. By the time women reach adulthood, they've been living in a world that implicitly and explicitly encourages female competition for almost two decades. Which is no accident. The catfight has endured because of this simple reality: when women fight against each other, the victors will always be men.

Bitchiness is a patriarchal construct. In almost every imaginable situation, its main benefactors are male. When women are busy competing against each other, their potential for collaboration, compromise, mutual support and collective bargaining is undermined. In the workplace, at the ballot box, and in our personal lives, competition with other women sets us against each other, when we'd most often be in a stronger position working alongside each other. Bitchiness saps the power of the sisterhood.

And yet, it enjoys a special kind of cred on social media and in pop culture. The film *Mean Girls* provides an illustration of the comedic power snark and malice can have. Though the movie was released in 2004, I still wouldn't go more than a couple of months without coming across a reference to it online ('You go, Glen Coco!', 'On Wednesdays, we wear pink', 'I'm a cool mom').

Mean Girls presents as its main characters a group of girls almost every kid in the Western World knows – the popular girls. As the beautiful arbiters of who is cool and who isn't, they wield enormous power in a school's social ecosystem. The hold they have on their peers is an odd mixture of idolatry and terror; they have the ability to raise your position in the school pecking order, but they also can also crush you into tiny pieces. It's a strange paradox that girls who demonstrate out and out cruelty to their peers somehow end up being idolised and admired. The physical beauty of the popular girls often disguises the ugliness of their actions, and they remain free to stalk the corridors with abandon, bestowing favour and breaking spirits as they see fit. We've all known girls like that. Though *Mean Girls* is satirical, some of the exaggerated actions of the 'plastics' aren't all that far from real life. Indeed, a group of popular girls in my year at school un-ironically adopted the 'plastics' moniker for themselves soon after the release of *Mean Girls*, treating the label almost as a badge of honour. Even teachers went along with it, though I now wonder whether there was a deeper layer of meaning in that which we didn't quite clock at the time.

Mean Girls is a study in bitchiness. And yet, the film forces us to rethink our complicity in a society that encourages and even expects nastiness between women. You might notice that there was no sequel called *Mean Boys*, although teen boys can be just as horrible as their female counterparts. Nevertheless, the popularity of the film certainly supports the idea that female nastiness holds great comic potential.

Another cultural icon that uses bitchiness and catfights to create dark and cruel comedy is Netflix's *Orange is the New Black*. While obviously no one expects women in prison to be holding hands and singing songs (which, ironically, the women of Litchfield sometimes do), the brutal laughs the show delivers sometimes make me feel like I'm watching a live action game of Cards Against Humanity. I sniggered at pampered and whiny Piper throughout most of season one. I cheered, roaring with laughter, when cancer-stricken Miss Rosa ran over sociopathic Vee, bringing about her certain death, at the end of season two. I've smiled at any number of delicious take-downs delivered by Taystee and her crew. I even laughed at the antics of a pair of 'meth-heads' brandishing a gun in season five. The inmates at Litchfield live in a punishing patriarchy, completely at the mercy of a patriarchal system and ordered around on a daily basis by mostly male guards. While the conflict between warring individuals and factions is hardly the only plot device the show uses – the deep, loving, imperfect and desperate relationships between inmates form the true heart of the show – there's no denying that the catfight trope is an important part of the comedy. As important as *Orange is the New Black* has become in telling the stories of marginalised groups in uncompromising ways, and as much as I love the show, I do sometimes wonder whether the fact that we laugh at the inmates' attempts to 'shade' and even kill each other says something unsettling about us.

Women being nasty to each other is hardly an uncommon storytelling device. *Mean Girls* and *Orange Is the New Black* use it satirically, drawing attention to its prevalence in pop culture. Other stories, like the horrific *Bride Wars,* simply play into the trope with little (if any) self-awareness. And don't even get me started on reality TV. The cumulative impact is that it remains a common stereotype under which female characters continue to be pitted against each other, making it easy to dismiss them as 'catty' and 'bitchy'. We may laugh at catfights on the screen, but they reinforce ideas about women that have a very real influence on women's lives.

Behind the screen, in the semi-real realm of Hollywood, prominent celebrity catfights emphasise the competitive paradigm women are forced to exist in. Take the apparent Jennifer Aniston/Angelina Jolie catfight over Brad Pitt. People divided into 'Team Jen' and 'Team Angelina', but Pitt may as well have been a trophy in a jelly-wrestling match. While Jolie was smeared as a 'home wrecker' and Aniston was created into a victim, Pitt's role in the supposed love triangle was minimised. He was simply the man the two women revolved around. He may have been the catalyst for the conflict, but the women were the ones who got burnt.

In music, one of the most famous feuds in recent times was that between Mariah Carey and Jennifer Lopez. Carey was asked about her fellow songstress and famously replied, 'I don't know her'. The line, which Carey later explained was more in reference to the fact that the two had never met, became one of the greatest put-downs of the early 2000s, and later became a popular meme. I wouldn't be surprised if there was tension between the two singers, but not for the reasons people might expect. In music, certainly during the time when Carey and Lopez were the biggest pop stars on the planet, there is only a certain amount of room allotted for female artists. There were (and still are) far more male than female acts in festival line-ups, and labels would often only want a handful of major female artists on their rosters. And so women were forced to compete against each other in order to survive in the male-dominated industry.

A modern equivalent of the Carey/Lopez feud could be seen between Katy Perry and Taylor Swift, though the two have since made peace after Perry sent Swift a literal olive branch. Not only have Perry and Swift been two of the biggest stars of the music world at the same time, they also share an ex-boyfriend. Their animosity, given the patriarchal world they live in, was hardly surprising.

In the real world, the comic potential of bitchiness has found a natural home on social media. It ranges from whole fandoms fighting against each other (and I have to confess, while I love both J. Lo and Mariah Carey, even I fell prey to the Perry/Swift feud; for the record, #TeamKaty) to teens bullying each other over Snapchat. 'Dragging', a term used to describe an intentional put-down, often for the purpose of encouraging others to laugh at the victim's expense, is rife across many social networks. It is part of a culture of snark (originally a portmanteau blend of 'snide' and 'remark'), which, in the cold light of day can be broken down as a desire to cruelly mock and ridicule others for one's own personal gratification. There's nothing particularly positive, intelligent or admirable about snark and shade, but they have become socially acceptable ways to bully others without it being termed bullying. And if the victim gets upset, then they just can't take a joke. I would be lying if I tried to tell you that I'd never indulged in snark, shade or dragging. I have. The temptation to ridicule others taps into the very worst of our human weaknesses, to which I am not immune. As I've grown older, I have attempted at least to be aware of that temptation so that I can try to counter it before I open my mouth or click 'post' and contribute to someone else's suffering. (Rightly or wrongly, I let myself off the hook somewhat with people who take time out of their days to send me nasty messages on social media. There's turning the other cheek, then there's being a doormat.)

My theory is that snark's appeal was conceived in school environments, incubated in the pages of tabloid magazines, nurtured through the lenses of reality television cameras, encouraged to try its strength on social media and has now grown up into a formidable, resilient monster that we don't know how to deal with. Its polar opposite, kindness, has fallen so far out of favour that it is often lost in a tide of bile, raising its head above the parapet in times of great need, but otherwise quietly minding its own business while snark romps around playing the class clown. Snark, however, doesn't serve women. Snark, when it is deployed against women, is merely bitchiness in a glittering little black dress. While snark may be funny, she's really a nasty bitch that sets out to make other women feel bad about themselves. She certainly ain't no feminist.

But while snark has become pervasive in online environments largely inhabited by digital natives, bitchiness is hardly the exclusive domain of the young. In fact, I'd argue that some of the most destructive bitchiness occurs in older generations of women. While young women have had the benefits, whether they're conscious of them or not, of growing up in a girl power-fuelled environment, older generations of women faced overt and biting sexism. The few who became successful in such an atmosphere often had to become ferociously tough in order to rise above seemingly impossible obstacles. Their achievements are inspirational, and many of them, upon reaching the top of the heap, have devoted considerable time, effort and money to helping to raise other women up around them. Some others, however, have taken the view that it's not fair for the younger women coming up behind them to have an easier ride than they did. Some of them will even stand in the way of other women, becoming unwitting henchwomen of the very system that oppressed them, while others will support other women with provisos and conditions attached, retaining a controlling hand in who ascends and who doesn't. Some women have become so adept at surviving and succeeding in patriarchal environments that they in turn recreate them.

I had an experience of this when I was asked to join a new women's group a few years ago. The organisation, helmed by a group of extraordinarily successful older women, seemed like a kind of intersectional feminist haven from the outside, but I found that the view was very different from the inside. To my surprise, I was asked to join the advisory board, becoming the youngest board member by, well, a lot. When I questioned the purpose of the group, its tiered structure, its non-charitable status and its out of the blue requirement for members to pay fees (after inviting women to join with no mention of any financial commitment), however, I was told to 'have some respect' and effectively given a dressing down in front of a group of other women. It quickly became clear that I was expected to know my place and that my concerns wouldn't be taken seriously. When I found that I couldn't get a straight answer on whether this new organisation would commit to tangibly changing the lives of not just those women who were already on the ladder of success, but those who had numerous obstacles to clamber over before even reaching the bottom rung, I realised that this wasn't the kind of sisterhood I could dedicate myself to. I was on the board for approximately three days before I resigned.

To my mind, creating an 'old girls' club' is just another way to create an oppressive structure. While it might feel satisfying to turn the tactics of the patriarchy back against it, forming groups of wealthy and successful women whose purpose is simply to help one another does little to improve the lives of the majority of women. In structures like that, the girl power seldom trickles down.

The irony in all of these situations is that kindness and collaboration are infinitely more powerful than bitchiness and division. When we view other women as competition, all we're really doing is creating another arbitrary binary; this time of winners and losers. By empowering a few but ignoring or disempowering the rest, we're ensuring that women will remain a marginalised group.

We're giving in to the fallacious idea that there's not enough success, kindness, resources or lovers to go around. That's simply not true. There is plenty for everyone, but the system we live in has created an illusion of scarcity in order to drive profit and division through fear. We hoard things – money, possessions and power – because we're afraid that sharing will mean we'll end up with nothing. In almost every realm – economically, socially, or even in our own communities – we can band together to change that. The power we have when we work together is extraordinary.

Women being kind to each other and working together are revolutionary ideas. So revolutionary that they have been discouraged for generations, likely for fear that they would bring about the almost certain toppling of several industries that derive profits from making women hate themselves and compete with each other. That's not to say that all women have to like and agree with each other, but it is possible to disagree with kindness.

A quick look at the broad church of feminism easily shows that wholesale agreement is utterly impossible, but there is no reason why we can't welcome differences of opinion within a united movement. Robust debate among feminists is vital, but sniping, uncompromising judgment and trying to out-feminist each other helps exactly no one – other than those who continue to benefit from patriarchal structures. There is no one way to be a feminist. The movement by its very nature and aims must be diverse, and that diversity should be supported rather than trampled upon. It may be frustrating, but part of changing the world around us will involve working with the imperfect people who live in it, and while some will have to be dragged kicking and screaming into the future, others could be encouraged to come along for the ride.

We can be angry without being mean. That's not to say that we all have to act like saints every second of the day, and it certainly shouldn't prevent us from speaking truth to power or standing up for ourselves, but we can have difficult discussions and speak up in support of our beliefs and opinions without giving in to nastiness. We can have fierce arguments without violating another human being's dignity. We can make the world a better place by remembering that it is possible to agree to disagree.

Which is not to say that I am a perfect person who gets it right all the time. I'm not. I get it wrong. I give in to temptation. I get hurt and lash out. But when it comes to altercations with other women particularly, I've become increasingly aware that fighting against each other is unlikely to serve either of us in the long run. I may disagree with my sister, but I try my best not to run her down.

In a society that is becoming increasingly polarised, where the very nature of reality is up for debate, it is more important than ever for us to be able to talk to each other, even when we disagree. But how do you talk to someone who makes you want to scream? While we're often told that having conversations with those who are on the opposite side of an issue or a spectrum is important, small steps may be more meaningful. If we can find common ground with those who we have mild disagreements with first, we'll likely be better equipped to talk to those who for all intents and purposes may as well live on another planet.

The stakes are too high for us not to try. If we can try to see the good in our sisters, understanding their perspectives and the events in their lives that may have led them to their particular view, rather than focussing solely on the bad, we'll be neutralising the patriarchy's power to divide us. We'll be striking back with kindness, collaboration and sisterhood against the system that has oppressed us – tools it has long despised.

As women, we don't always need to agree with each other in order to work together. We can agree to disagree and still stand alongside each other as sisters in arms, empowered by sharing the load and fighting the battles together from many different fronts. If there's one feminist resolution we all should make, it's to support and uplift women whenever possible, particularly those whose oppressions are heavier than our own. If we all raise each other up, we all rise.

CHAPTER SIXTEEN

Bringing down the invisible man

Do I hate men? – A love poem.

L. Marvelly

Do you hate men? the nice man asked.
Don't you know that not all men are monsters?
Why are you so angry? What happened in your past
To make you such a sour and spiteful bitch?

Why do you hate men? the nice man asked.
Did your father not give you enough attention?
I wouldn't fuck you if you were the last
Woman on earth. You make me sick.

Do I hate men? I pondered to myself.
Then I bit my tongue.
Hard.
The blood tasted bitter.

People are very curious about why I hate men. They demand that I explain myself and then make up their own reasons anyway. Reasons that usually involve me not having enough sex or having too much sex or having the wrong kind of sex or having some deeply held 'daddy issues'. Of course, no response that I could ever give them would deter them from their deeply held view that LIZZIE MARVELLY IS A MAN-HATER. So I've largely given up trying to reason with them. They seem to enjoy spending their time inventing fictitious histories for me, so why spoil their fun? I once wrote in a column that I assessed the risk (of being catcalled, jeered at or groped) when I walked past a group of men – especially a group of drunk men – and that, as far as the forensic man-hater hunters were concerned, was that: case closed. You may as well call me Man Hater In Chief.

The idea that feminists supposedly hate men is such a tired trope that you'd think it would've been debunked by now, but it remains depressingly common. For example, I spoke about feminism at a high school last year, and at the conclusion of my talk, a Year 12 girl put her hand up and asked me whether I had a boyfriend. The implication echoed throughout the school hall, and I laughed, but only barely succeeded in not rolling my eyes. She wasn't the first (and nor will she be the last) person to imply that my feminist beliefs and values may exclude me from liking, or being liked by, men, and her question provides an important illustration of an obvious aspect of feminism that yet proves too nuanced for many people to grasp. Just because you are a supporter of one thing, doesn't mean that you hate its opposite. Just because I support and advocate for women, doesn't mean that I hate men, or people of any other gender for that matter. Or, to illustrate – and as I put it to her – just because I'm a supporter of hokey pokey ice cream, doesn't mean that I hate chocolate.

The issue of man-hating is one that I want to address up front in this chapter, entitled, as it is, 'Bringing down the invisible man'. The invisible man is, of course, patriarchy, but it seems that an understanding of symbolism is not our societal strongpoint, so it's important to point out the differences between hating men and hating a system that requires people to put themselves into two rigidly constrained cages and take on a series of arbitrary expectations and responsibilities unique to each of those two imaginary prisons that we call 'male' and 'female'.

For the record, I don't hate men. And my father has been present throughout every stage of my life. I can say with some certainty, however, that a small minority of women do hate men, and often have very good reason to. You only need to take a look at our sexual violence statistics to be able to imagine the kind of experiences that could lead women to feel negatively about men. I am not going to take it upon myself to tell a woman who has been harassed, beaten, raped or otherwise brutalised by a man that she should squash her quite understandable feelings of aversion because they make some men feel uncomfortable. I would suggest that perhaps the men who feel uncomfortable when confronted with women who don't like men should spend a bit of time reflecting on just why that may be, and then strive to change the shitty culture that condones violence against women by becoming active allies, but I suspect that suggestion would go down like a cup of cold sick.

What I *do* hate is a system that penalises women, puts unfair pressure on men and makes life for people who don't identify as male or female difficult. Patriarchy, 'a system in which men have all or most of the power and importance in a society or group'[1], is a structure that doesn't really work for anyone, but it does reward those who adhere to it stringently, especially if they are male and white. But even white men are forced to make trade-offs. While men may generally receive a better deal than women under a patriarchal system, they too suffer, but often without recognising it in such terms. From the pressure to stifle any display (or indeed, sensation) of emotion, to the long-established reality that men are more likely than women to die in road accidents[2], men also get shafted by the patriarchy. Men are more likely than women to die in workplace accidents, a fact that could be connected to the traditional male role of 'breadwinner', and the risky types of work that have conventionally been male-dominated[3]. Outside of the workplace, men are more likely to willingly engage in risky behaviour, like binge-drinking and smoking[4] – behaviours that researchers have theorised can sometimes be enacted in an attempt to appear masculine[5]. Men are also less likely to seek help for both physical and mental illnesses, both because they may see health and wellbeing as being 'feminine' and because they may view illness as a sign of weakness that may threaten their masculinity[6]. Patriarchy, which relies on rigid and oppositional definitions of masculinity and femininity, basically screws us all – just in different ways.

It's important though to pare back that generalisation. Patriarchy isn't a kind of one-size-fits-all power differential in which all people are set on predetermined paths determined by their gender. As writer and activist Natasha Walter explains:

> *People often misunderstand patriarchy as a totalitarian system, in which all the women feel powerless all the time, and all the men feel powerful all the time. That isn't how it works, a lot of women do feel powerful and a lot of men don't.*[7]

The idea of patriarchy is instead that broader structural, cultural, social, sexual and economic norms and expectations exist in our society that dictate that people should act in certain ways, that certain people should be more powerful than others, and that society should be organised in a certain fashion (for example, patriarchy prescribes that society's primary unit should be the heterosexual nuclear family, with Dad at the head).

It's not hard to see the ways in which patriarchy pits us against each other. Under a traditional patriarchal system, men are in control, while women are controlled. Men are the heads of the household and the masters of industry. They shoulder both the burden of providing for their families and the power that comes with being the one to possess what others need. Men set the rules and women follow them. Women take care of the domestic chores and raise the children. Men are tough, while women are emotional. Men provide, while women nurture. Men are promiscuous while women crave relationships. Thankfully our modern society has secured at least some concessions from the punishing patriarchy of old. Women no longer need men to protect them (and let us remember that needing and wanting are very different concepts) but still the influence of patriarchy endures in our society, dividing men and women into segregated classes of people, and often still casting women in the role of 'dependant'.

Throughout my adult life, I've been surprised to discover how prominently patriarchal ideas have featured in some of my own relationships. Over the years, I have dated men around my own age (and even younger) who have had very strong ideas about gender roles. On a few memorable occasions, men I have dated have brought up marriage very early in a relationship – as a topic of conversation, not as the precursor to a proposal – and been shocked when I've expressed ambivalence to the idea. The response 'I'm not sure how I feel about the institution of marriage' was clearly not the reply they expected. Similarly, men I've dated have expressed views about women, motherhood and work that would have been totally normal in the 1950s. There's nothing quite like going out on a date with someone you quite like and realising that a side of patriarchy is on the menu.

Under patriarchal systems, women depend on the magnanimity of men, and must adhere to the conditions of such an arrangement lest they displease their male partners, colleagues or family members (which is one of the reasons why I don't dig it).

Outside of marriage and family relationships, patriarchy extends its tentacles into wider social codes, punishing its subjects if they should dare to break free from its shackles. For a man to be seen as feminine, or a woman to be viewed as masculine, is the ultimate transgression in a patriarchal society. Under a patriarchal system, there is no room for collaboration or role-swapping; for example, families in which a mother is the main breadwinner while a father stays at home to raise their children are still rare in our society. I recently saw an article that talked about how worried men were that taking parental leave may affect their careers, and the depth of the irony made me choke on my tea. For one, no shit. It's hilarious that men now see what we've been talking about for all these decades – when it might impact upon them. And two, this very example is patriarchy in action. By threatening men with repercussions for daring to step outside of the strictly defined boundaries of 'the male role' in society, patriarchy tries to ensure that everything will stay the way it's always been, staving off a threat of a more egalitarian and collaborative society that would divide power evenly. The ideas that some men actually *want* to stay at home with their children, and that some women would rather work than be stay-at-home parents, have been actively ignored and stifled by patriarchy for as long as possible. But, faced with a society that is rapidly evolving, patriarchy is fighting a losing battle. One it will fight, viciously, to the death.

It will fight, because to the proponents of patriarchy, a society organised in any other way is alarming. While I'm sure I'll be cast as a radical lunatic for saying this (what's new?), I find it very difficult to understand why some people are so scared of the idea of a society in which there are no defined gender roles. What is so scary about men who cry when they feel sad and women who are unashamedly ambitious? What is so frightening about people deciding that actually they don't feel comfortable being defined as either 'male' or 'female' and deciding to live their lives in a way that allows them to be true to themselves? What is wrong with the idea of men who are the primary caregivers for their children and women who pursue careers in firefighting? Or little boys who like playing with dolls and little girls who play with trucks? A boy dressed up as Elsa! WHAT IS THIS WORLD COMING TO? Hilariously, those who are most utterly terrified by the idea of a boy engaging in any stereotypically feminine activity are often those who go to pains to assert their big, strong masculinity. We are literally living in an age when 'big, tough men' are petrified of tiny boys dressed as princesses. And that should provide a clear illustration of just how ludicrous this whole situation is.

I'll be accused of ignoring 'biological truths', but the reality is that the genitalia and chromosomes we possess have very little to do with whether it's socially acceptable for us to wear dresses or not. It's not like little boys are born with skirt-repelling enzymes. They are, however, born into a society that has some very strong ideas about what they should and should not do.

The impact of patriarchy is all around us, and has been defended as a 'natural' organisation of human relationships. This is bullshit. Contrary to what evolutionary psychologists have been suggesting ad nauseum for decades, patriarchy is not some kind of biological fait accompli. It may have been established in a time when life expectancy was so low and child mortality so high that women were almost constantly giving birth to and raising children, when it made sense for men to hunt and gather and women to focus solely on propagating the tribe, but the fact that it remained the dominant structure as society progressed beyond breeding to beat the Grim Reaper is little more than a historical hangover. As historian Gerda Lerner explains:

> *Anatomy once was destiny. But it no longer is, and it should not be in the future. Patriarchy is a human creation, it is not functioning very well now, and it can be ended.*[8]

There is no longer any biological need for patriarchy, as even the impact of childbirth (which remains a largely female activity) can be mitigated by other human constructions like paid parental leave and supportive workplaces. It persists simply because it has been the dominant societal structure for generations.

I am neither a scholar nor a historian, so I won't demean either profession by going into the history of patriarchy in any great depth but I will point out the obvious: at no point in our human history were 'men' and 'women' homogenous groups of clones who all thought and acted the same way. For example, there are many cases throughout history of women engaging in trades[9], and even dominating some now masculinised crafts (such as brewing beer)[10], even if the expectations of women at the time were for them to stay at home, sign over their individual identity to a man and produce offspring. There have always been women who have broken the patriarchal mould. Cumulatively, across the centuries, there have been many of them. That in itself negates the idea that patriarchy is biological. It's not. It's socially conditioned. And it's a scam.

For those wedded to the idea of patriarchy, people who do not fit into patriarchal categories can easily become 'them' – those weirdos who threaten the worldview of 'us'. They become the 'other', while traditionalists are the 'natural' default. The 'abnormal' who must be stopped, lest they alter the restrictive boundaries of 'normality'.

Being an 'other' is an interesting experience, and it is one that is tied to the concept of patriarchy. 'Othering' someone allows for them to be treated as different, and when someone is different, they can be assigned a lesser value. History is littered with examples of exactly this concept, with some of the most glaring being the treatment of Jewish people by the Nazis and the treatment of African American people in the United States. The treatment of Māori by British settlers was also made possible by othering. Othering is a key component of any system that manifests as a hierarchy. Patriarchy, as a system that relies on the power of the patriarch – most often in the form of a straight white man – does its best to crush any threat to that power.

The historic and continuing oppression of women through pay inequality, sexual harassment and abuse, discriminative hiring practices, domestic violence, tokenistic representation at governance and executive levels, unequal divisions of domestic labour, unconscious bias and misogyny merely continues the pattern of male dominance. Only now we also have to contend with patriarchal gaslighting, as the henchmen and women of tradition try to convince us that sexism doesn't exist anymore. That it's not the 1950s and we should stop complaining. If only.

How much healthier would we be as a society if we allowed people to define themselves, without conditioning them to feel like they have to think and act in certain ways or casting them as 'others'? My radical idea of a healthy society is one in which people can be authentically themselves without having to adhere to preconceived ideas of who they should be, whether consciously or subconsciously. A place where people can love who they love, regardless of their gender; where they can feel free to identify with any gender or none at all. To be clear, I don't advocate for a completely genderless society, both because I think it would be frankly impossible and because I think that gender identity can be an important part of some people's overall concept of self. Feelings about being a woman, a man, a non-binary person, a trans woman or a trans man are all intensely private and individual, and can bring comfort and/or stability to some people. What I do advocate for is a society in which people can be the masters of their own identity. A place where the concept of 'fitting in' is redundant, because there are no restrictive constraints to force anyone to be anything other than themselves. While I understand that the urge to categorise is a common and often unconscious tactic to try to understand people in relation to ourselves, our beliefs, and what we know of the world, I believe that it's one that we should resist, or at least be very conscious of. The only identity we should concern ourselves with is our own. Freedom of identity should be a basic human right.

Why? Because outside of the cookie-cutter mould of the 1950s nuclear family, identities can be refreshingly complex and multi-faceted. Although traditionalists may struggle to believe this, it is actually possible for individuals to express seemingly contradictory attributes and be unharmed by them. I am one such individual. While I've never felt uncomfortable about my gender identity as a woman (quite the opposite), my personality is made up of a collection of stereotypically feminine and masculine traits. I am affectionate (feminine), compassionate (feminine), communicative (feminine), ambitious (masculine), stubborn (masculine), and forthright (masculine), among many other things. I'm also a woman with fair skin and Māori whakapapa, who is attracted to men and women, who doesn't have a conventional 'day job', who has been deliberately single for a good portion of her adult life, and who makes no apologies for any of that. I am a walking contradiction, and I'm fine with that. I understand, however, that hodgepodge identities such as my own can be challenging for some people to grasp. What I don't understand is why. Even more perplexing is why someone else's identity should be any concern of theirs.

Rigidly defined gender identities and the need to divide people into male-female units that will produce children are the building blocks of the patriarchy, so it's no surprise that there has been a significant backlash to feminism. But while patriarchy hates difficult women, it *loathes* people who refuse to play by the rules of the gender binary. As a cisgender woman, I cannot and will not speak for transgender, gender queer and non-binary people, but as an ally I will stand up and say that for every sucker-punch patriarchy has delivered to women, it has turned next to people who have rejected the gender binary and thumped them too. No feminist battle can ignore the injustices that have been inflicted upon non-cisgender people.

Indeed, when we're fighting against the patriarchy, we need to view its problems with a very wide lens. Patriarchy is linked in both overt and less obvious ways to racism, transphobia, homophobia, Islamophobia, white supremacy, xenophobia and any number of other discriminative practices and belief systems. I am not automatically saying that every supporter of patriarchal society is a bigot. I am saying that patriarchy has created an environment in which white, heterosexual, Christian, cisgender men are held to be supreme above all others, which has had obvious repercussions for people who do not fit that description. When we strike back against patriarchy, we are fighting against the idea that some people are more important than others by virtue of their genitalia, skin colour, religion, socio-economic standing, able-bodiedness or other arbitrary markers of identity. We are fighting for the idea that we are all equally valuable and equally deserving of human rights, regardless of what 'category' we fall under, if we can be categorised at all.

In New Zealand, as in most other countries around the globe, we still live in a patriarchy. Men still hold the bulk of the power in almost every realm, from our Parliament, where 61.6 per cent of MPs are men, to our boardrooms, where 83 per cent of board members are men[11], to our families, where working mothers are paid 17 per cent less than working fathers[12] – and the term 'working father' stands out as being odd, because a man being a father is thought to have little or no bearing on his ability to work. While we have certainly made gains in the fight against a male supremacist society, we are nowhere near equality. We have, however, achieved a kind of momentum that patriarchy and its advocates regard as a deadly threat. And so, with every inch of ground gained, patriarchy fights back with increasing ferociousness. It can be seen in the election of Donald Trump. In the disgustingly misogynistic comments splattered across the internet. In the initial attempts to blame of women for the repugnant behaviour of Harvey Weinstein and men like him. In the dismantling of women's rights to access abortion and birth control in the United States. In the infantilising and misogynistic comments made about female leaders. In the reprehensible 'No' campaign launched during Australia's horrific marriage-equality plebiscite to scare people into voting to prevent same-sex couples from being able to marry. In the fierce resistance to the idea of gender quotas and the lack of action by the previous New Zealand Government to actually do something to reduce the gender pay gap (until, of course, it was threatened with a tidal wave of court case; that seemed to spur it into action). Patriarchy knows that it is under threat, and it has begun to fight back more and more viciously.

The conflation of patriarchy with men as individuals is nothing new, but it has recently been advanced with increasing levels of hysteria. When any discussion about the ways in which patriarchy is harmful can be dismissed as 'man-hating' or 'misandry', patriarchy defends itself against the probing analysis it deserves. Indeed, I fight back against patriarchy daily, but I very rarely refer to it by name. To do so is to invite instant dismissal of your arguments, because having a discussion about patriarchy marks you as both a feminist and a man-hater (and it's very clear that to some people, those two very different things seem identical). In that way it is the noxious ghost that hides in plain sight. While people believe that any anti-patriarchy sentiment can essentially be boiled down to the hatred of men, the conversation cannot turn to the ways in which patriarchy hurts men too. While the danger of patriarchy is seen as some kind of feminist conspiracy, we can't talk about the ways in which it influences serious global issues like war and climate change, even though we have illustrations of both right before our eyes. Watching Donald Trump and Kim Jong-un goading each other from their respective sides of the dying ocean like two overgrown toddlers fighting over who gets to be the king of the castle provided a striking example of the worst excesses of toxic masculinity, bred and nurtured by patriarchy and then manifesting as a nuclear threat to millions of innocent people. And yet patriarchy was mentioned in few, if any, discussions of the escalating tensions, despite the fact that the patriarchal ideal of machismo – to which both men have clearly fallen victim – suggests that backing down means suffering a disastrous loss of face. When doing the right thing and walking away from a fight to defuse a terrifyingly serious situation amounts to a threat to fragile masculinities, patriarchy has a lot to answer for.

Similarly, our continued lack of significant action to stop climate change demonstrates how patriarchy and capitalism work together to reinforce an ideology of competition, possession and control – with disastrous effect. Patriarchy places men at the top of the food chain, as masters of the environment. It's no accident that countries that became colonies of European superpowers were described as 'virgin land', ripe for 'conquering'. It's also no surprise that said virgin lands (and their indigenous populations) were later raped and pillaged. The environment, under a patriarchal worldview, exists to be exploited by men. Perhaps if the natural world was instead referred to as 'Father Nature' it would be afforded the basic respect it deserves.

Patriarchy also views empathy, kindness and caring as feminine behaviours and thus treats them with condescension. When we talk about 'caring' for the environment, it flies in the face of patriarchy's desire towards staunchness and control. We live in a world where boardrooms and executive teams are dominated by men. I wonder, if the macho drive for profit and one-upmanship was balanced by an equal number of women in those decision-making positions, whether the situation would be different. I suspect it would take more than that, and that we'd need to undergo a radical rethinking of our priorities as a society to break away from our current obsession with individualistic greed. Cynically, I also wonder if we may have to wait for powerful men to be negatively affected – by which time it will be almost certainly too late. Patriarchal approaches are failing when it comes to climate change. I suspect it may be time to start viewing the problem through a more female lens. If collaboration and concern for the health of communities and the environment were valued more highly by corporations, governments and global bodies than a constant need for economic growth, I think we'd find that many of our most challenging problems would become solvable.

And on that note – it's no surprise that Donald Trump removed the United States from the historic Paris Climate Agreement. Working together for the greater good instead of competing against one another for private profit is incomprehensible to a man who is a walking embodiment of the patriarchy. In Donald Trump, many of the worst tenets of patriarchy intermingle to produce a truly gob-smacking individual. The allegations of sexual abuse, his derogatory remarks about women, his childish habit of trying to 'out-handshake' anyone he meets, his bravado, his habit of baseless boasting and his comically thin skin are merely the tip of the iceberg. Yet, I don't hate Donald Trump. I loathe almost everything he stands for and I despair for those who have suffered at his hand, but I also pity him. Patriarchy may have built him up and paid him huge dividends, but it has also robbed him of any meaningful way of dealing with his emotions, mitigating conflict or protecting himself against the insults that he appears to feel so keenly. Unfortunately, those personal tragedies are now very much our problem. In Trump, the pitfalls of patriarchy are on display for all to see, if they only care to look.

So how do we take it down? Patriarchy, I mean – not Trump. That would be another book entirely. In advocating for the destruction of patriarchy, we're asking for a radical reorganisation of the way our world is structured. There is no silver bullet, and such a drastic change will take time, but the way I see it, the first step is to focus on the end game. What is it that we want? What does a post-patriarchal society look like? That vision should be collaboratively assembled, and communicated widely. While I could write another whole book outlining my ideas for a post-patriarchal society, I'll focus in on just a few here.

The first is a society in which the positions of power are held equally by women and men. The good news is that we have in our grasp an extremely simple way to make that a reality, if we'd only get over our squeamishness around quotas. The bad news is that I don't think that quotas go far enough. If we embed gender quotas into the existing structures of governance and production throughout our society, I believe that we will see many better outcomes (research supports this too: the most significant effect of gender quotas is that they get rid of mediocre men)[13] but essentially still deal with many of the same problems. Gender quotas alone won't fix climate change and poverty. They won't overcome a system of inequality and privilege. Gender quotas won't suddenly make the workplace family-friendly, value unpaid work, or automatically fix the pay gap. By implementing gender quotas, we're still forcing women to operate in a system that was designed by and for men. It's hard to even imagine the possibilities that may be available to humankind if we were to reimagine that system through a truly gender-equal lens.

The second idea that I think is key to a post-patriarchal society is a pervasive feeling that women are cool. It may sound reductive on the surface, but when you deconstruct some commonly held attitudes in our society you find that there are a number of men who don't think that women are cool; unless, that is, they're having sex with them, and even then, there's a difference between thinking a woman is sexually attractive and admiring her as a human being.

While high-profile manifestations of contempt towards women include things like the reluctance of many men to watch women play professional sport, the degradation of female musicians (in every genre – 'Oh, she's only successful because she's hot, she's not even that good, she probably slept her way into that gig/record deal/hit single'), and the ridicule of 'chick flicks' and 'chick lit', the idea that women are deserving of scorn and condescension is pervasive throughout our society. We don't raise our boys to think that girls are cool. We raise them to think the opposite. We say 'Don't be such a *girl*!', suggesting to little boys that girls are inferior. As a society we generally don't encourage boys to be friends with girls, to engage in activities that have traditionally been seen as 'girly', or to be inspired by female role models. I remember having a male friend at primary school who played with the girls during many lunchtimes. As the only boy in a group of girls, he stood out. He was kind and caring. I was a slow reader when I first started school, while he was more advanced. He would often choose to read to me during reading time, happily reading the 'girly' stories that I loved so that we could share them together. He thought that girls were cool. He still does. The other boys regarded him as an oddity. They couldn't understand why he would want to play with us. They were only five or six years old, but they'd already been influenced by the patriarchy. This boy, who is now a man, grew up to be a great guy, with lots of friends – male and female. And no, to debunk yet another stereotype, he's not gay.

Under our patriarchal system, boys grow up being wary of girls, disparaging of anything labelled as feminine, and as a result find it difficult to relate to girls. At the extreme end, this becomes especially apparent when men react to stories of violence against women by saying, 'as a husband/father/son/brother of a woman', as if it is only because they are somehow related to a woman that they can understand that treating women badly is unacceptable. If we as a society thought that women were cool and held them in high regard, the whole paradigm would shift.

The third great vision I have for the post-patriarchal age is a world in which we collectively told the 'isms' and 'phobias' to fuck off. While sexism is the obvious lowest-hanging fruit to be plucked first from the tree of dickwaddery and squashed to a pulp, racism, homophobia, transphobia, ableism, classism and all other retrograde morally bankrupt mindsets can also go and jump off a cliff. All of the isms are products of hierarchical thinking, and they're all related to patriarchy. While a world free of prejudice seems like exactly the kind of utopian dream a snowflake like me would have, we need to examine why oppression is still an ingrained feature of our society. It largely comes down to fear. We fear what is different. We divide people into 'us' and 'them', because the idea that we might all be equal would require us to rethink the way that we treat each other. Those of us who come from privileged positions can be particularly susceptible to prejudice, as acknowledging our unfair advantages makes us feel uncomfortable and guilty, but no one is born sexist, racist or homophobic. Even if we are tribal animals, that doesn't mean that we can't be harmonious and generous in our treatment of others. Our hatred is learnt, and we can unlearn it. A post-patriarchal society would be built on the idea that no human being is more valuable or less worthy than another. What a radical notion.

I could go on. And on. The idea of a society in which we've moved beyond patriarchy and dismantled the structures of oppression excites me. But while that lofty goal is still a fair way off, there is plenty that we can do in the here and now. Most importantly, we can speak boldly and unapologetically about the kind of future we want. We can make plans to fight for change, and we can support each other. We can call patriarchy for what it is – an out-dated, regressive, ill-fitting, discriminatory, and harmful human invention that we should've abandoned generations ago.

The day patriarchy picked a fight with feminism, it messed with the wrong women.

CHAPTER SEVENTEEN

One last rant

As women, we are often looked at, but rarely seen. So many elements of our identities are smelted by external influences that it's hard to know what originates within and what is cast upon us. For those of us who become fed up with the reflections we're supposed to imitate, it can become our lives' work to unpick and unravel the tangled jumble of truth and falsehood that is womanhood to find the flesh-and-blood woman underneath.

Being our true selves is not easy. There will inevitably be parts of ourselves that we find distasteful or dangerous and that we try to hide lest we find ourselves shamed in some way. Shame is constantly within arm's reach of womanhood, ready to pounce whenever we cross the invisible boundary from good woman to bad.

I am a bad woman. I am too much and not enough. I don't fit neatly into anyone's idea of what a woman should be. I am one of those bloody women who refuses to march to anyone's drum but her own. One of those infuriating women who draws attention to uncomfortable things, and has the audacity to suggest that the status quo should change. One of those impudent women who declines to apologise for her behaviour. While the house of mirrors I grew up in casts me in a particular light, I prefer to see myself with my own eyes.

The truth is that the mirrors we see ourselves in, and the eyes that gaze at us through subjective lenses, lie. They reflect an unreality that has been repeated so many times it is thought of as real. The things we *must* be. The transgressions we must not commit. The femininity that we must uphold at all times is an illusion. An imaginary house of cards. A stone wall we've been pushing up against, willing it to move just a little, when we should've blown the bloody thing up.

The time has come for us to smash the mirrors, suspicions and curses be damned. It's time for us to look at ourselves with piercing eyes, and to insist on being the only ones who have the right to define ourselves. I have a T-shirt emblazoned with the phrase 'The future is female'. As much as it has become a cliché, I read it as a challenge. This is our time. We've waited patiently for centuries and now it's our turn to shape the future.

In writing this book, I'll admit that I allowed myself to fantasise about the kind of future that I hope I'll live to see, as I alluded to in the last chapter. Some of my recurring daydreams included:

- A sell-out crowd at Eden Park gathered to watch the Black Ferns win the World Cup.
- The destruction of the diet industry.

- A Parliament that has an equal number of male and female MPs, serving alongside a number of non-binary members.
- A Māori female CEO leading the largest and most successful NZX 50 company. A Pasifika woman CEO joining her in the group of top Kiwi Chief Executives. An Indian woman CEO joining them. Women of colour running some of our most successful organisations and changing the shape of the business world for employees and consumers alike.
- A future in which the stale, pale, male old boys' club is a broken relic. A mere symbol of a time long past.
- A New Zealand in which both the Prime Minister and the Deputy Prime Minister are female. Not forever, but for at least a few terms. It would make up for the many, many decades in which political leadership teams were exclusively male.
- A female President of the United States.
- A world in which no sexual harasser or abuser will ever be elected or appointed to a position of power. Actually, fuck it, it's *my* fantasy. How about a world in which sexual harassers and abusers actually feel the wrath of the justice system for their troubles?
- Free or affordable day-care centres in all large organisations, allowing parents the convenience and peace of mind of being close to their children while they work.
- Equal and generous allocations of paid parental leave for both parents that could be taken concurrently or separately without affecting the overall amount of leave each parent could take.

- Organisations that allow parents to work flexible hours.
- A living wage paid to every New Zealander.

And so on and so forth.

In order to achieve any of these marvellous visions, however, we would have to become comfortable with the very uncomfortable idea that the meritocracy is a fantasy. One of the most pervasive beliefs of our modern capitalistic society is that those who work hard succeed and those who don't, fail. I can understand its potent, intoxicating allure. I work hard and I have achieved success in my life. It would be very easy for me to link the two together, adding two and two and getting five, and mistaking correlation for causation. I would feel pretty good about myself if I could claim full responsibility for my good fortune, but while my hard work has certainly contributed to my success, it is not the only factor at play. Hard work and success, in most cases, and contrary to popular opinion, do not exist in a simple two-party causative relationship.

In my case, I started life a few steps ahead, and have maintained that advantage for much of my journey. I was born able-bodied, with fair skin, into a family that nurtured me and could afford to give me access to opportunities that were out of the reach of some of my peers. I had a rare musical talent that was handed down through my genetics. I was able to pursue a tertiary education. I've always known that whatever happened I wouldn't be left destitute and starving.

I am privileged, and my privilege has contributed to my success. Even with a few curveballs thrown in. I'm a woman, a person of Māori descent, a member of the LGBTQ+ community, someone who has experienced sexual violence, a person who has suffered mental illness; but at every step of the way I've been able to access the support I've needed to mitigate the impact of any of these factors. I have struggled, but the struggles I faced would've been much worse had I not had a level of privilege to begin with.

I am not arrogant enough to believe that I'm somehow special, or that I work harder than, say, a miner or a cleaner. I simply won a couple of metaphorical lotteries in the nature and nurture departments. The meritocracy has served me well, because I was in a position where I was able to focus on excelling rather than surviving, and as such, it is my responsibility to use my privileges to serve others whenever I can.

While the meritocracy remains the dominant ideology of our society, many of the fabulous feminist dreams we have for the future will remain just that – dreams. While the meritocracy thrives, society will still be able to argue that the CEOs of the NZX 50 companies are almost all male because they're the 'best people for the job', rather than acknowledging the truth – that they're the people who have risen to the top of a system that has rewarded them almost every step of the way. They're the people who have not been viewed as sexual objects for their entire lives until they're old and suddenly invisible, they haven't had to deal with unconscious biases and 'benevolent' sexism, haven't been called 'shrill' or 'aggressive' for voicing their opinions, haven't had to navigate 'emasculating' their partners by being more successful, and haven't had to take time out of their careers to raise families. They're the people who have been supported by old boys' networks, made lucrative deals over golf and in strip clubs, easily found mentors (whose wandering hands they didn't have to worry about), and been encouraged to be ambitious and competitive.

The above are, of course, sweeping generalisations, but for most successful men there will be at least a few kernels of truth hiding in a painful sea of denial. The old adage that women must work twice as hard to be thought half as good as men is excruciatingly real, and the meritocracy doesn't reward our extra effort with double points. The meritocracy is a nice idea, but it doesn't work. It won't work until we address the many inequalities that exist within our society.

None of this is to blame anyone for being privileged. I don't blame myself for the arbitrary advantages that were bestowed upon me at birth; if anything, they make me work harder. I recognise that my receipt of those benefits seals my social contract to help others. But if you did read those last few paragraphs and feel deeply unsettled, I'd gently encourage you to ask yourself why. There's much to be learned from inconvenient facts. Even when we wish they were fictions.

Asking why is a tool that's fallen out of fashion lately. Probing, analysing and thinking critically isn't exactly encouraged in the time of Trump and Twitter. If there's one thing that would've saved me an enormous amount of frustration and grief over the years, however, it's asking the question 'why'? Why should I have to be skinny? Why is feminism a dirty word? Why do they say that boys who are mean and/or violent towards you are just doing it because they like you? Why are there 13 blue jersey prefects who are boys, and only three who are girls? Why do I feel like a misfit for not being in a relationship? Why does it matter 'how Māori' I am? Why do some people have a problem with me having an opinion? Why, to this day, do men continue to run the planet, when women are beating them resoundingly at educational institutions? Why do I feel scared to admit that I am ambitious? Why do I feel that I have to make myself smaller so I don't intimidate a man?

If I'd started asking the question earlier, I would've treated myself more kindly. I would've both gained some important insights into my thought patterns, and been forced to conclude that many of the answers to my questions made very little sense, which, in fact, meant that I was dealing with a load of bullshit that wasn't worth wasting my energy on. For example, why do I feel that I have to make myself smaller so that I don't intimidate a man? Because toxic masculinity has made it very difficult for men to be able to accept not being the most powerful one in a relationship, and women have been taught to compensate for that by taking a step back to become lesser versions of themselves. It's definitely bullshit, and there's not much I can do about it at this stage, other than spend time with men who are strong enough to not have to be the strongest one all the time. Or date women. There's the silver lining …

Asking why isn't just a tool for better understanding our personal beliefs and impulses, it's an increasingly vital device for investigating the world around us. Why, for example, is an alleged serial sexual harasser the President of the United States? Why do we see many more penises than vulvas on screen? Why did male founders receive $58.2 billion in venture capital funding in 2016, when female founders received only $1.46 billion[1]?

The answers to some of these questions may be ugly. They may be depressing and disheartening, but if we don't ask them, we may be inclined to believe that the reasons for the kinds of shitty states of affairs mentioned above may be just because *that's the way things are.* Yes, that is the way things are, and it's not good enough, and we shouldn't stop squawking about how it's not good enough until things actually change.

And they will change. They're already changing. Slowly, and reluctantly, but in such a way that the idea that gender inequality is just a fact of life has been dealt a fatal blow and is gasping for air. I'd like to take this opportunity to cordially invite you to dance upon its grave. I'll bring the wine, you bring the chips and dip. I'll see you there.

POSTSCRIPT

I started writing this book when I was 27 years old, and I'll be (at least) 29 by the time you're reading this. Over the nine months it took to pour my guts out onto these pages, I laughed, I cried and I raged. I found the bossy little girl inside me and felt her indignation at being punished for being bold and forthright. I reconnected with the young woman wracked with depression and marvelled at the depth of her self-hatred. I discovered a reflective woman, turning over old events and gleaning new meanings. Then I went to therapy to try to make sense of it all.

When everything is said and done, however, I'm just a kid from Rotorua. I don't profess to possess any profound, life-altering wisdom – or, for the sake of my 40-year-old self, looking back on this book and rolling her eyes – none that I'll admit to at the tender age of not-yet-30. I do hope, though, that there was something in these pages – even just one little morsel – that you found interesting, heartening, affirming, motivating or even frustrating. I hope that there was a spark in there that will add to the fire within.

ACKNOWLEDGMENTS

Writing a book is simultaneously a privilege, a joy, a frustration, an exhaustion and an utterly amazing experience. I feel such gratitude to so many people, without whom this book would never have been written, let alone published.

First, to Alex Hedley at HarperCollins. Thank you for having the vision and belief in me to make this book a reality. Your dedication, gentle guidance and wisdom have been immensely valuable and reassuring. It has been a privilege to work with you.

To Sandra Noakes and the rest of the team at HarperCollins, thank you for giving me this wonderful opportunity.

To Leonie Freeman, who took this book under her wing when it was a ranty brain dump, and turned it into something readable. Thank you for 'getting it' so thoroughly, and polishing my words so masterfully.

To Niki Schuck, thank you for believing in me from the get go, always giving me excellent advice, putting up with me for all these years, AND reading this book when it was little more than word salad. I cannot put into words how grateful I am.

To Kate Barron, for being the voice of reason, always having my back, and gently helping me to murder my darlings, thank you so much.

To Miriyana Alexander, who took a leap of faith in putting me in her newspaper. Your support, belief and encouragement played an enormous role in making me the writer (and tough cookie) that I am today. I will be forever grateful.

To Jo Raj, my co-conspirator. I am so lucky that I get to do cool stuff with you. Thank you for supporting me right throughout the process of writing this book, and for being the kind of friend that shows up late at night with wine and open arms when I need to cry. You are so special to me.

To Alison Mau. You are an inspirational mentor and a good friend. Thank you for all of your support and guidance.

To Barbara Brookes, for making sure I gave an accurate retelling of herstory. Thank you for your advice, conversation and help with this book.

To Hilary Barry and Miriama Kamo, thank you for sharing your stories with me so generously.

To Mick Sinclair, for your wise counsel (as always).

To my beautiful, beloved friends. You have been fiercely in my corner since I was a baby feminist and I am so grateful.

To Anna, my sister. Thank you for loving me unconditionally and keeping me sane.

To my long-suffering parents. I would not be the woman I am today without your tireless support, love, and guidance. I'm sorry I talk about sex in public so much. I love you. You're the best parents in the whole wide world.

And last, but certainly not least, to the bossy little girls and strong young women reading this. Thank you for inspiring me, energising me and making me excited about the future. You are so powerful. You give me hope. You are the bright, blazing light this world needs.

HELP AND SUPPORT

Sexual and Domestic Violence

Te Ohaakii a Hine – National Network Ending Sexual Violence Together (Toah Nnest)

Phone: 0800 88 33 00

Web: toah-nnest.org.nz

Women's Refuge

Phone: 0800 733 843 (0800 REFUGE)

Web: womensrefuge.org.nz

Shine

Phone: 0508 744 633

Web: 2shine.org.nz

NZ Police

Phone: 111

Web: police.govt.nz

Depression and Suicide

Suicide Crisis Helpline
Phone: 0508 828 865 (0508 TAUTOKO)

Lifeline
Phone: 0800 543 354 (0800 LIFELINE)
Web: lifeline.org.nz

Samaritans
Phone: 0800 726 666
Web: samaritans.org.nz

Depression Helpline
Phone: 0800 111 757
Text: 4202
Web: depression.org.nz

Anxiety

Anxiety New Zealand
Phone: 0800 269 4389
Web: anxiety.org.nz

Eating Disorders

Mental Health Foundation of New Zealand
Web: mentalhealth.org.nz/get-help/a-z/resource/37/eating-disorders

Ministry of Health
Phone: 0800 611 116 (Healthline)
Web: health.govt.nz/your-health/conditions-and-treatments/mental-health/eating-disorders

Alcohol and Drugs

Alcohol Drug Helpline
Phone: 0800 787 797
Web: alcoholdrughelp.org.nz

Support for Young People

Youthline
Phone: 0800 376 633
Text: 234
Web: youthline.co.nz

The Lowdown
Text: 5626
Web: thelowdown.co.nz

What's Up?
Phone: 0800 942 8787 (0800 WHAT'S UP)
Web: whatsup.co.nz

Kidsline
Phone: 0800 54 37 54
Web: kidsline.org.nz

ENDNOTES

Preface

1 New Zealand Family Violence Clearinghouse, 'United Nations report on status of women released', nzfvc.org.nz/news/united-nations-report-status-women-released, accessed 23 March 2018.

2 Ministry for Women, 'Gender pay gap', women.govt.nz/work-skills/income/gender-pay-gap, accessed 3 December 2017.

3 'Pay gaps by ethnicity and gender', cevepnz.org.nz/Gender%20pay%20gap/gender-ethnicity.htm, accessed 3 December 2017.

4 Statistics New Zealand, '2013 Census quickstats about national highlights, archive.stats.govt.nz/Census/2013-census/profile-and-summary-reports/quickstats-about-national-highlights/age-and-sex.aspx, accessed 24 March 2018.

5 Aimee Shaw, 'Only one woman running a large public company in New Zealand', nzherald.co.nz/business/news/article.cfm?c_id=3&objectid=11895649, accessed 24 March 2018.

6 'Main activity of people who are not in the labour force in New Zealand', figure.nz/chart/ZmxpeujUBCQ2EmIF, accessed 2 April 2018.

7 Tina Law, 'National suicide numbers rise three years in a row', stuff.co.nz/national/health/96217175/national-suicide-numbers-rise-three-years-in-a-row, accessed 24 March 2018.

Chapter 2 – Boys don't cry

1 Daphna Joel, Zohar Berman, Ido Tavor, Nadav Wexler, Olga Gaber, Yaniv Stein, Nisan Shefi, Jared Pool, Sebastian Urchs, Daniel S.

Margulies, Franziskus Liem, Jürgen Hänggi, Lutz Jäncke, and Yaniv Assaf, 'Sex beyond the genitalia: The human brain mosaic', *PNAS*, 2015, vol. 112, no. 50, pp. 15,468–15,473.

Chapter 4 – Herstory

1 R. Busch, N. Robertson, and H. Lapsley, 'Protection from family violence; A study of breaches of protection orders', *Victims Task Force: Wellington,* 1992, p.1.

2 'Roast Busters victim asked to "re-enact" alleged rape', newshub.co.nz/nznews/roast-busters-victim-asked-to-reenact-alleged-rape-2013110618, accessed 9 July 2017.

3 'Consent at heart of cricketer Scott Kuggeleijn's rape trial', stuff.co.nz/national/crime/82437492/Consent-at-heart-of-cricketer-Scott-Kuggeleijns-rape-trial, accessed 9 July 2017.

4 Catriona MacLennan, 'Finally, hope for victims of domestic violence', newsroom.co.nz/2017/07/07/37783/catriona-maclennan-template, accessed 9 July 2017.

5 New Zealand History, 'Women and the vote', nzhistory.govt.nz/politics/womens-suffrage/brief-history, accessed 14 September 2017.

6 Barbara Brookes, *A History of New Zealand Women*, Bridget Williams Books, Wellington, 2016, p. 50.

7 New Zealand History, 'Treaty signatories and signing locations', nzhistory.govt.nz/politics/treaty/making-the-treaty/signing-the-treaty, accessed 14 September 2017.

8 Michael King, *The Penguin History of New Zealand Illustrated*, Penguin Books, Auckland, 2007, p. 77.

9 Ibid, p. 78.

10 Barbara Brookes, *A History of New Zealand Women*, Bridget Williams Books, Wellington, 2016, p. 176.

11 Te Ara, 'Story: Herangi, Te Kirihaehae Te Puea', teara.govt.nz/en/biographies/3h17/herangi-te-kirihaehae-te-puea, accessed 14 September 2017.

12 Ibid.

13 Michael King, *The Penguin History of New Zealand Illustrated*, Penguin Books, Auckland, 2007, pp. 407–408.

14 Te Ara, 'Story: Rout, Ettie Annie', teara.govt.nz/en/biographies/3r31/rout-ettie-annie, accessed 27 November 2017.

15 Te Ara, 'Story: Sheppard, Katherine Wilon', teara.govt.nz/en/biographies/2s20/sheppard-katherine-wilson, accessed 27 November 2017.

16 Barbara Brookes, *A History of New Zealand Women*, Bridget Williams Books, Wellington, 2016, p. 57.

17 Ibid, pp. 66–67.

18 Hazel Petrie, 'Colonisation and the Involution of the Māori Economy', 2002, news.tangatawhenua.com/wp-content/uploads/2010/10/24Petrie75.pdf, accessed 15 September 2017.

19 Barbara Brookes, *A History of New Zealand Women*, Bridget Williams Books, Wellington, 2016, pp. 57–82.

20 Married Women's Property Protection Act 1860 (24 Victoriae 1860 No 9), nzlii.org/nz/legis/hist_act/mwppa186024v1860n9535/, accessed 15 September 2017.

21 Divorce and Matrimonial Causes Act 1867 (31 Victoriae 1867 No 94), nzlii.org/nz/legis/hist_act/damca186731v1867n94402/, accessed 15 September 2017.

22 Te Ara, 'Story: Gender inequalities', teara.govt.nz/en/gender-inequalities/page-2, accessed 15 September, 2017.

23 Barbara Brookes, *A History of New Zealand Women*, Bridget Williams Books, Wellington, 2016, p. 120.

24 Married Women's Property Protection Act 1870 (33 and 34 Victoriae 1870 No 37), nzlii.org/nz/legis/hist_act/mwppa187033a34v1870n37551/, accessed 15 September 2017.

25 Te Ara, 'Story: Gender inequalities', teara.govt.nz/en/gender-inequalities/page-3, accessed 15 September 2017.

26 Barbara Brookes, *A History of New Zealand Women*, Bridget Williams Books, Wellington, 2016, p. 120.

27 Te Ara, 'Story: Gender inequalities', teara.govt.nz/en/gender-inequalities/page-2, accessed 15 September 2017.

28 Te Ara, 'Story: Gender inequalities', teara.govt.nz/en/gender-inequalities/page-3, accessed 15 September 2017.

29 Te Ara, 'Story: Gender inequalities', teara.govt.nz/en/gender-inequalities/page-2, accessed 15 September 2017.

30 Te Ara, 'Story: Women's movement', teara.govt.nz/en/womens-movement/page-4, accessed 15 September 2017.

31 Te Ara, 'Story: Te mana o wāhine – Māori women', teara.govt.nz/en/te-mana-o-te-wahine-maori-women/page-5, accessed 15 September 2017.

32 Divorce Act 1898 (62 VICT 1898 No 42), nzlii.org/nz/legis/hist_act/da189862v1898n42167/, accessed 15 September 2017.

33 Ibid.

34 Te Ara, 'Story: Gender inequalities', teara.govt.nz/en/gender-inequalities/page-3, accessed 15 September 2017.

35 Ibid.

36 Ibid.

37 Government Service Equal Pay Act 1960 (1960 No 117), nzlii.org/nz/legis/hist_act/gsepa19601960n117335/, accessed 15 September 2017.

38 Equal Pay Act 1972 (1972 No 118), nzlii.org/nz/legis/hist_act/epa19721972n118138/, accessed 15 September 2017.

39 Katarina Williams, 'Kristine Bartlett: "This is going to be the biggest pay rise we'll ever get"', stuff.co.nz/national/politics/91678514/Kristine-Bartlett-This-is-going-to-be-the-biggest-pay-rise-we-ll-ever-get, accessed 15 September 2017.

40 Te Ara, 'Story: Te mana o wāhine – Māori women', teara.govt.nz/en/te-mana-o-te-wahine-maori-women/page-7, accessed 15 September 2017.

41 Matrimonial Property Act 1976 (1976 No 166), nzlii.org/nz/legis/hist_act/mpa19761976n166287/, accessed 15 September 2017.

42 Te Ara, 'Story: Gender inequalities', teara.govt.nz/en/gender-inequalities/page-2, accessed 15 September 2017.

43 Crimes Act 1908, enzs.auckland.ac.nz/docs/1908/1908C032.pdf, accessed 15 September 2017.

44 Crimes Amendment Act 1977 (1977 No 113), nzlii.org/nz/legis/hist_act/caa19771977n113189/, accessed 15 September 2017.

45 Contraception, Sterilisation, and Abortion Act 1977 (1977 No 112), nzlii.org/nz/legis/hist_act/csaaa19771977n112447/, accessed 15 September 2017.

46 Domestic Protection Act 1982 (1982 No 120), nzlii.org/nz/legis/hist_act/dpa19821982n120253/, accessed 15 September 2017.

47 Te Ara, 'Story: Gender inequalities', teara.govt.nz/en/gender-inequalities/page-2, accessed 15 September 2017.

48 Crimes Amendment Act (No 3) 1985 (1985 No 160), nzlii.org/nz/legis/hist_act/caa319851985n160216/, accessed 15 September 2017.

49 Crimes Act 1961 (1961 No 43), nzlii.org/nz/legis/hist_act/ca19611961n43109/, accessed 15 September 2017.

50 Prostitution Reform Act 2003 (2003 No 28), nzlii.org/nz/legis/hist_act/pra20032003n28301/, accessed 16 September 2017.

51 Barbara Brookes, *A History of New Zealand Women*, Bridget Williams Books, Wellington, 2016, p. 473.

52 'Farah Palmer first woman appointed to New Zealand Rugby', stuff.co.nz/sport/rugby/87587298/farah-palmer-first-woman-appointed-to-board-of-new-zealand-rugby, accessed 15 September 2017.

Chapter 5 – The media told me I was fat

1 Elly Strang, 'A look at plus-sized retailing in New Zealand', theregister.co.nz/news/2015/12/look-plus-sized-retailing-new-zealand, accessed 28 March 2018.

2 The American Society for Aesthetic Plastic Surgery, '2015 Cosmetic Surgery National Data Bank Statistics', surgery.org/sites/default/files/ASAPS-Stats2015.pdf, accessed 23 July 2017.

3 Ibid.

4 'I had plastic surgery to change my vagina', fq.co.nz/missfq/life-love/sex-relationships/i-had-plastic-surgery-to-change-my-vagina, accessed 23 July 2017.

5 'Why I had labiaplasty at just 16', stuff.co.nz/life-style/life/66633138/why-i-had-labiaplasty-at-just-16, accessed 23 July 2017.

Chapter 6 – Take back the media

1 Susan Fountaine, New Zealand Global Media Monitoring Project 2015 National Report, cdn.agilitycms.com/who-makes-the-news/Imported/reports_2015/national/New_Zealand.pdf, accessed 5 November 2017.

Chapter 7 – The crime of opining whilst female

1 Virginia Myers, *Head and Shoulders*, Penguin, Auckland, 1986.

2 'PM's pants prove problematic', tvnz.co.nz/content/83922/2591764.xhtml, accessed 2 December 2017.

3 Antony Green, 'NZ Labour hears echoes of Howard's election loss', abc.net.au/news/2008-11-06/nz-labour-hears-echoes-of-howards-election-loss/197292, accessed 9 July 2017.

4 Mike Moore, 'Return to Muldoonism?', nzherald.co.nz/opinion/news/article.cfm?c_id=466&objectid=10460368, accessed 30 September 2017.

5 'The real Helen Clark', stuff.co.nz/national/politics/2607353/The-real-Helen-Clark, accessed 9 July 2017.

6 Audrey Young, 'Bitter Clark savages rumours', nzherald.co.nz/nz/news/article.cfm?c_id=1&objectid=10401769, accessed 2 December 2017.

7 Margie Comrie, 'Helengrad and other epithets: Aspects of Helen Clark's third term media coverage', anzca.net/documents/2008-conf-

papers/95-helengrad-and-other-epithets-aspects-of-helen-clark-s-third-term-media-coverage-1/file.html, accessed 9 July 2017.

8 Ian Wishart, 'The Siege of Helengrad', investigatemagazine.com/nov03paradise.htm, accessed 9 July 2017.

9 Louisa Peacock, 'New Zealand's former woman PM: Margaret Thatcher set the tone for women in politics', telegraph.co.uk/women/womens-politics/10587999/Margaret-Thatcher-set-the-tone-for-women-in-politics-says-woman-Prime-Minister-of-New-Zealand.html, accessed 9 July 2017.

10 Geoff Kemp (ed.), *Politics and the Media,* Auckland University Press, Auckland, 2016.

11 Bernadette Luciano and David G. Mayes (eds), *New Zealand and Europe: Connections and Comparisons*, Rodopi, 2005, p. 236.

12 twitter.com/JarrodGilbertNZ/status/873720857381580801, accessed 11 June 2017.

13 Claudia Pond Eyley and Dan Salmon, *Helen Clark: Inside Stories*, Auckland University Press, Auckland, 2015, p. 172.

14 Gabrielle Chan, 'Julia Gillard explains "misogyny speech"', theguardian.com/world/2013/sep/30/julia-gillard-explains-misogyny-speech, accessed 2 December 2017.

15 'Transcript of Julia Gillard's speech', smh.com.au/federal-politics/political-news/transcript-of-julia-gillards-speech-20121009-27c36.html, accessed 9 July 2017.

16 'PM must apologise to Abbott women: Bishop', smh.com.au/federal-politics/political-news/pm-must-apologise-to-abbott-women-bishop-20121011-27g0o.html, accessed 9 July 2017.

17 Jonathan Milne, 'Nicola Kaye vs Jacinda Ardern', noted.co.nz/archive/listener-nz-2011/nicola-kaye-vs-jacinda-ardern/, accessed 9 July 2017.

18 '"Zip it sweetie" Bennett to Ardern', youtube.com/watch?v=Mk-Yva9nnwg, accessed 9 July 2017.

19 'Jacinda Ardern a "pretty little thing", would "look good" as PM – Graham Lowe', stuff.co.nz/national/politics/71471800/Jacinda-

Ardern-a-pretty-little-thing-would-look-good-as-PM-Graham-Lowe, accessed 9 July 2017.

20 'Jacinda Ardern responds to being called "pretty bloody stupid"', stuff.co.nz/national/politics/73319715/Jacinda-Ardern-responds-to-being-called-pretty-bloody-stupid, accessed 9 July 2017.

21 Fran O'Sullivan, 'Jacinda Ardern needs to put in the hard yards', nzherald.co.nz/business/news/article.cfm?c_id=3&objectid=11811602, accessed 9 July 2017.

22 'Bill English's new attack: Jacinda "Stardust" Ardern', stuff.co.nz/national/politics/96622994/Bill-Englishs-new-attack-Jacinda-Stardust-Ardern, accessed 30 September 2017.

23 'Newstalk ZB host Leighton Smith calls Jacinda Ardern "chicky babe"', stuff.co.nz/entertainment/tv-radio/98023842/newstalk-zb-host-leighton-smith-calls-jacinda-ardern-chicky-babe, accessed 7 November 2017.

24 'Jacinda Ardern laughs off "pretty communist" protest sign', newshub.co.nz/home/election/2017/09/jacinda-ardern-laughs-off-pretty-communist-protest-sign.html, accessed 30 September 2017.

25 twitter.com/Hilary_Barry/status/636273505554665472, accessed 9 July 2017.

26 twitter.com/jacindaardern/status/636276238844235776, accessed 9 July 2017.

27 twitter.com/Hilary_Barry/status/892295268808273920, accessed 1 August 2017.

28 'Jacinda Ardern: It is "totally unacceptable" to ask women about baby plans, newshub.co.nz/home/election/2017/08/jacinda-ardern-it-is-totally-unacceptable-to-ask-women-about-baby-plans.html, accessed 2 August 2017.

29 twitter.com/thetvnews/status/892649240740024320, accessed 3 August 2017.

30 'Hooton: Ardern "will fail, I think she's a flake", newstalkzb.co.nz/news/vote2017/matthew-hooton-ardern-will-fail-i-think-shes-a-flake/, accessed 1 August 2017.

31 'Andrew Little pulls out of all media minutes before live TV appearance', newshub.co.nz/home/election/2017/07/andrew-little-pulls-out-of-all-media-minutes-before-live-tv-appearance.html, accessed 1 August 2017.

32 Michael Field, 'Eleanor Catton's problem with New Zealand', stuff.co.nz/entertainment/books/65463098/eleanor-cattons-problem-with-new-zealand, accessed 9 July 2017.

33 Andrew Dean, 'The Catton conundrum: What attacks on the novelist say about public debate in NZ', thespinoff.co.nz/featured/18-03-2016/the-catton-conundrum-what-attacks-on-the-novelist-say-about-public-debate-in-nz/, accessed 9 July 2017.

34 Siobhan Downes, 'Radio host Sean Plunket stands by calling Eleanor Catton a "hua"', stuff.co.nz/entertainment/books/65493542/radio-host-sean-plunket-stands-by-calling-eleanor-catton-a-hua, accessed 9 July 2017.

35 'New Zealand PM John Key rejects author Eleanor Catton's criticism of his government', abc.net.au/news/2015-02-02/john-key-rejects-eleanor-cattons-criticism-of-his-government/6063814, accessed 9 July 2017.

36 Lizzie Marvelly, 'When did New Zealand become so sexist?', villainesse.com/girl-power/when-did-new-zealand-become-so-sexist, accessed 9 July 2017.

Chapter 8 – Someone please shoot this bitch. NZ fucking hates her.

1 Harmful Digital Communications Act 2015, legislation.govt.nz/act/public/2015/0063/latest/DLM5711810.html, accessed 30 March 2018.

2 'Norton study shows online harassment at epidemic proportions for young New Zealand women', symantec.com/en/au/about/newsroom/press-releases/2016/symantec_0720_01, accessed 9 July 2017.

3 'Rates of cyber bullying in New Zealand alarming', nzherald.co.nz/nz/news/article.cfm?c_id=1&objectid=11612551, accessed 9 July 2017.

Chapter 9 – Pornication

1 'Best Friends Fuck Together', pornhub.com/view_video.php?viewkey=ph55ddb463aab3d, accessed 13 August 2017.

2 'Porn use on the rise among teens, researchers find link with mental health problems', abc.net.au/news/2017-06-30/teenagers-porn-use-on-the-rise-research-says/8664842, accessed 14 August 2017.

3 American Psychological Association, 'Age of first exposure to pornography shapes men's attitudes toward women', eurekalert.org/pub_releases/2017-08/apa-aof072717.php, accessed 14 August 2017.

4 'Pornography reinforces sexist attitudes among a subgroup of heterosexuals', sciencedaily.com/releases/2013/09/130906102536.htm, accessed 14 August 2017.

5 Sandra Laville, 'Most boys think online pornography is realistic, finds study', theguardian.com/culture/2016/jun/15/majority-boys-online-pornography-realistic-middlesex-university-study, accessed 14 August 2017.

6 C. Marston and R. Lewis, 'Anal heterosex among young people and implications for health promotion: a qualitative study in the UK', *BJM Open*, 2014, bmjopen.bmj.com/content/bmjopen/4/8/e004996.full.pdf, accessed 15 August 2017.

7 'Sex robot display model molested so much it breaks before anyone can actually use it', mirror.co.uk/news/weird-news/expensive-sex-doll-molested-much-11251239, accessed 30 September 2017.

8 'Women searching for women', pornhub.com/insights/women-searching-for-women, accessed 19 August 2017.

9 Michael Castleman, 'How common is masturbation, really?', psychologytoday.com/blog/all-about-sex/200903/how-common-is-masturbation-really, accessed 17 August 2017.

10 Lizzie Marvelly and Jo Raj, 'My body, my terms', villainesse.com/mybodymyterms/mybodymyterms, accessed 20 August 2017.

11 Amanda Lenhart, Michele Ybarra, Myeshia Price-Feeney, 'Nonconsensual image sharing: one in 25 americans has been a victim of "revenge porn"', *Data & Society Research Institute*, 2016, datasociety.net/pubs/oh/Nonconsensual_Image_Sharing_2016.pdf, accessed 27 August 2017.

12 'Netsafe warns New Zealanders against sharing "revenge porn"', scoop.co.nz/stories/PO1707/S00272/netsafe-warns-new-zealanders-against-sharing-revenge-porn.htm, accessed 27 August 2017.

Chapter 10 – The possessed body

1 'Chiefs sponsor supports players after stripper scandal', nzherald.co.nz/sport/news/article.cfm?c_id=4&objectid=11687082, accessed 9 July 2017.

2 Madeleine Chapman, '"Were you saying no but not meaning no?": On the tactics of Scott Kuggeleijn's lawyer', thespinoff.co.nz/society/24-02-2017/were-you-saying-no-but-not-meaning-no-on-the-tactics-of-scott-kuggeleijns-lawyer/, accessed 9 July 2017.

3 'Mike Hosking's opinion on the pony tail waitress', youtube.com/watch?v=oxBx6RfVc_A, accessed 12 August 2017.

4 'BSA upholds "ponytail" complaints against Seven Sharp's Mike Hosking', tvnz.co.nz/one-news/new-zealand/bsa-upholds-ponytail-complaints-against-seven-sharp-s-mike-hosking-q13158, accessed 12 August 2017.

5 'John Key to release "ponytail" saga text message from gossip columnist', stuff.co.nz/national/politics/77076492/john-key-to-release-ponytail-saga-text-message-from-gossip-columnist, accessed 12 August 2017.

6 'The ineptitude of the left', whaleoil.co.nz/2015/04/the-ineptitude-of-the-left/, accessed 12 August 2017.

7 'Face of the day', whaleoil.co.nz/2015/04/face-of-the-day-671/, accessed 12 August 2017.

8 Greg Bruce, 'Paul Henry reveals why he hates people', nzherald.co.nz/entertainment/news/article.cfm?c_id=1501119&objectid=11737753, accessed 12 August 2017.

9 Aimee Cronin, 'Paul Henry is next-level creepy', stuff.co.nz/entertainment/tv-radio/85897555/paul-henry-is-nextlevel-creepy--aimie-cronin, accessed 12 August 2017.

10 'Roast Busters case: "Where was the respect?" – police', nzherald.co.nz/nz/news/article.cfm?c_id=1&objectid=11350007, accessed 9 July 2017.

11 'Research & data: Sexual violence', justice.govt.nz/justice-sector-policy/research-data/nzcass/survey-results/results-by-subject/sexual-violence/, accessed 9 July 2017.

12 The Law Commission, 'The justice response to victims of sexual violence: Criminal trials and alternative', processesr136.publications.lawcom.govt.nz/Chapter+6+-+The+fact-finder+in+sexual+violence+cases/Juror+decision-making+in+sexual+violence+cases+the+issues, accessed 5 August 2017.

13 'Sexual violence courts to be trialled', lawsociety.org.nz/news-and-communications/latest-news/news/sexual-violence-courts-to-be-trialled, accessed 9 July 2017.

14 New Zealand Ministry of Justice, '2014 New Zealand crime and safety survey', justice.govt.nz/assets/Documents/Publications/NZCASS-201602-Main-Findings-Report-Updated.pdf, accessed 9 July 2017.

15 Eva McGauley, '"This is what it's like for us" – a teenager on Wellington College Facebook comments and rape culture', thespinoff.co.nz/society/10-03-2017/this-is-what-its-like-for-us-a-teenager-on-wellington-college-facebook-comments-and-rape-culture/, accessed 9 July 2017.

16 Ministry of Justice, 'Sexual violence', justice.govt.nz/justice-sector-policy/research-data/nzcass/survey-results/results-by-subject/sexual-violence/#reported, accessed 30 March 2018.

17 ASA, 'Code for people in advertising', asa.co.nz/codes/codes/code-for-people-in-advertising/, accessed 1 August 2017.

18 New Zealand Herald, 'Northern Districts cricketer's rape trial: "She was dressed provocatively"', nzherald.co.nz/nz/news/article.cfm?c_id=1&objectid=11683185, accessed 1 August 2017.

19 Contraception, Sterilisation, and Abortion Act 1977, legislation.govt.nz/act/public/1977/0112/latest/DLM18510.html, accessed 1 August 2017.

20 Henry Cooke, 'Hundreds of Kiwi women told their abortions were "not justified"', stuff.co.nz/national/health/90390584/hundreds-of-kiwi-women-told-their-abortions-were-not-justified, accessed 5 August 2017.

21 Susan Strongman, 'Antiquated abortion law a $20 million "box ticking exercise"', thewireless.co.nz/articles/antiquated-abortion-law-a-20-million-box-ticking-exercise, accessed 30 March 2018.

22 'Sci-fi writer baffles abortion foes with simple question: Would you save 1,000 embryos or one child in fire?', rawstory.com/2017/10/sci-fi-writer-baffles-abortion-foes-with-simple-question-would-you-save-1000-embryos-or-one-child-in-fire/, accessed 19 November 2017.

Chapter 11 – The possessed mind

1 NZQA, 'Are there gender differences in achievement rates?', nzqa.govt.nz/qualifications-standards/qualifications/ncea/understanding-ncea/the-facts/factsheet-9/, accessed 15 July 2017.

2 Ministry for Women, 'Qualification attainment', women.govt.nz/work-skills/education-and-skills/qualification-attainment, accessed 15 July 2017.

3 Lisa Appignanesi, *Mad, bad and sad: Women and the mind doctors,* W. W. Norton & Company, United States of America, 2008.

4 World Health Organisation, 'Gender disparities and mental health: The facts', who.int/mental_health/prevention/genderwomen/en/, accessed 9 July 2017.

5 Ibid.

6 C. Brems, 'Women and depression: A comprehensive analysis', in *Handbook of Depression* (2nd edition), Guilford, New York, 1995, pp. 539–566, cited in Ann M. Kring, Sheri L. Johnson, Gerald Davison, John Neale, *Abnormal Psychology* (12th edition), John Wiley & Sons, Inc., United States of America, 2012.

7 S. Seedat, K. M. Scott, M. Angermeyer, P. Berglund, E. Bromet, T. Brugha, ... R. Kessler, 'Cross-national associations between gender and mental disorders in the World Health Organisation world mental health surveys', *Archives of General Psychiatry*, 2009, vol. 66, no. 7, pp. 785–795, cited in Ann M. Kring, Sheri L. Johnson, Gerald Davison, John Neale, *Abnormal Psychology* (12th edition), John Wiley & Sons, Inc., United States of America, 2012.

8 S. Nolen-Hoeksema, 'Gender differences in depression', *Current Directions in Psychological Science*, 2001, vol. 10, pp. 173–174, cited in Ann M. Kring, Sheri L. Johnson, Gerald Davison, John Neale, *Abnormal Psychology* (12th edition), John Wiley & Sons, Inc., United States of America, 2012.

9 Ibid.

10 B. L. Hankin and L. Y. Abramson, 'Development of gender differences in depression: An elaborated cognitive vulnerability-transactional stress theory', *Psychological Bulletin,* 2001, vol. 127, pp. 773–796, cited in Ann M. Kring, Sheri L. Johnson, Gerald Davison, John Neale, *Abnormal Psychology* (12th edition), John Wiley & Sons, Inc., United States of America, 2012.

11 Ann M. Kring, Sheri L. Johnson, Gerald Davison, John Neale, *Abnormal Psychology* (12th edition), John Wiley & Sons, Inc., United States of America, 2012, p. 350.

12 Barbara L. Fredrickson, Tomi-Ann Roberts, Stephanie M. Noll, Diane M. Quinn, Jean M. Twenge, 'That swimsuit becomes you: Sex differences in self-objectification, restrained eating, and math performance', *Journal of Personality and Social Psychology*, 1998, vol. 75, no. 1, pp. 269–284.

13 'Perfectionism hits working women', news.bbc.co.uk/2/hi/health/8072739.stm, accessed 9 July 2017; 'More than third of teenage girls in England suffer depression and anxiety', theguardian.com/society/2016/aug/22/third-teenage-girls-depression-anxiety-survey-trend-truant, accessed 9 July 2017.

14 Cameron Slater, 'Proof most men have a bigger IQ than Lizzie Marvelly', whaleoil.co.nz/2017/07/proof-men-bigger-iq-lizzie-marvelly/, accessed 15 July 2017.

Chapter 12 – That F word

1 'Ethical Fashion Fast Finder', baptistworldaid.org.au/resources/2017-ethical-fashion-guide/, accessed 3 December 2017.

Chapter 13 – Hashtag feminism

1 J. K. Rowling, *Harry Potter and the Goblet of Fire*, Scholastic, New York, 2000, p. 196.

Chapter 14 – The non-feminist

1 'Womanist', thoughtco.com/womanist-feminism-definition-3528993, accessed 1 April 2018.

Chapter 16 – Bringing down the invisible man

1 Collins Dictionary, collinsdictionary.com/dictionary/english/patriarchy, accessed 8 October 2017.

2 L. Doyal, 'Gender equity in health: debates and dilemmas', *Social Science & Medicine*, 2000, vol. 323, pp. 1061–1063, cited in Poul Rohleder, *Critical Issues in Clinical & Health Psychology*, SAGE Publications, India, 2012, p.125.

3 L. Doyal, *Gender and health: A technical document*, World Health Organisation, Geneva, cited in Poul Rohleder, *Critical Issues in Clinical & Health Psychology*, SAGE Publications, India, 2012, p. 125.

4 I. Waldron, 'Contributions of changing gender differences in behaviour and social roles to changing gender differences n mortality', in D. Sabo & D. F. Gordon (eds), *Men's health and illness: Gender, power and the body*, Sage, California 1995, cited in Poul Rohleder, *Critical Issues in Clinical & Health Psychology*, SAGE Publications, India, 2012, p. 127.

5 W. H. Courtenay, 'Constructions of masculinity and their influence on men's well-being: A theory of gender and health', *Social Science & Medicine*, 2000, vol. 50, pp. 1385–1401. Cited in Poul Rohleder, *Critical Issues in Clinical & Health Psychology*, SAGE Publications, India, 2012, p.125.

6 E. Cameron and J. Bernardes, 'Gender and disadvantage in health: Men's health for a change', *Sociology of Health & Illness*, 1998, vol. 20, no. 5, pp. 673–693, cited in Poul Rohleder, *Critical Issues in Clinical & Health Psychology*, SAGE Publications, India, 2012, p. 126.

7 Zoe Williams, 'Sexual harassment 101: what everyone needs to know', theguardian.com/world/2017/oct/16/facts-sexual-harassment-workplace-harvey-weinstein?CMP=twt_gu, accessed 17 October 2017.

8 Glenn Collins, 'Patriarchy: is it invention or inevitable?', *New York Times*, nytimes.com/1986/04/28/style/patriarchy-is-it-invention-or-inevitable.html, accessed 21 October 2017.

9 Karl Bücher, *Die Frauenfrage im Mittelalter*, Hansebooks, 2016, cited in Martha C. Howell, *Women, Production, and Patriarchy in Late Medieval Cities*, University of Chicago Press, Chicago, 1986.

10 Judith M. Bennett, *History Matters: Patriarchy and the Challenge of Feminism*, University of Pennsylvania Press, 2006, cited in Leila J. Rupp, 'Revisiting Patriarchy (book review)', *Journal of Women's History*, 2008, vol. 20, no. 2, pp. 136–140.

11 Holly Ryan, 'Women on boards — NZ lagging behind', nzherald.co.nz/business/news/article.cfm?c_id=3&objectid=11780512, accessed 8 October 2017.

12 Statistics New Zealand, 'Effects of motherhood on pay', stats.govt.nz/browse_for_stats/income-and-work/Income/motherhood-penalty-summary.aspx, accessed 8 October 2017.

13 Tim Beasley, Olle Folke, Torsten Persson, Johanna Rickne, 'Gender quotas and the crisis of the mediocre man', LSE Business Review, blogs.lse.ac.uk/businessreview/2017/03/13/gender-quotas-and-the-crisis-of-the-mediocre-man/, accessed 21 October 2017.

Chapter 17 – One last rant

1 'Venture capital's funding gender gap is actually getting worse', fortune.com/2017/03/13/female-founders-venture-capital/, accessed 21 November 2017.